The Ethical, Legal and Social Issues of Pandemics

Iñigo de Miguel Beriain

The Ethical, Legal and Social Issues of Pandemics

An Analysis from the EU Perspective

 Springer

Iñigo de Miguel Beriain
Faculty of Law
University of the Basque Country
Leioa, Bizkaia, Spain

Ikerbasque
Basque Foundation for Science
Bilbao, Bizkaia, Spain

ISBN 978-3-031-03820-4   ISBN 978-3-031-03818-1   (eBook)
https://doi.org/10.1007/978-3-031-03818-1

This Springer imprint is published by the registered company Springer Nature Switzerland AG
The registered company address is: Gewerbestrasse 11, 6330 Cham, Switzerland

To my dear aunt Mariaje

Foreword

This Time Is Different? A New Book on the Ethical, Legal and Social Issues of Pandemics

I imagine a book written 100 years from now. A person looking back at the first half of our century, what would their judgement be in terms of how we handled the COVID-19 pandemic, and how the world changed as a result?

When I read books about large disease outbreaks in the past, I am struck by both the similarities and the differences to what we are currently experiencing. In terms of the similarities, those who proposed measures to improve hygiene or restrict people's movements have often faced accusations of conspiracy. Another constant is the exclusion—and sometimes even demonisation—of marginalised and vulnerable groups. In terms of differences, for centuries, pandemic management used to focus on socio-economic determinants. They were not called that, of course, but up until the first half of the twentieth century, the focus of pandemic control was on the circumstances in which people lived and worked. When and where antibiotics and other biomedical therapies were more widely available, the emphasis changed. As pointed out by historians such as Silverstein (2021), individuals increasingly became the focus of intervention. Responsibility for preventing health crises shifted from collective actors—local communities, religious entities, or "the state"—to individual people and families, who were supposed to behave healthily and carefully to reduce risks. This current pandemic is a stark illustration of this.

During COVID-19, in much of the rich world, there has been a striking disconnect between pandemic measures aiming at regulating individual behaviour on the one hand, and the embodied experiences of people on the other. While mask mandates, rules for physical distance or calls to use contact tracing apps suggested to people that they were individually responsible for helping to end the pandemic, their own daily experience told a different story. Even if they did everything "right", if they were careful and obeyed all rules, they could still get infected, or lose their job or income as a (direct or indirect) result of the pandemic. Whether we were ready for this or not, during the pandemic almost everyone of us experienced how risk is a collective practice. Everyone else's actions or non-actions shape our personal risk, and vice versa. Especially for those of us who were told from early childhood on that we should and could control life's risks through our own, individual behaviour—by working hard in school, by getting good job training, by living healthily and choosing a "good" partner—the experience that no matter what we do, we can still suffer from the pandemic, was a narcissistic injury. I believe that this factor accounts for at least part of the resistance and protests against pandemic measures.

For many people in the less privileged world, the suggestion that they could control the pandemic through adapting their individual behaviour must have sounded like a bad joke. While the rich world agonised over how they could convince enough people to get vaccinated, societies in Global South did not even get enough vaccines to immunise their most vulnerable members. While many cities in North America, Europe and Australia experienced protest against face masks, low-income countries did not have enough protective equipment for health-care staff. At the same time as leaders in the Global North kept emphasising that "we are all in the same boat", they keep deciding over life and death of people in the Global South.

This is the status at the end of the second year of COVID-19, when Iñigo de Miguel Beriain finished his important new book. Restrictions on movement, immunity certificates, vaccination and triage were hardly discussed 2 years ago, but they are now in the centre of attention by ethicists and policy makers and give rise to serious—sometimes even violent—disputes. By addressing these topics, the author does not set himself an easy task: Positions on these topics are entrenched and have become markers of identity. Those who carry an immunisation certificate, get boosted, and who accept restrictions on their movements often consider these practices as necessary to protect society and especially the most vulnerable. Those who reject these practices, in contrast, see themselves as fighting for freedom and autonomy, and against over-surveillance and an overbearing state. It important to see, however, how these positions, on both sides, bear the marks of privilege. Being able to get vaccinated, to restrict one's movements or to work from home, for example, requires that one has the means and choice to do so. Similarly, for someone to reject vaccination against COVID-19, to protest mask wearing or to drive their car or truck to a capital to protest pandemic measures means that they have access to vaccines, cars, and face masks in the first place. And they will still receive medical care if they get sick.

Against this backdrop, those who hold nuanced positions in between the opposites often receive criticism from both sides. Iñigo de Miguel Beriain's book is one such contribution "in the middle": It analyses four fields of practice and technology that have become important during COVID-19 and is free from preconceptions about what a supposedly "liberal" or "communitarian" position should be. The author explores these topics on the basis of values such as solidarity, equity and autonomy, in full acknowledgement of the fact that these values cannot guide policy making in the abstract. They need to be discussed and evaluated in connection with concrete practices. Freedom is a good example: When it comes to limits on the freedom of movement, whose freedoms require protection, the freedom of low-risk groups to move around as freely as possible, or the freedom of high-risk groups to be protected from avoidable danger of infection? And if both are worthy of protection, how do we solve this dilemma?

Iñigo de Miguel Beriain's answer is typically more pragmatic than principled. This is one of the key strengths of this book: Weighing different risks, stakes and goods, he either points out the advantages and disadvantages of several scenarios or develops a new approach that attends to the needs of as many different groups as possible (the "venue tagging" approach in Chap. 1 is an example). Such a pragmatic approach, informed by social values yet without any ideological commitments, is exactly what is needed in this moment of time. Whether or not readers find themselves agreeing with the author's conclusions, one of the things they will learn from this book is what we can gain if we consider pandemic measures in a deliberative manner. Pandemic measures touch upon the big, constitutional (in the literal sense of the word) questions: What kind of society do we want to live in? How do certain measures affect the distribution of rights and responsibilities, benefits and costs within and across societies? Given that poverty is both a medical and a social risk factor (e.g. Abedi et al., 2021; Agrawal et al., 2021; Bambra & Lynch, 2021; Delaporte et al., 2021), what steps need to be taken to abolish poverty and to reduce social and economic inequalities? How can we move social determinants back into the focus of pandemic management and prevention? This book is an important step in finding answers to these questions.

Department of Political Science   Barbara Prainsack
University of Vienna
Vienna, Austria

References

Abedi, V., Olulana, O., Avula, V., Chaudhary, D., Khan, A., Shahjouei, S., Li, J., & Zand, R. (2021). Racial, economic, and health inequality and COVID-19 infection in the United States. *Journal of Racial and Ethnic Health Disparities, 8*(3), 732–742.

Agrawal, S., Cojocaru, A., Montalva, V., Narayan, A., Bundervoet, T., & Ten, A. (2021). *COVID-19 and inequality: How unequal was the recovery from the initial shock?*. World Bank. Retrieved from https://openknowledge.worldbank. org/handle/10986/35867. License: CC BY 3.0 IGO.

Bambra, C., & Lynch, J. (2021). *The unequal pandemic: COVID-19 and health inequalities*. Policy Press.

Delaporte, I., Escobar, J., & Peña, W. (2021). The distributional consequences of social distancing on poverty and labour income inequality in Latin America and the Caribbean. *Journal of Population Economics, 34*(4), 1385–1443.

Silverstein, S. (2021). *What do we learn from past pandemics? Invited lecture at the Pandemic Forum 2021*. Retrieved December 15, 2021, from https://www. meduniwien.ac.at/web/en/ueber-uns/events/2021/pandemic-forum-2021/

Preface

On December 30, 2019, the health authorities in the Chinese city of Wuhan notified that 27 people had been diagnosed with a severe acute respiratory syndrome of unknown origin. At the time, it was hard to anticipate how much our lives would change in the coming months. As I write these lines, we are still dealing with the consequences of the pandemic caused by SARS-CoV-2, and it is not yet clear what the end of this story will be. What we do know for sure, however, is that it will take a lot of time and effort to analyse what has happened. Nor will it be easy to figure out how to improve our response to the pandemics that at some point in the—hopefully distant—future will succeed this one.

This book aims to contribute to this debate by providing ideas to stimulate public discussion. It is based on a multidisciplinary analysis, encompassing ethical, legal and social issues. Its contents cover the issues that are likely to be most controversial in any public health crisis. Its first chapters deal with the appropriateness of containment, how to control compliance with public health measures or the ethical, legal and social acceptability of health certificates. Those pages, therefore, are devoted to dealing with the response to a situation of this kind through non-pharmacological measures. The subsequent chapters, on the other hand, focus on issues related to the production, distribution and administration of vaccines, taking into account that, in general, whatever is said about them will be applicable to medical treatments against pathogens that cause infectious diseases. Finally, the last part of this book will analyse one of the most controversial—and probably least explored—issues regarding the response to a crisis of these dimensions: the most appropriate criteria to develop a triage, when the situation brings us to this terrible scenario.

My analysis is restricted, however, to the framework of some specific political institutions, the liberal democracies. Unlike other "democracies" and, above all, those countries where it is not possible to speak of the rule of law, our systems—fortunately for us—have to reconcile the defence against a public health crisis together with a respect for fundamental rights and freedoms. Hence, our legal systems have developed a number of conceptual tools designed to ensure that there is no room for arbitrariness in the restrictions introduced by the political power in emergency situations. Of these tools, the principle of proportionality, which is constantly present in the conceptual framework on which this work has been built, undoubtedly stands out. Originally developed by the Prussian Oberverwaltungsgericht (Prussian Supreme Court of Administrative Law) at the end of the nineteenth century (Grimm, 2007), it ultimately shaped the legal systems of most democratic countries. It is currently expressed in Article 52.1 of the EU Charter of Fundamental Rights.

The principle of proportionality states, synthetically, that for a measure to be acceptable, it must meet three fundamental requirements: suitability, necessity and "proportionality stricto sensu". The first implies that any measure adopted must be effective for the intended purpose, assuming that this purpose can be reconciled with the values of the legal system in which the measure is inserted. The second requirement, necessity, means that, of all the possible alternatives for achieving the same objective, the one selected entails the least restriction of rights and freedoms. Hence, this sub-principle is also often referred to as the *least restrictive alternative*. Thirdly, the principle of "proportionality stricto sensu" dictates that, while a measure is suitable and less restrictive than others, the harm it causes to rights and freedoms must not be disproportionate to the end it seeks to achieve. Only when a proposal satisfies these three conditions may it be considered legitimate. Hence the importance of applying this test to many of the debates that underlie this book.

This is, on the other hand, a work focused on the European Union arena. This, of course, does not mean that it will not include information on how other political structures combat public health crises, but my focus will be primarily on how we should construct our responses from a European perspective. The reason for this constraint is simple: the European Union is a unique phenomenon in the international scene. Unlike the United States, for example, it is not a single country. This has important consequences in that it does not possess many of the key competencies in a situation such as the one I discuss below. Indeed, according to the EU Treaties, responding to public health emergencies, such as SARS-CoV-2 pandemic, is primarily a responsibility of the Member States (De Ruijter & Weimer, 2021). However, neither is it an international organisation of the type of the African Union, for example. In contrast to such institutions, the EU does have adequate structures for the efficient coordination of many of the policies of its Member States and sufficient competences to implement some of the necessary actions.

In addition—and this is fundamental—the EU possesses common values, which are expressed in the Charter of Fundamental Rights of the European Union (2000/C 364/01). Initially proclaimed by the European Parliament, the Council of the European Union and the European Commission on 7 December 2000 in Nice, the Charter is now a binding legal instrument for all Member States. Its importance is therefore fundamental, since it does not merely list a series of values or principles, but establishes a conceptual framework to be implemented even in times of crisis. Moreover, it is precisely at these times that the Charter and its fundamental values—freedom, equality, solidarity, justice, etc.—acquire greater relevance.

Of all of these values, ideological freedom and freedom of expression stand out, since it is the value that ultimately provides us with the capacity to make criticisms. Those who admire the authoritarian response to the pandemic forget that, in contrast to what happens in many Western countries, in authoritarian regimes there will be no public debate on the measures adopted and their costs in lives, rights and freedoms. Nor will they reach social compromises to determine which rights and freedoms will have to give way to duties and obligations in future pandemics. The strength of liberal democracy lies in being able to create structures capable of subverting the prioritisation of values and goods when society is at risk, but as a result of free choice, not imposition. This, precisely, is what should ensure that the loss is not irrevocable and that the relationship between freedom and security does not lose the balance that is necessary for our lives to be truly livable. This is only feasible thanks to the freedom of expression that makes it possible to ask uncomfortable questions.

However, beyond this, what differentiates the EU from, for example, the United States is a preferential approach to solidarity, which is the value that should mark our policies in times of crisis. Moreover, this approach is certainly right, as Prainsack (2020) has repeatedly argued. Solidarity is best defined as a practice that expresses the willingness to support others with whom we recognise similarity in a relevant respect (Prainsack & Buyx, 2017). In times of tribulation, it should be the basis of our discourse, because the reasonable thing to do is to appeal to solidarity rather than freedom, when circumstances make ourselves a mortal threat to those around us. Therefore, the EU's own vision is, of course, suitable for tackling the titanic task of dealing with a public health crisis while respecting our fundamental rights.

In addition, if it is reasonable to focus on the geopolitical scope of the EU as a frame of reference, it is because, in general, its Member States have a socio-political structure that is similar to each other and vastly different from that of other political entities. They all have public health systems based on free health-care or common regulations in terms of data protection or limitation of fundamental rights, such as the right to freedom of movement. This is not only because many of them derive from rules approved by the Union itself, such as the mandatory and directly enforceable regulations, but also because they have all ratified the European Convention on Human Rights. Hence, many of the problems that may affect other places—such as inequitable access to health resources, for example—have a different nature at the European level.

I would like to clarify that in writing this text, by necessity, I have had to restrict the topics to what the limitations of a work of this type demands. I would have liked to talk more about the repercussions that the strategies implemented by the most developed countries have on others, or the role that European institutions could play, to give just two examples. However, I am sorry that this was not possible. I can attest that in the topics I have dealt with I have tried to be intellectually honest. In some of them, I have made my position clear. In others, I have necessarily been more descriptive, for the simple reason that I am not certain which is the right position. In all cases, however, I have tried to be objective in the presentation of the facts and the arguments. I hope I have succeeded, so that this is what it is intended to be, namely material for a discussion, and not what books sometimes end up being, that is to say, secular homilies.

Finally, I would like to introduce a disclaimer. This book was written in early 2022. Probably, some of the facts it contains will be out of date or will have been contradicted by reality in the following months. I regret these dyssynchronies. I am afraid they are inevitable in books that often refer to current circumstances.

Leioa, Bizkaia, Spain   Iñigo de Miguel Beriain

References

De Ruijter, A., & Weimer, M. (2021). The COVID-19 crisis: Lessons from risk regulation for EU leaders. In D. Utrilla & A. Shabbir (Eds.), *EU Law in times of pandemic* (pp. 199–205). EU Law Live Press/Comares.

Grimm, D. (2007). Proportionality in Canadian and German constitutional jurisprudence. *University of Toronto Law Journal, 57,* 383.

Prainsack, B. (2020). Solidarity in times of pandemics. *Democratic Theory, 7*(2), 124–133.

Prainsack, B., & Buyx, A. (2017). *Solidarity in biomedicine and beyond* (Vol. 33). Cambridge University Press.

Acknowledgements

I am indebted to a great many people, colleagues and friend who have helped me to make this book possible. First and foremost, to Mónica Loyo Menoyo and Shane Reilly, who made the English of the original edition really English, and to my admired colleague Barbara Prainsack, who honoured me by writing the foreword for this book.

Some of the texts included in it come from works elaborated in cooperation with Pepe Alcami, Miguel Ángel Ramiro, Jorge Ramos, Jon Rueda, Mario Santisteban or Begoña Etxeberría. Many of the ideas it contains have emerged in conversations and debates with people such as Federico de Montalvo, Vicente Bellver, Joaquín Cayón de las Cuevas, Pilar Nicolás, Emilio Armaza, Itziar Alkorta, Ana Marcos, Pablo de Lora, Ione Isasa, Emma Fernández de Uzquiano, José A. Castillo, Txetxu Ausín, David Rodríguez-Arias, Adrian Hugo Aginagalde, Vera Lucía Raposo, Carlos Álvarez, J.J. Gómez Cadenas, Daniel Jové, Gorka Orive, Ugo Mayor, Juan Ignacio Pérez Iglesias, Javier Gil, David Alvira, Jacobo Baselga, Ignacio Estalés, Luis Arrechea and Ignacio Gascón.

I would also like to publicly acknowledge the input received over the years from multiple experts with whom I have established a unique relationship through different channels, most notably Twitter. Our discussions have helped me enormously to refine my knowledge of the science behind pandemic responses. Thank you, therefore, @YoryoBass, @mariaitapia, @jmanclus60, @Virusemergents, @OscarGenomics, @gomez_rial5, @Miss_Salmonella, @microbio, and many others that I'm surely leaving out.

José Luis Martí (the first, as far as I remember who had the audacity to defend sanitary passports when no one else did), Ivó Coca Vila, César Cierco and Angel Puyol reviewed some of the parts of this book. Last but not least, Ricardo de Lorenzo and my colleagues from the Asociación Española de Derecho Sanitario were a fundamental source of inspiration (thanks so much to you all!). Thanks to their invaluable comments, it was possible to improve many of its contents. Obviously, the errors that remain are, without a doubt, of my exclusive authorship.

Finally, this research is part of the Participatory Approaches to a New Ethical and Legal Framework for ICT (Panelfit) project. This project received funding under the European Union's H2020 research and innovation programme under grant agreement No 788039. Those who are interested in data protection issues will probably enjoy our web page at panelfit.eu.

Contents

Chapter 1
Confinement, Isolation and Tracking

1.1 Introduction

The occurrence of any disease outbreak caused by a pathogen poses a threat to public health that needs to be averted as soon as possible. This need will be more or less urgent depending on the type of threat we face. The pathogenicity (ability to cause serious or lethal disease) or infectivity (ability to be transmitted) of the agent is likely to be the key factor in determining the level of intervention required at any given time. If it can be anticipated that it will produce a situation that overwhelms the available care capacity (and any emergency capacity that may have been added), it is not possible to remain inactive. The role of the State as guarantor of public health obliges it to introduce measures to control the situation. This, however, is often not easy. The most reasonable approach is to adopt the strategy that has traditionally been used to stop an epidemic outbreak: testing to identify those who are infectious, tracing their direct contacts (i.e. people who are at risk of infection due to their proximity), isolating the former and quarantining the latter (*test-trace-isolate*).

Unfortunately, this strategy is not always feasible. There are times when there are too many cases, and it is not possible to identify them all. Suddenly, tracers find people who are **not sure how and where they got infected.** This is called community transmission. When it happens, confinement is necessary. If it is not possible to know who is infectious and who is not in the outbreak area, the best way to deal with the situation is to treat everyone in that area as infectious, extending quarantine to the entire population of it. This is called containment, which is basically a community quarantine. This is what China did in Wuhan in the COVID-19 case, with great success. The scenario becomes much more complicated when community transmission is not limited to a particular city or region. In that case, it becomes necessary to enact a nationwide containment.

I. de Miguel Beriain, *The Ethical, Legal and Social Issues of Pandemics*,
https://doi.org/10.1007/978-3-031-03818-1_1

Up to this point, the ethical discussion should not be too acrimonious. When the dead are piling up and triage has replaced the resource allocation practices we normally use, there are few other courses of action available than to resort to confinement. Where the discussion really begins is when cases are substantially reduced and a decision has to be made as to which of these two options to adopt: either to continue confinement until the agent is eradicated (or, at least, until a return to a traceability system is possible) or, conversely, to replace it with a battery of measures designed to mitigate the consequences of living with the pathogen (Bramble, 2020). In the case of COVID-19, the latter strategy was proposed by a group of infectious disease epidemiologists and public health scientists in the Great Barrington Declaration published on 4 October 2020. This document gave birth to the concept of "Focused Protection", which basically proposes to focus our protective measures on those people who are really vulnerable to a threat, the elderly over 70 in the case of COVID-19, leaving the rest of the population to go about their daily lives (Lenzer, 2020). This option was adopted more openly by some countries, such as Sweden, at first, and more covertly by many other EU members later on. There was a strong reaction to this proposal in the form of the John Snow Memorandum, drafted by a group of experts who strongly disagreed with the idea of Targeted Protection, which advocated avoiding the free circulation of the virus at all costs. Instead, the Memorandum appeals that governments should delay complete reopening until everyone, including adolescents, have been offered vaccination and uptake is high and until mitigation measures, especially adequate ventilation (through investment in CO_2 monitors and air filtration devices) and spacing (e.g. by reducing class sizes), are in place in schools. The signatories of the document consider that this strategy ensures that everyone is protected and makes it much less likely that we will need further restrictions or lockdowns in the autumn (Gurdasani et al., 2021, p. 298).

Basically, both manifestos reflect the differences between two completely opposing ways of dealing with a pandemic. The first is reactive, aimed at mitigating transmission, so that it decrees confinement as soon as cases are recorded and then gradually relaxes measures restricting rights and freedoms as long as it is possible to trace contagions. The second, on the other hand, is proactive, aimed at eliminating transmission, so that measures are introduced as the number of cases increases (Priesemann et al., 2021). The responses by different countries to the pandemic can be associated, with varying nuances, with one or other position. It is therefore important to understand, first, what are the facts, what factors play in favour of one position or the other, and second, what ethical, legal or public health policy arguments can be made for, or against, these positions. This is precisely what I will do next. Then I will outline some guidelines on how to approach this dilemma from an ethical point of view.

1.2 Mitigation and Eradication: The Facts

1.2.1 Introduction

Confinement is the most extreme measure to stop the transmission of a pathogen. Since time immemorial, it has been the last line of defence, with which terrified survivors in every age tried to escape from various pests and plagues. However, for over a century, that is, since the end of the Spanish influenza pandemic, it had not been used. The appearance of SARS-CoV-2 brought it back first in Eastern countries, with considerable success, and then in Western countries. By 18 March 2020, there were already more than 250 million people confined to their homes in the EU. This was an obvious shock, bearing in mind that, despite what had already happened in China, our authorities had assured the population that nothing remotely similar would happen here.

Generalised confinement is of varying degrees, but it never causes slight harm. At its best, it implies preventing people from leaving their place of residence for no more than a few brief moments. People cannot leave their homes except to make essential purchases; to attend health centres, services and establishments; to travel to work when it is a necessary activity and it is impossible to work from home; or to care for the elderly, minors, dependants, disabled or particularly vulnerable people. Schools and kindergartens remain closed, while homes for the elderly are isolated. In one of its cruelest consequences, the sick die alone because their relatives are not allowed to enter overcrowded health facilities. Moreover, we bury them clandestinely, as if they had been murdered by a secret society. In cases of even stricter confinement, such as the one China decreed in Wuhan, sacrifices are even greater. The population is not allowed to leave their homes for any reason whatsoever, with designated and authorised workers taking care of supplies. Those who rebel, or who do not understand, or those who do not manage to live in this isolation are hunted down like serial killers and neutralised carelessly. Confinement, in short, involves an enormous effort that entails great losses. There are, at the very least, economic costs, health costs and costs related to children's education that we must bear in mind when debating the morality of the measure and its proportionality in relation to the ends to be achieved.

1.2.2 The Economic Cost

Confinement always entails a significant, or even absolute, paralysis of economic activity, depending on whether it is more or less strict. The consequences are not insignificant. The stoppage causes the closure of some companies, which increases unemployment figures. It often leads to a temporary reduction in the workers' income, which is particularly serious for those who work by themselves. In all these cases, moreover, problems of equity arise, since it is often the most disadvantaged social classes that are the most affected by the circumstances. At first sight, therefore, it seems to make sense to avoid them or at least to try not to prolong them from an economic point of view. Some authors, such as Sewell, have tried to determine whether this cost outweighed the savings made in return by estimating the number of years of quality life saved as a result. Their conclusion was that this was not the case (Sewell, 2020). Other studies, such as Baqaee et al. (2020), drew cost/benefit comparisons between different types of reopenings, concluding that a partial reopening provided little advantage over a more generalised reopening.

Against this, there are arguments stating that the implementation of confinements would be perfectly justified for several reasons. Firstly, we cannot compare costs and benefits only based on lives saved. It should be borne in mind that "the economic costs of the great lockdown, while very high, might still be lower than the medical costs that an unchecked spread of the virus would have caused" (Gros, 2020). Against this argument, some authors have in turn stressed that this overlooks the fact that it does not appear that States or regions that have opted for stricter containment have achieved much better results than those that adopted the opposite alternative (Lemoine, 2021), with the obvious exceptions of Australia or New Zealand, which are not easily comparable to other Western countries that are less isolated.

Another strong argument is that the losses by an economy that subjects several sectors to multiple constraints over the medium to long term are likely to be much greater than those by one that shuts down all activity but for a short period of time. After all, there are sectors, such as tourism and leisure, that maintain only minimal activity when different waves impose consecutive restrictions. They are the paradigmatic example of the fact that it is better to have one very strong impact than many smaller-scale blows.

1.2.3 Health Costs

Confinements also have a cost in terms of health. Isolation leads to loneliness and lack of physical exercise, potentially resulting in high blood pressure, heart diseases, disability or impaired cognitive functions (Gerst-Emerson & Jayawardhana, 2015; Ganesan et al., 2021). It is estimated that within the excess deaths that occurred during the pandemic in high-income countries, 20–50% were not directly due to COVID-19 (Kontis et al., 2020; Woolf et al., 2020). In addition, according to some authors, strict containment prevents a pathogen from reaching those parts of the population that could, in principle, generate natural immunity without putting their health at serious risk. Viewed in population terms, this would pose a danger to the most vulnerable, as it would deprive them of a formidable protective shield, the one created by herd immunity.

Mental health is another major victim of a confinement that substantially alters our lifestyles and personal relationships. The severity of the damage is, however, debatable. Some studies have argued that confinement may cause an increase in suicide rates (Yling, 2020). Some available data, however, do not seem to support this (Appleby, 2021; John et al., 2020; Mourouvaye et al., 2021). However, it is more than likely that the real impact of COVID-19 will be seen in the medium to long term (AMA, 2020). It is then later on that we will be able to quantify the real number of suicides it may have caused. In any case, there are many other mental disorders that are clearly associated with confinement, such as emotional disturbances, depression, stress, low mood, irritability, insomnia, post-traumatic stress symptoms, anger and emotional exhaustion (Brooks et al., 2020). It is also the case that these disorders typically affect vulnerable populations to a greater extent. As Joffe writes:

> Unequal structural determinants of health meant that disadvantaged minorities have experienced a greater toll from the COVID-19 "Great Lockdown" (117), with contributors including lower income (e.g., economic and job insecurity), homelessness or crowding at home (and in transportation), worse health care (and pre-existing health disparities), and inability to work from home (e.g., for essential, manual, and temporary workers) (Joffe, 2021).

All this, of course, goes against every human being's right to health, proclaimed by Article 25 of the Universal Declaration of Human Rights and enshrined in many international treaties, such as the European Social Charter (Article 11). The question, however, is whether a strategy based on less stringent confinement, which avoids some of the effects I have just mentioned, will be better in the medium or long term. It is not easy to evaluate. Certainly, as I am writing these lines, at least one factor has become clear: the idea of defeating a pathogen by creating herd immunity in a more or less controlled way is weak. The emergence of the Omicron variant, capable of re-infecting those who had already overcome the Delta infection in the SARS-CoV-2 pandemic, is the most tangible proof. In addition, the very fact of multiplying contacts favours the emergence of new variants capable of escaping the immunity provided by the previous ones. Moreover, a mitigation strategy that avoids confinement will cause much more workload for health professionals, because there will be more infections and more hospitalisations. This, on the one hand, will put them at greater risk and, on the other hand, will cause them considerable deterioration in terms of health, due to the stress and exhaustion that continuous effort produces. Finally, we must not forget the obvious: objectively, more infections mean more deaths and more physical consequences (think of the "long COVID" case). It is also important to consider that dying in the company of loved ones is not the same as dying alone in hospital. Not to mention what it means not to be able to say goodbye in a public funeral. These, in fact, are some of the great dramas caused by COVID-19. The fact that many of us did not experience this suffering (nor was it shown to us) does not mean it did not have an intensity difficult to measure. Hence, by choosing an eradication strategy, we are not only trying to reduce deaths but also much suffering. However, how can we recognise when we should consider one scenario a failure and switch to another?

1.2.4   Costs for Minors

Finally, strict confinement entails particular suffering for those who, in principle, should be especially protected, namely, children and adolescents. In the case of COVID-19, the closure of schools and the prohibition to go out or to socialise with other people in their age range placed a considerable burden on these age groups. This is not easily reconcilable with the best interests of the child as declared by the *Convention* on the *Rights of the Child*, proclaimed and adopted by the UN General Assembly on 20 November 1989. Therefore, it seems reasonable to allow minors to resume their activities as soon as possible (Bell et al., 2020).

However, those who suggest the eradication strategy have a good counter-argument. While accepting that the suffering of children is enormous in confinement, limiting ourselves to mitigating contagion will be even worse for them, for several reasons. The first is that schools and colleges are a major focus of mass transmission, which we cannot deal with except by isolating those infected and confining their close contacts. Second, if we agree only to mitigate the effects of contagion, then minors become a reservoir of infection, thus fuelling the spread of a pathogen. Third, it must be stressed that this approach entails a clear risk for children who are particularly vulnerable to the pathogen. Their health would be more exposed than if we were to opt for an eradication strategy, with confinement when there is community transmission and severe isolation and quarantine measures in the event of any cases. It is, of course, difficult to know which of the two approaches offers the best guarantees for children's rights.

1.3   Ethical, Legal, Political Analysis

Confinements are, in sum, a devastating measure, which not only seriously harm the development of minors but also jeopardise our system of coexistence, causing terrible effects on the economy and on people's health. So much that the famous trade-off between the two factors comes down to which of the two should bear the brunt of the damage. As Singer and Plant (2020) state, one has to be somewhat naïve to think that it is possible to preserve both. From this observation, the question inevitably arises as to whether public policies that promote confinement are legitimate or at what point they cease to be so. This, of course, will depend first and foremost on whether we are able to justify that the introduction of lockdown passes the cost/benefit test. No one doubts that the use of this tool is harmful. Nonetheless, this does not determine its ethical qualification. A pandemic often forces us to choose between different evils of enormous magnitude. Having to choose the weaker evil is an ethical obligation, even if it means subordinating individual interests to those of the population.

The problem, as I have shown in the previous section, is that it is extraordinarily complex to value whether a mitigation policy is more or less successful than a restriction policy in terms of cost/benefit, not only because there are serious doubts about what is less harmful in terms of the major assets affected—economy, health, right to education and emotional development, etc.—but also because the different variables to be compared are not expressed in common units (Singer & Plant, 2020). Some authors, such as Paul Frijters (2020), have tried to do this by appealing to concepts such as quality-adjusted *life years* (QALYs). This is not convincing, especially for those who do not consider life as a trade-off commodity. Moreover, the specific characteristics of a new pathogen, how they will affect each other, their resistance to eradication strategies, etc., will change markedly from one crisis scenario to another. This implies that any analysis should be treated with the necessary caution.

It is therefore likely that in every pandemic decisions will have to be made on the basis of weak data. We will hardly know if the selected path is the right one when we choose it. In any case, there are some ethical considerations worth introducing. Whatever the decision, the point is to try to minimise the harm caused to the individuals concerned. Thus, for example, in the case of their mental health, it is undeniable that "a lockdown that has left survivors mentally unhealthy is not necessarily unjustifiable from a public mental health ethics perspective, insofar as the responsible authorities have taken real steps to substantially neutralize threats to population mental health by effective ex ante prevention and ex post intervention measures" (Cheung & Ip, 2020, p. 506).

Similarly, governments can provide financial support to maintain jobs or mitigate the situation of those who have already lost them. They can also freeze rents or prohibit evictions to prevent individuals and businesses from being seriously harmed by the situation. These and other measures could work to reduce the economic crisis caused by lockdown (Bramble, 2020). Finally, we must not forget that if the mitigation strategy is chosen, it must be accompanied by the adoption of measures that actually serve to reduce risks, such as (in the case of COVID-19) subsidies for air renewal equipment or the provision of affordable diagnostic tests. The key to an ethical judgement, in summary, will depend not so much on the decision taken, but, to a large extent, on the appropriate introduction of safeguards aimed at alleviating the harm caused as a result.

The debate becomes even more complex if the threat is not evenly distributed among all social groups. In such a scenario, it is necessary to ask what amount of sacrifice we can impose on one part of society to protect another. In the case of SARS-CoV-2, confinement meant considerable harm to all, but the benefit of this strategy to children, young people and the elderly was certainly not the same. The logic behind the "Focused Protection" proposal is precisely to avoid this imbalance by minimising the restrictions imposed on those who will least enjoy its consequences. Moreover, it was assumed that we would thus be promoting a long-term benefit for all at the same time, thanks to a group immunity acquired in an accelerated manner. As I have already mentioned, this latter belief has been profoundly discredited by the practical impossibility of achieving such immunity. Nevertheless, the consistency of the underlying objection remains. In addition, it is not bad that it does. What this debate really brings to the table is what the objective of a confinement should be. For, in reality, there can be two. The first is to prevent the most vulnerable population from becoming infected. The second is simply to buy time to prevent a high number of infections in a narrow time interval from collapsing health care or to buy time for science to develop efficient vaccines or remedies against the pathogen. It is, of course, also possible that the introduction of lockdowns may seek to achieve both ends. However, it is clear that the more ambitious the objectives to be achieved, the harsher (longer or more repeated) the confinement will be, hence the attitudes adopted, for example, by the governments of China and Australia during the SARS-CoV-2 pandemic, which managed to eradicate the virus and keep its spread under control but only in exchange for great sacrifices in terms of public freedoms. Whether this is always worth it or not is complicated. Assuming that confinement causes a net harm to a social group, not only in the short term but also in the long one, it will involve deciding whether the benefits to one part of society justify the sacrifices to another. If not, compensation mechanisms will have to be introduced, and determining what these will be is another problem of considerable dimensions. This seems particularly relevant if we bear in mind that those who suffer most from the economic effects of a closure are often the most disadvantaged social classes (Bell et al., 2020). Equity demands that, if we are not going to reopen first, which implies a sacrifice of their interests, we should at least offer them some compensation.

Worse still, if the interests of some of those affected (children, people with disabilities) do not coincide with those of their representatives, it will be difficult to know whether our decisions will be disinterested. As can be seen, there is no easy answer to these questions, but it is good to know from the outset that balancing the interests of the various stakeholders is likely to be one of the dilemmas we will have to face. Better to do so before the crisis erupts, when we do not yet know what role each social group will have to play.

However, there will be those who do not accept these initial reflections as valid, on the grounds that public intervention cannot be based on causing harm deliberately to some people in order to safeguard others. Indeed, from a deontological ethical point of view, it is controversial to place the harm caused by a natural catastrophe and that by a public authority's action at the same level. If we were to draw a parallel with the well-known tram dilemma, we could say that a pandemic is the train that is heading towards several people and the public health intervention is the hand that pulls the lever to divert it towards the track where it will end up ramming a lone individual (Frijters, 2020). A strict deontologist would probably consider this action that changes the course of events to be morally unacceptable, since it involves using human beings—the person we divert the tram towards, the victims of the confinement—as mere means to save the interests of other people. This, according to their argument, would be a violation of human dignity.

The problem with such statements is, first of all, that they give too much weight to the action/omission distinction. This, as I will underline in other sections of this work, can lead to counter-intuitive consequences. We should be wary of this apparent dilemma. On the other hand, the utilitarian objection inevitably arises: by avoiding the harm caused by a preventive intervention on certain individuals, those who omit to adopt it end up causing disproportionate harm to the health of other individuals who, although not identifiable at the time of adopting (or not) the preventive measure, will eventually suffer its consequences (Quigley & Harris, 2008). This does not match well with the logic that we usually apply to the reaction to outbreaks. In such cases, we have no problem confining some people, sometimes for prolonged periods of time, in order to stop the outbreak, even if this constitutes considerable harm to their interests or health. If we were to accept the logic of my rejoinder, these policies would have to be changed. This is unreasonable, given that a State's duty is to protect its citizens from threats such as those posed by a public health crisis.

It should also be borne in mind that those making the decision on whether to declare lockdown or its duration should try to avoid basing it on opinion polls. If anything, we know that there are multiple biases that favour the introduction of measures that may provide us with a short-term benefit, even if they are detrimental in the long term, or that will lead us to favour action over inaction (Joffe, 2021). This, of course, is compounded by the fact that it is easier for us to identify the victims and the causes of their suffering. This, again, creates a biased effect in favour of taking measures such as confinement that is hardly ethically justifiable (Singer & Plant, 2020). From the other side of the colour spectrum, as time goes on, pandemic fatigue (Michie et al., 2020) makes it more difficult for a ruler to adopt measures that may be necessary, but which clash with the wishes of the majority of the population. In such scenarios, there is a particular need for science in the decision-making, so that policy-makers are able to overcome the pressure from citizens who are neither optimally informed nor able to avoid bias. Only in this way will it be possible to deal with such a complex scenario. Therefore, what ethics demands in these cases are appropriate procedures rather than concrete answers.

Finally, I would like to end this section by making two considerations that I believe to be essential. The first is to point out that lockdowns, for all the reasons I have already mentioned, should be conceived as a last resort, a tool which, if implemented, means that everything else has failed. By this I mean that we should not be tempted to ignore the necessary improvement of our health systems and planning for such situations on the basis of an over-reliance on this measure. This is not an unfounded fear (Joffe, 2021). As is well-known, public health spending is not so popular. If it does its job, the result will be barely noticeable. If it fails, however, it will be easy to conclude that we have taken away resources needed for clinical care (Quigley & Harris, 2008), causing serious problems for the person responsible for this expenditure. We must, however, manage to steer clear of electioneering considerations. The awareness of the harm that confinement entails demands an adequate preparation for situations such as that posed by COVID-19. This is the least we owe to the generations that have suffered the consequences of what we have experienced the most.

The second has to do—more than ever—with ethics. As I have already reiterated, there is too high an uncertainty to be able to apply the principle of proportionality correctly to a situation involving confinement. Beyond its appropriateness, it is extremely complex to know whether it will be the least restrictive alternative. It will also be hard to identify whether the balance between the rights and freedoms suspended and the assets protected is always in favour of the latter. What is important, in any case, is to base our decisions on reasons of which we are proud, after a public discussion with perfect transparency. When we do this, we are going one step further than simply responding to a contemporary challenge: we are making a commitment to the kind of ethics we want to prevail in the future. Awareness of this is absolutely essential, because it will condition (for the better, I hope) the debate. It will make us aware that, if we make decisions on the basis of ideas, for example, that the vulnerable are expendable, we will be creating a world of which we will not be proud. If, on the other hand, the choice is precisely to defend the interests of those in greater need of protection, even if it turns out to be unsuccessful, this is something we will be able to explain to our children without being ashamed of ourselves. We cannot be sure that we will get the best possible results, but we must make sure that we choose the right reasons for taking the measures to achieve them, because they will define what we will become as a society when the storm subsides.

1.4   Test, Isolation and Adherence

The response to a pandemic, in the absence of community transmission, is based on identifying those affected and their direct contacts so that they can be isolated or quarantined, respectively. This is undoubtedly the most efficient strategy to eliminate the problem: less polemic and probably more successful than mass vaccination (think of New Zealand, China or Japan, which controlled the pandemic well without resorting to this mechanism) and much less costly than confinement, moreover, with hardly any moral problems. I am aware that there are those who consider even the obligation to undergo a test capable of determining their infectivity to be an unacceptable intrusion upon their right to bodily integrity or privacy. This makes no sense at all, unless they are prepared to accept that breathalyser or drug tests to control dangerous driving should not be allowed either. I do not know many people who are capable of taking that position seriously.

   The problems with the testing strategy do not stem from its moral acceptability, but from the real possibility of implementing it. Of course, this is only feasible if, first of all, we have the capacity to correctly identify infectious people, or at least, those who are seriously likely to be infectious. This requires even earlier tests with sufficient specificity and sensitivity to distinguish who is infectious and who is not. This is extremely complicated. Sometimes we do not use the available tests in the most appropriate way. In the case of COVID-19, some authors have hypothesised that the reference test (the gold standard), i.e. PCR, is overly sensitive, leading us to consider people as infectious when they are not. Hence, their proposal is to use less sensitive tests more frequently (Mina et al., 2020; Larremore et al., 2021). Clearly, this requires careful consideration for the future. In a public health crisis caused by a pathogen, there is a need for tests that are sensitive and specific, identifying as positive only those who are actually infectious, not the infected who do not transmit the agent. Too many false positives lead to unnecessary loss of rights and freedoms and avoidable economic damage. If, on the other hand, there are too many false-negative results, infections will spread, because there will be people with a high infectious load who will act with a false sense of security. The same, of course, applies to serological tests, hence the importance of promoting technological improvement on this point.

However, the issue that raises the greatest complexity both from an ethical and legal point of view, and from a public health policy perspective, is that of adherence to isolation and quarantine measures. This is a crucial issue, because there is little point in having adequate testing if we cannot ensure compliance with isolation and quarantine. In principle, one might think that this should not be a major problem. The assumption is that in a pandemic situation everyone will try to do what they can to prevent avoidable infections from occurring. In reality, multiple studies show that this does not happen in practice, especially as time passes and the situation does not improve definitively (SPI-B, 2020).

Why does this happen? Why do infected people avoid isolation? Why do their contacts not quarantine themselves? In principle, this is a strange behaviour. We usually assume that citizens behave in solidarity in an emergency situation. Several factors come together to prevent this idyllic scenario from becoming a reality. To begin with, isolation is simply impossible if we are unaware of our infectious status because we are asymptomatic. Moreover, it may be that, even if we are aware of our own dangerousness, we may prefer not to behave as expected. Indeed, the prospect of having to isolate oneself for at least 10 days is not a pleasant one. It is a home arrest that many people cannot afford (because they might see their salary reduced or be fired) or do not want to face (because they do not want to deprive themselves of their freedom for that length of time). In countries where there is a high degree of social solidarity, or where the State is able to adequately compensate citizens who have to be separated from others, those affected are more likely to put aside their own interests and behave in solidarity (Patel et al., 2021; Bodas & Peleg, 2020). If this is not the case, there will be many instances of non-compliance with isolation or quarantine, especially among the most economically vulnerable population groups (Denford et al., 2021). As the economic situation worsens and fatigue with restrictions increases, this number rises. Even more so, if the behaviour of those who are to exercise leadership tasks is not exemplary, as the "Cummings effect" in the UK shows. Dominic Cummings, the chief adviser to British Prime Minister Boris Johnson, travelled 264 miles from London to Durham with his sick wife and son to visit his parents, despite official advice not to visit any non-cohabitant. When the press revealed this, the prime minister backed his adviser. This greatly reduced public confidence in the response to the crisis and solidarity in the effort (Fancourt et al., 2020). Moreover, if citizens do not cooperate with public health authorities, the classical epidemiological surveillance and control system collapses.

One might think that this would be solved by the coercive imposition of tests and quarantines or supervised isolation when necessary. Unfortunately, this is legally complex, as it implies the introduction of invasive surveillance systems that are not compatible with our fundamental rights framework (I will return to these issues in the next section). For instance, police officers could knock on the door of an isolated person's home, but if they do not open, this would only demonstrate that they had not received the police officers. Proving that they are not at home would require a warrant and forcible entry into their houses. Clearly, this is out of the question. The more feasible alternative—for the police to carry out random checks on the population, penalising those who breach quarantine or isolation in some way (in the UK, e.g. with a fine of £10,000)—would require, among other things, that law enforcement agencies access databases of those affected held by the health authority. This would in my view constitute a surely disproportionate measure, a hardly justifiable attack on the right to informational self-determination of individuals, enshrined in the General Data Protection Regulation (Regulation (EU) 2016/679 of the European Parliament and of the Council of 27 April 2016 on the protection of individuals with regard to the processing of personal data and on the free movement of such data and repealing Directive 95/46/EC, GDPR),[1] to which I will refer at length below.

Moreover, we must consider that such initiatives would probably not be suitable to achieve their original objectives. If we impose strict surveillance and control measures on people who test positive, we will create a greater problem than the one we wish to avoid (Independent SAGE, 2021). Many will skip testing if they believe it will result in isolation. Unless their health is truly dire, they will try to keep away from seeking medical attention at all costs. If they do, the consequences could be dramatic. Not only will they put their own health at risk, but they will also expose others to contagion. In addition, many people will no longer cooperate efficiently in tracing efforts in order to ensure that those they cite as contacts may avoid the probable loss of freedom. The closer the relationship between those affected, the more likely this effect is to occur. Thus, citizens will do their "private" tracing, informing those concerned of the situation, but without notifying the authorities, harmfully superimposing their private interest on the public interest. The more precarious the situation of those affected, the more likely that all this may happen, of course.

Escaping from this web of interests is complicated. So much so, I fear, that the reasonable action to take is to plan the strategy on the assumption that these situations will occur more and more frequently. Alternatives to mere sanctions must be sought when the main weapon—conviction, support, complicity—does not work. In the next chapter, I will discuss the possibilities offered by immunity certificates to respond to systemic failures. They will not allow us to keep those affected at home, but they will prevent them from entering particularly sensitive spaces where contagion is likely. As we shall explain, they can be an effective remedy. After all, it is much easier to prevent someone from entering my home than to keep them locked up in theirs. Before we get to it, however, I would like to end this chapter with a particularly interesting topic in the context of identifying contagion in a pandemic scenario: the use of location and contact data through applications linked to mobile devices.

---

[1] Regulation (EU) 2016/679 of the European Parliament and of the Council of 27 April 2016 on the protection of natural persons with regard to the processing of personal data and on the free movement of such data, and repealing Directive 95/46/EC, GDPR.

1.5   Technology to Our Aid: Geospatial Data as a Response Tool

1.5.1   Introduction

One of the most hopeful contributions at the beginning of the SARS-CoV-2 pandemic was technological developments using personal data, to be more precise, geospatial data, which can be divided into two specific types, proximity data and location data. These two are not the same. Proximity data reveals information about how close one device is to another. It does not tell us where they are actually located. It only focuses on the fact that they share a nearby location. Wallet alerts that notify you if you have left something behind are excellent examples of tools that use this data. They do not process any information about the whereabouts of your phone or wallet. They simply work based on the distance between the two. They do not need to know your specific location. They only need to alert you when they are too far away from you. Proximity data therefore only provides information about the relative position of the user (rather their device), i.e. their position in relation to another person's (or their device). Location data, on the other hand, reports position in absolute terms: where you are or have been, but reveals nothing about your social interactions.

The "good" news is that our mobile devices continuously emit geospatial data, which is captured by different devices, whether we are using GPS (Global Positioning System), connecting to a Wi-Fi signal or using a Bluetooth beacon. We therefore have an inordinate amount of information that can be used in the response to a pandemic. Proximity data helps to trace contacts by indicating who has been near whom at any given time. Location data, on the other hand, can serve to discover outbreaks or track their evolution. It can also, of course, be used to determine whether a person who needs to be placed in isolation or confinement is actually where he or she is supposed to be. For instance, this is what we use them for when we force people under security measures or home arrest to wear a bracelet. In the case of COVID-19, there were numerous examples of the use of this data to monitor compliance with isolation and quarantine measures, especially in East Asian countries. As described by Costica Dumbrava in a European Parliament Policy Report prepared by (EPRS | European Parliamentary Research Service 2020):

> China obliges citizens to use an app that tracks their movement. The Alipay Health Code system combines location data and other information (e.g. a health survey) to score persons based on their contagion risk, and restrict mobility. Taiwan rolled out a phone-based electronic fence that monitors individuals' movements and alerts police if quarantine is not respected. In Hong Kong, persons who have been placed in quarantine must carry a location-tracking wristband. South Korea has launched an app to monitor people on lockdown and uses a public database of known patients (with additional information about their age, gender, occupation, and travel routes). In Thailand, people arriving at airports are obliged to download an app to help monitor their movements.

In Western countries, the use of proximity data is admissible under certain conditions. However, imitating the initiatives taken by East Asian countries based on the use of location data is clearly impossible nowadays, as it clashes head-on with the importance attributed to the right to informational self-determination and/or privacy by our legal systems. Their use, once anonymised for epidemiological purposes, is another matter. Let me clarify this aspect in the following section.

1.5.2   The Use of Location Data and in the EU Context

The use of location data regime in the European context is based on the General Data Protection Regulation,[2] which provides the general legal framework, as well as on the so-called ePrivacy Directive,[3] now in the process of being replaced by a regulation, which specifically refers to the data at hand. According to its Article 9(1):

Where location data other than traffic data, relating to users or subscribers of public communications networks or publicly available electronic communications services, can be processed, such data may only be processed when they are made anonymous, or with the consent of the users or subscribers to the extent and for the duration necessary for the provision of a value added service. The service provider must inform users or subscribers, before obtaining their consent, of the type of location data other than traffic data that will be processed, the purpose and duration of the processing and whether the data will be transmitted to a third party for the purpose of providing the value-added service. Users and subscribers shall be given the possibility to withdraw their consent to the processing of location data other than traffic data at any time.

Under this clause, in principle, public authorities could only process personal geospatial data if the user had given consent. However, derogations to these rights and obligations are possible pursuant to Art. 15, when they constitute a necessary, appropriate and proportionate measure within a democratic society for certain objectives (*"to safeguard national security* (i.e. *State security), defence, public security, and the prevention, investigation, detection and prosecution of criminal offences or of unauthorized use of the electronic communications system, as referred to in Article 13(1) of Directive 95/46"*).

In light of this legal framework, the European Data Protection Board (EDPB), which is an independent European body that contributes to the consistent application of data protection rules across the European Union, produced, in April 2020, some guidelines.[4] Its main recommendations were as follows:

---

[2] Regulation (EU) 2016/679 of the European Parliament and of the Council of 27 April 2016 on the protection of natural persons with regard to the processing of personal data and on the free movement of such data, and repealing Directive 95/46/EC.

[3] Directive 2002/58/EC of the European Parliament and of the Council of 12 July 2002 concerning the processing of personal data and the protection of privacy in the electronic communications sector, Directive on privacy and electronic communications.

[4] Guidelines 04/2020 on the use of location data and contact tracing tools in the context of the COVID-19 pandemic on how to use geospatial data in cases of public health crises.

- Location data collected by electronic communications providers may only be transmitted to authorities or other third parties if they have been anonymised by the provider or, in the case of data indicating the geographical position of a user's terminal equipment, which are not traffic data, with the prior consent of the users (point 10).
- The storage of information on the user's device or access to already stored information is only allowed if (a) the user has given his consent or (b) the storage and/ or access are strictly necessary for the information society service explicitly requested by the user (point 11).
- As regards the re-use of data collected by an information society service provider for modelling purposes, further conditions must be met. Indeed, where data have been collected in accordance with Art. 5(3) of the ePrivacy Directive, they may only be further processed with the additional consent of the data subject or on the basis of a Union or Member State law which constitutes a necessary and proportionate measure in a democratic society to safeguard the purposes referred to in Article 23(1) of the GDPR (point 13).

From these indications, it is clear that European data protection regulations make it difficult for the authorities to use our location data to monitor our movements. It will be even more complex (impossible, I would say) to authorise their use if this means using bracelets or similar devices to prevent us from resorting to the simple trick of leaving our mobile phone at home or to make up for the lack of it, as was done in Hong Kong (Pollicino & Gregorio, 2021).

What the rule does allow, however, is the use of pre-anonymised aggregated data to monitor the evolution of a crisis. This has become increasingly important in recent years, as big data analysis tools have reached a certain maturity (Wirtz et al., 2021). A model built using AI tools by companies such as BlueDot and Metabiota not only anticipated but also explored the impact of the virus in China in 2019, long before any disease control centre (Allam et al., 2020). Indeed, AI-based systems using this data make it possible to detect, identify and track outbreaks in real or nearly real time to help contain the spread of disease (Ghayvat et al., 2021; Mitchell, 2018).

European regulations, as I have just mentioned, allow the use of anonymised data for these purposes, but their use entails some issues that should be considered. Firstly, it is possible that the data may be de-anonymised, which poses an obvious risk to the privacy of those involved, especially since most people are not even aware that they are sharing them. Hence, their range of vulnerability is high. This should force us to be extremely cautious in determining who would access this information. Indeed, the European Data Protection Supervisor, Wiewiorowski, has stressed that access to anonymised data should be limited to authorised experts in spatial epidemiology, data protection and data science. Furthermore, he underlined that "such developments usually do not contain the possibility to step back when the emergency is over. I would like to underline that such a solution should continue to be recognised as extraordinary".[5] This is especially important considering that data aggregation needs someone to collect the raw data and blend it. In principle, this could be done by means of privacy protection software embedded in the collection mechanisms. However, in practice data is often channelled through a data broker (Stanley & Granick, 2020). This is not a perfect scenario. Strong safeguards should be implemented to reinforce privacy protection.

Second, depending on the origin of the aggregated data, it is likely that its degree of social representation is inaccurate. Indeed, context and marginalisation matter with location data (Graham & Zook, 2013). This creates issues of inequality, as some social classes (especially those who do not use the specific devices or capabilities that enable the data) would be under-represented in the analysis and subsequent decision-making (Frith & Saker, 2020). Making public health decisions on datasets that do not represent populations and demographics correctly "could leave out whole populations, and misrepresent others, and lead to a deployment of health care resources that is not only biased and unfair—skewed towards wealthy neighbourhoods, for example—but ineffective from a public health perspective" (Stanley & Granick, 2020).

In summary, although the use of anonymised data does not create fundamental social, ethical and legal issues, there are some conditions that must be properly adopted if any potential danger to citizens' privacy is to be avoided: data aggregators must disclose sufficient information about the protocols and procedures used to anonymise the data and allow independent, external researchers to check whether they are effective. In addition, data controllers and policy makers must disclose how they draw conclusions from these data or how they are used to inform public health interventions and the limits and risks associated with this analysis. There must also be a filter capable of uncovering major biases that emerge, and policies to counteract these must be implemented. Finally, public authorities should ensure that they do not share too much information, to avoid stigmatisation of specific citizens or social groups.

1.5.3 Proximity Data

More controversial, of course, is the use of proximity data for tracking purposes through apps. At the beginning of the SARS-CoV-2 pandemic, this appeared to be an extremely useful development to overcome the limitations of human-developed tracking. In the EU context, the Commission supported the use of proximity data for traceability purposes very early on. In April 2020, the Commission adopted a Recommendation[6] aimed at promoting a coordinated pan-European approach to the

---

[5] https://www.reuters.com/article/us-health-coronavirus-telecoms-eu/vodafone-deutsche-telekom-6-other-telcos-to-help-eu-track-virus-idUSKBN21C36G

[6] Recommendation (EU) 2020/518 of 8 April 2020 on a common Union toolkit for the use of technology and data to combat and overcome the COVID-19 crisis, in particular as regard mobile applications and the use of anonymised mobility data.

use of mobile applications for contact tracing, among other purposes. The document included in its Recital 25 some concrete ideas on the main ethical and legal issues at stake: "public health authorities and research institutions should process personal data only where adequate, relevant and limited to what is necessary, and should apply appropriate safeguards such as pseudonymisation, aggregation, encryption and decentralization".

This paragraph clearly shows some of the general recommendations by the European institutions on app localisation, which, moreover, reflect the considerations introduced by *Digital Rights Ireland*, the landmark decision of the Court of Justice of the EU (CJEU) in these matters.[7] Shortly afterwards, on 17 April 2020, the European Parliament adopted a resolution,[8] generally adopting the Commission's recommendations.

The EDPB's position was reflected in the Guidelines 04/2020 that I mentioned earlier. There is no draconian stance in favour of a decentralised management system, even though it is probably the one that best fits the data minimisation principle of the GDPR. However, from the general context of the Guidelines, there is a strong concern to ensure that there is never any data processing incompatible with the rights proclaimed in the GDPR and that its legitimacy is ensured. Particularly relevant is that document's point 29, which recommends the processing of such data on the basis of the need to fulfil a task carried out in the public interest, i.e. Article 6(1) (e) of the GDPR, when public authorities provide a service based on a mandate conferred by law and in accordance with the legal requirements in force. However, the possibility to process data without the data subject's consent does not represent a serious infringement of the data subject's autonomy, as point 24 of the GDPR underlines that the installation and use of the applications must be voluntary. This implies that individuals who choose not to use such applications, or are unable to use them, should not be disadvantaged. So if someone does not want a State to process their data without their consent, they could simply not install the app. In any case, moreover, point 31 of the same Guidelines specified that, in case of recourse to the public interest as a source of legitimacy, specific safeguards should be introduced. Textually:

The lawful basis for the use of contact tracing applications should, however, incorporate meaningful safeguards including a reference to the voluntary nature of the application. A clear specification of purpose and explicit limitations concerning the further use of personal data should be included, as well as a clear identification of the controller(s) involved. The categories of data as well as the entities to, and purposes for which, the personal data may be disclosed should also be identified. Depending on the level of interference, additional safeguards should be incorporated, taking into account the nature, scope and

---

[7] Judgment of the Court (Grand Chamber), 8 April 2014. Digital Rights Ireland Ltd. v Minister for Communications, Marine and Natural Resources and Others and Kärntner Landesregierung and Others. Joined Cases C 293/12 and C 594/12. ECLI:EU:C:2014:238.

[8] European Parliament Resolution of 17 April 2020 on coordinated Union action to combat the COVID-19 pandemic and its consequences (2020/2616(RSP)) (2021/C 316/01).

purposes of the processing. Finally, the EDPB also recommends including, as soon as practicable, the criteria to determine when the application shall be dismantled and which entity shall be responsible and accountable for making that determination.

Member States proceeded to develop their own applications along these lines. Almost all of them chose a decentralised system and all opted to allow citizens to decide whether or not to notify their positive to the system. This, of course, was a decisive move in favour of a balance between privacy and the defence of public health. Unfortunately, even in such a rights-respecting framework, the implementation of these technologies will always present some considerable ethical problems. To begin with, the use of digital technology opens up a considerable equity gap between middle/high-income and low-income social strata or those living in better or worse connected regions. Parts of the population will not have access to broadband signals, smartphones or wearable technology such as smartwatches (Whitelaw et al., 2020). In the specific case of the apps developed by most European countries in the COVID-19 case, the situation was aggravated because they were designed for the latest generations of mobile devices and did not work with older ones (Poillot et al., 2021, p. 149). This is not ethically acceptable. To this, of course, it must be added the classic considerations of the need to respect users' privacy. I do not think, however, that they are of particular importance in a system as protective as the EU's, which, as I have expressed, in addition to granting the data subject a wide range of rights, provides for essential guarantees, such as the systematic deletion of data every 2 weeks or the pseudonymisation of data.

Beyond these issues, the system's apparent uselessness is of particular concern even if fundamental rights were not violated. Overall, the operation of apps was a painful failure in Western countries, a defeat that contrasts with the successes of Asian countries. Although it was initially considered (Fraser Group, 2020) that the necessary rate of downloading and use to ensure the success of the measure was 60% of the population (it was later shown that much lower percentages were also reasonably useful), this figure was only ever achieved in Ireland. In the rest of the Member States, it was rare to exceed 30%, the norm being around 20% (Poillot et al., 2021, p. 147). In such conditions, it is inevitable to ask what was the reason for such a disparate result. The problem is that it is not easy to give an answer to this question, not least because many of the Asian nations combined the use of these applications with other measures in the same time period. This makes it more complex to determine how much of their success was due to the use of this tool and not others (Poillot et al., 2021, p. 146).

In any case, it seems clear that the effectiveness of the use of tracking apps depends, first and foremost, on the percentage of the population that uses them. Besides, this is closely related, in turn, to the ability to adequately communicate their virtues or to the introduction of incentives to encourage the most reluctant part of the population to implement them. Some studies have shown that even small amounts of money would be sufficient for this purpose (Munzert et al., 2021). If this is not achieved, there is always the option of imposing sanctions on those who do not use them, assuming that we are able to give everyone the possibility to access a suitable terminal.

In the light of what I have just mentioned, one might think that choosing not to make the systems compulsory was a mistake, especially since it would not be easy to convince Europeans to use systems that were born in haste, with serious technical and organisational shortcomings. Things, I am afraid, are not that simple. There is little point in chasing people to use a tracking application if the data on who is infected and who their direct contacts are does not flow to the pandemic response managers. This, as I have already pointed out, is hard to accept on the basis of our data protection rules. Nonetheless, even if we were to overcome this difficulty, it would still be absurd to curtail our freedoms to an extreme in order to know who should be isolated or quarantined if no one is going to monitor their compliance afterwards. At this juncture, the policy suggested by the European institutions becomes coherent: if there will finally be no effective monitoring of compliance with restrictions on freedom in the face of a possible (or certain) contagion, it makes more sense to provide a tracking tool that the population can use or not at its own free will than to impose it through rigorous control. In fact, in the East Asian countries I have mentioned, the mandatory use of the app was combined with the transfer of data to databases controlled by health authorities, the use of health certificates or the use of location data to ensure compliance with strict regulations in terms of isolation and quarantine. All of this would be impossible here.

So what is left for us to do? To give up our data protection regime? I doubt whether it makes sense if we are not going to monitor the compliance by infected persons and their contacts with the appropriate measures (either through encouragement or sanctions), as I have merely pointed out above. Besides, I do not believe that this is possible unless the transmission rate is low enough to be able to use the necessary resources for this purpose. My suggestions, in short, are twofold: firstly, to strengthen information and support policies for tracking apps by (greatly) simplifying their operating system. In many countries, the difficulty involved in reporting a positive made the tool extremely difficult to use. This can and should be solved, if we need it again in the future. Secondly, I understand that it makes much more sense to change the focus of tracking from people to places. I will explain this idea carefully in the next section.

1.5.4 Tagging Venues

There is an alternative use of geospatial data to what I have explained so far, which I find much more promising: to use it for labelling spaces.[9] What is this idea about? Actually, it is relatively easy to understand with an example. Let us consider the hypothetical case of public health authorities that have identified an outbreak in a restaurant. In such cases, they usually go to the restaurant's reservation book to

---

[9] This text was originally written by Jorge Ramos and myself and published in El Mundo on 19 June 2021. It can be found here https://www.elmundo.es/ciencia-y-salud/salud/2021/06/19/60ccf2 fae4d4d8487f8b4670.html (Accessed November 22 2021).

identify who was present at the time of the contagious event and notify them via the mobile phones that the clients used to make their reservations. Obviously, this is a laborious process and not very respectful, by the way, of the GDPR. Moreover, it is impracticable when there are no bookings involved. Proper tagging of spaces would be of great help in these circumstances, as it would allow all those who have shared an infectious environment to receive a warning of danger without the human tracker ever intervening. Technically, it would work like this: venues would make a code (a QR) available to their users that they could store on their devices with an app. Public health would send on a daily basis the QRs of the venues where an outbreak has occurred, so that the user would receive the corresponding message. From there, it would be up to the user to act responsibly, of course.

The advantages of implementing such a system would be obvious. Firstly, it would allow users to have much more accurate information about any possible danger with minimal effort (swiping the QR on the device). This is especially important if we take into account that it is not the same to be in direct contact with an infected person on a terrace as inside a bar or in a well-ventilated room as in a hovel that looks more like a submarine than a restaurant. It would be much easier for the user to find out what to do if he or she knew where the danger had arisen. Moreover, we would avoid false alarms, such as contact warnings that occur, for example, in close proximity on a beach or in a park. For public health authorities, it would allow them to know, in turn, how many people were in the infectious venue (they would not know who, but how many, thanks to the structure of the system, which allows the data to be provided anonymously, i.e. without compromising the privacy of the people concerned). For human trackers, it would save many hours of work, and for hotel and catering establishments, it would allow them to offer a service that would give their customers a great deal of peace of mind. Finally, it would give us all, in general, a better understanding of where contagions are occurring. Moreover, all of this would be obtainable at almost no cost.

There are at least three objections to this system. The first is that this model would completely neglect contagion in offices or private homes. This does not seem to be consistent. Experience shows that when an outbreak occurs in a place where the people who coincide have regular contact with each other, the warning reaches its recipients without major problems. The second objection has to do with the more than likely resistance by those who have no interest in locating outbreaks. However, this does not outweigh the strength of an information policy that explains why space labelling would benefit us all in the medium and long term. Besides, for the most refractory, an administrative measure could always be passed threatening closure on any business that refuses to cooperate. The third objection is, in my view, more substantial. It would be clearly wrong, for example, if everyone visiting a department store on a given day were to receive a notice of possible infection just because someone who had never been less than 5 m away from them had entered a warning into the system. This observation is certainly pertinent. Too many cautions would cause unnecessary fatigue, leading the user, again, to switch off the system. However, this could be avoided by introducing different QRs in different parts of an establishment (e.g. in each section of a department store, or in different rooms of a restaurant). This would avoid this kind of confusion. On the basis of the reflections I have introduced, it is clear that the system offers many advantages and the obstacles to its implementation are weak. In short, it is easy to understand why this tool should be used.

References

Allam, Z., Dey, G., & Jones, D. S. (2020). Artificial intelligence (AI) provided early detection of the coronavirus (COVID-19) in China and will influence future urban health policy internationally. *Artificial Intelligence, 1*(2), 156–165.

AMA. (2020). *Joint Statement—COVID-19 impact likely to lead to increased rates of suicide and mental illness.* Retrieved December 19, 2021, from https://www.ama.com.au/media/joint-statement-covid-19-impact-likely-lead-increased-rates-suicide-and-mental-illness

Appleby, L. (2021). What has been the effect of covid-19 on suicide rates? *British Medical Journal, 372,* n834.

Baqaee, D., Farhi, E., Mina, M. J., & Stock, J. H. (2020). *Reopening scenarios* (No. w27244). National Bureau of Economic Research.

Bell, R., Butler-Jones, D., Clinton, J., Closson, T., Davidson, J., Fulford, M., et al. (2020). *Dealing with COVID-19: An open letter to Canada's Prime Minister and provincial and territorial premiers.* Retrieved October 11, 2020, from https://healthydebate.ca/opinions/an-open-letter-to-pm-covid19

Bodas, M., & Peleg, K. (2020). Income assurances are a crucial factor in determining public compliance with self-isolation regulations during the COVID-19 outbreak—Cohort study in Israel. *Israel Journal of Health Policy Research, 9*(1), 54. https://doi.org/10.1186/s13584-020-00418-w. Retrieved December 19, 2021.

Bramble, B. (2020). *Pandemic ethics: 8 big questions of COVID-19.* Bartleby Books.

Brooks, S. K., Webster, R. K, Smith, L. E., Woodland, L., Wessely, S., Greenberg, N., & Rubin, G. J. (2020). The psychological impact of quarantine and how to reduce it: Rapid review of the evidence. *The Lancet, 395*(10227), 912–920. https://doi.org/10.1016/S0140-6736(20)30460-8

Cheung, D., & Ip, E. C. (2020). COVID-19 lockdowns: A public mental health ethics perspective. *Asian Bioethics Review, 12*(4), 503–510.

Denford, S., Morton, K. S., Lambert, H., Zhang, J., Smith, L. E., Rubin, G. J., Cai, S., Zhang, T., Robin, C., Lasseter, G., Hickman, M., Oliver, I., & Yardley, L. (2021). Understanding patterns of adherence to COVID-19 mitigation measures: A qualitative interview study. *Journal of Public Health, 43*(3), 508–516.

EPRS | European Parliamentary Research Service. (2020). *Tracking mobile devices to fight coronavirus.* Retrieved December 19, 2021, from https://www.europarl.europa.eu/RegData/etudes/BRIE/2020/649384/EPRS_BRI(2020)649384_EN.pdf

Fancourt, D., Steptoe, A., & Wright, L. (2020). The cummings effect: Politics, trust, and behaviours during the COVID-19 pandemic. *Lancet (London, England), 396*(10249), 464–465. https://doi.org/10.1016/S0140-6736(20)31690-1. Retrieved December 19, 2021.

Fraser Group. (2020). *Digital contact tracing can slow or even stop coronavirus transmission and ease us out of lockdown.* University of Oxford. Retrieved December 21, 2021, from https://www.research.ox.ac.uk/Article/2020-04-16-digital-contact-tracing-can-slow-or-even-stop-coronavirus-transmission-and-ease-us-out-of-lockdown

Frijters, P. (2020). *The Corona Dilemma. Club Troppo.* Retrieved October 11, 2020, from https://clubtroppo.com.au/2020/03/21/the-corona-dilemma/

Frith, J., & Saker, M. (2020). It is all about location: Smartphones and tracking the spread of COVID-19. *Social Media + Society, 6*(3), 2056305120948257.

Ganesan, B., Al-Jumaily, A., Fong, K. N., Prasad, P., Meena, S. K., & Tong, R. K. Y. (2021). Impact of coronavirus disease 2019 (COVID-19) outbreak quarantine, isolation, and lockdown policies on mental health and suicide. *Frontiers in Psychiatry, 12*, 565190.

Gerst-Emerson, K., & Jayawardhana, J. (2015). Loneliness as a public health issue: The impact of loneliness on health care utilization among older adults. *American Journal of Public Health, 105*(5), 1013–1019. https://doi.org/10.2105/AJPH.2014.302427. Retrieved December 19, 2021.

Ghayvat, H., Awais, M., Gope, P., Pandya, S., & Majumdar, S. (2021). Recognizing suspect and predicting the spread of contagion based on mobile phone location data (counteract): A system of identifying covid-19 infectious and hazardous sites, detecting disease outbreaks based on the internet of things, edge computing, and artificial intelligence. *Sustainable Cities and Society, 69*, 102798.

Graham, M., Zook, M., & Boulton, A. (2013). Augmented reality in urban places: Contested content and the duplicity of code. *Transactions of the Institute of British Geographers, 38*(3), 464–479.

Gros, D. (2020). The great lockdown: Was it worth it. *CEPS Policy Insights, 11*.

Gurdasani, D., Drury, J., Greenhalgh, T., Griffin, S., Haque, Z., Hyde, Z., Katzourakis, A., McKee, M., Michie, S., Pagel, C., Reicher, S., Roberts, A., West, R., Yates, C., & Ziauddeen, H. (2021). Mass infection is not an option: We must do more to protect our young. *The Lancet, 398*(10297), 297–298.

Independent SAGE. (2021). *Independent sage briefing note on use of punishments in the covid response*. Retrieved December 19, 2021, from https://www.independentsage.org/wp-content/uploads/2021/02/Crime-and-punishment-John-4.1-1.pdf

Joffe, A. R. (2021). COVID-19: Rethinking the lockdown groupthink. *Frontiers in Public Health, 9*, 98.

John, A., Pirkis, J., Gunnell, D., Appleby, L., & Morrissey, J. (2020). Trends in suicide during the covid-19 pandemic. *British Medical Journal, 371*, m4352.

Kontis, V., Bennett, J. E., Rashid, T., Parks, R. M., Pearson-Stuttard, J., Guillot, M., Asaria, P., Zhou, B., Battaglini, M., Corsetti, G., McKee, M., Di Cesare, M., Mathers, C. D., & Ezzati, M. (2020). Magnitude, demographics and dynamics of the effect of the first wave of the COVID-19 pandemic on all-cause mortality in 21 industrialized countries. *Nature Medicine, 26*(12), 1919–1928.

Larremore, D. B., Wilder, B., Lester, E., Shehata, S., Burke, J. M., Hay, J. A., Tambe, M., Mina, M. J., & Parker, R. (2021). Test sensitivity is secondary to frequency and turnaround time for COVID-19 screening. *Science Advances, 7*(1), eabd5393.

Lemoine, P. (2021, March 11). The lockdowns weren't worth it. *Washington Post*. Retrieved December 19, 2021, from https://www.wsj.com/articles/the-lockdowns-werent-worth-it-11615485413?reflink=desktopwebshare_permalink

Lenzer, L. (2020). Covid-19: Group of UK and US experts argues for "focused protection" instead of lockdowns. *British Medical Journal, 371*, m3908. https://doi.org/10.1136/bmj.m3908

Michie, S., West, R., & Harvey, N. (2020) The concept of "fatigue" in tackling covid-19. *British Medical Journal, 371*, m4171. https://doi.org/10.1136/bmj.m4171

Mina, M. J., Parker, R., & Larremore, D. B. (2020). Rethinking Covid-19 test sensitivity—A strategy for containment. *New England Journal of Medicine, 383*(22), e120.

Mitchell, S. S. (2018). "Warning! You're entering a sick zone": The construction of risk and privacy implications of disease tracking apps. Online Information Review.

Mourouvaye, M., Bottemanne, H., Bonny, G., Fourcade, L., Angoulvant, F., Cohen, J. F., & Ouss, L. (2021). Association between suicide behaviours in children and adolescents and the COVID-19 lockdown in Paris, France: A retrospective observational study. *Archives of Disease in Childhood, 106*(9), 918–919.

Munzert, S., Selb, P., Gohdes, A., Stoetzer, L. F., & Lowe, W. (2021). Tracking and promoting the usage of a COVID-19 contact tracing app. *Nature Human Behaviour, 5*(2), 247–255.

Patel, J., Fernandes, G., & Sridhar, D. (2021). Maximising public adherence to COVID-19 self-isolation in Europe. *The Lancet Regional Health-Europe, 4*, 100089.

Poillot, E., Lenzini, G., Resta, G., & Zeno-Zencovich, V. (2021). *Data protection in the context of covid-19. A short (hi)story of tracing applications* (Vol. 12). Rome TrE-Press.

Pollicino, O., & Gregorio, D. (2021). Fighting COVID-19 and protecting privacy under EU law: A proposal looking at the roots of European Constitutionalism. In D. Utrilla & A. Shabbir (Eds.), *EU law in times of pandemic* (pp. 163–176). EU Law Live Press/Comares.

Priesemann, V., Balling, R., Bauer, S., Beutels, P., Valdez, A. C., Cuschieri, S., Czypionka, T., Dumpis, U., Glaab, E., Grill, E., Hotulainen, P., Iftekhar, E. N., Krutzinna, J., Lionis, C., Machado, H., Martins, C., McKee, M., Pavlakis, G. N., Perc, M., ... Willeit, P. (2021). Towards a European strategy to address the COVID-19 pandemic. *The Lancet, 398*(10303), 838–839.

Quigley, M., & Harris, J. (2008). Personal or public health? In *International public health policy and ethics* (pp. 15–29). Springer.

Sewell, M. (2020). *The UK lockdown: Was it worth it?* Retrieved from https://hectordrummond.com/2020/06/09/martin-sewell-the-uk-lockdown-was-it-worth-it/

Singer, P., & Plant, M. (2020). *When will the pandemic cure be worse than the disease?* Project Syndicate. Retrieved October 11, 2020, from https://www.project-syndicate.org/commentary/when-will-lockdowns-be-worse-than-covid19-by-peter-singer-and-michael-plant-2020-04?barrier=accesspaylog

SPI-B. (2020). *The impact of financial and other targeted support on rates of self-isolation or quarantine.* Retrieved December 14, 2021, from https://www.gov.uk/government/publications/spi-b-impact-of-financial-and-other-targeted-support-on-rates-of-self-isolation-or-quarantine-16-september-2020

Stanley, J., & Granick, J. S. (2020). *The limits of location tracking in an epidemic.* American Civil Liberties Union.

Whitelaw, S., Mamas, M. A., Topol, E., & Van Spall, H. G. (2020). Applications of digital technology in COVID-19 pandemic planning and response. *The Lancet Digital Health, 2*(8), e435–e440.

Wirtz, B. W., Müller, W. M., & Weyerer, J. C. (2021). Digital pandemic response systems: A strategic management framework against Covid-19. *International Journal of Public Administration, 44*(11–12), 896–906.

Woolf, S. H., Chapman, D. A., Sabo, R. T., Weinberger, D. M., Hill, L., & Taylor, D. D. (2020). Excess deaths from COVID-19 and other causes, March-July 2020. *Journal of the American Medical Association, 324*(15), 1562–1564.

Yling, L. (2020). *The silent COVID-19 death toll: Far more Australians will kill themselves because of coronavirus lockdown than those who die of the virus, experts say.* Retrieved December 19, 2021, from https://www.dailymail.co.uk/news/article-8293233/Far-people-Australia-predicted-die-suicide-coronavirus-lockdown.html

Chapter 2
Immunity Certificates: The New Frontier

2.1 Introduction

In late 2020 and early 2021, when SARS-CoV-2 was at its peak, some governments, such as Israel, and private actors, such as IATA (the International Air Transport Association), proposed the creation of certificates to facilitate the orderly movement of people. These would attest to the fact that the people carrying them would have a reduced ability to transmit the virus, so that the risks of transporting them would be drastically reduced. This initiative was soon imitated by some EU Member States, such as Greece. The reaction of the European institutions was not long in coming. On 17 March 2021, the European Commission presented its intention to launch a legislative initiative on this issue. Shortly afterwards, Regulation (EU) 2021/953 of the European Parliament and of the Council 14 June 2021 on a framework for the issuance, verification and acceptance of interoperable COVID-19 vaccination, diagnostic test and recovery certificates (EU digital COVID certificate) to facilitate free movement during the COVID-19 pandemic was adopted.[1] This tool was implemented with the stated purpose of "facilitating the exercise, by its holders, of their right to free movement during the COVID-19 pandemic" and "the gradual lifting of restrictions on free movement put in place by the Member States, in accordance with Union Law, in order to limit the spread of SARS-CoV-2, in a coordinated manner".

With hindsight, the reality is that this idea of requiring a certificate to travel was not new. A similar tool, the International Certificate of Vaccination (Carte Jeune), had been around for a long time. This was an official document obtained from the international vaccination centres, authorised and approved by the World Health

---

[1] Regulation (EU) 2021/953 of the European Parliament and of the Council of 14 June 2021 on a framework for the issuance, verification and acceptance of interoperable COVID-19 vaccination, test and recovery certificates (EU Digital COVID Certificate) to facilitate free movement during the COVID-19 pandemic (Text with EEA relevance).

I. de Miguel Beriain, *The Ethical, Legal and Social Issues of Pandemics*,
https://doi.org/10.1007/978-3-031-03818-1_2

Organization. It was obligatory for travel to certain countries where there is a high risk of contracting diseases such as yellow fever or meningococcal meningitis. This was intended to prevent the spread of these kinds of diseases to those who were not immune to them. The International Health Regulations (IHR), revised in 2005, expanded the scope of international concerned diseases to include all "events that may constitute public health emergencies of international relevance" (16). The former "International Certificate of Vaccination or Revaccination against Yellow Fever" was revised to become the "International Certificate of Vaccination or Prophylaxis", which now includes documentation not only on yellow fever but also on any vaccination or prophylaxis (Schlagenhauf et al., 2021).

The problem we have had to face in the context of the SARS-CoV-2 pandemic is that the use of the digital certificate envisaged by the EU Regulation (the EU digital COVID Certificate) soon extended far beyond its original scope. As early as autumn 2021, many of the Member States were turning them into real safe conducts without which it was impossible to gain access to certain places, such as entertainment venues, health centres or retirement homes. As might be expected, this generated strong controversy, including mass demonstrations against their use in most of the countries where they were introduced.

In the following pages, I will focus on the legal-ethical analysis of this tool from a much less visceral perspective than the public debate usually inspires. In order to focus the discussion, I will start by delimiting what exactly a health certificate is and what are the different types of certificates that exist, at least conceptually. I will then focus my attention on one type of health certificate in particular, certificates of immunity, i.e. those that provide assurances that their bearers have little or no ability to spread a contagious pathogen, which is the one that is really an interesting novelty. I will later outline the ethical and legal issues raised by this tool, both at a time when tests or vaccines are available and at earlier stages. At the same time, I will address the complex issue of data processing for these purposes, complementing what has already been said in the section on the use of geospatial data.

2.1.1   Definition and Typologies of Health Certificates

What is a health certificate? This is an essential question, as many of the controversies that have accompanied this tool arise from a poor understanding of the concept. As such, a health certificate is only a tool that attests that its bearer fulfils certain conditions relevant in terms of his or her health or public health. For example, a vaccination certificate is a health certificate proving that a person has been vaccinated against a specific disease. In contrast, a certificate of immunity is one that provides evidence that a person has a particular immunological condition. It may show, for example, that he or she will not develop the severe form of a disease or that they are unable to transmit a pathogen. If we accept the latter sense, a certificate of vaccination may or may not also be a certificate of immunity. If, for example, it is a pathology such as measles, the identification is plausible, because the vaccine prevents the disease and the transmission of the virus. In the case of COVID, on the other hand, the identification is much more debatable, because it ultimately depends on whether we consider that vaccination substantially reduces the contagiousness of the virus, which is complex to determine. Conceptually, however, they will always be different things: one (the certificate of immunity), the evidence of the low risk of infectivity, and the other (vaccination) the factual evidence that allows this to be assumed.

What should be clear, in any case, is that different health certificates state different things. With this in mind, they should be obtained through separate channels. In the context of COVID-19, if the aim is to ensure that a person has actually a low probability of transmitting the virus, it would make sense to make obtaining the certificate conditional on a very sensitive and specific test with a negative result within the last few hours. If, on the other hand, the aim is to reduce the risk of infection without reaching that level of certainty, other tests and other time windows would be admissible. If, however, the goal is to use the health certificate to stimulate vaccination, evidence of having been vaccinated should be required for its possession, so that the health certificate used will be, in reality, a vaccination certificate, regardless of what we are told, given the low sterilising action of the vaccine, which I have already pointed out above.

Table 2.1 Types of health certificates

Type of certificate	Eligibility requirements	Likely purpose
G1a	Complete the recommended vaccination schedule	Stimulating vaccination
G1b	Having overcome an infection	Promoting the recovery of rights for the infected
G1c	Have had a recent negative test result	Reduce or eliminate risks (depending on the characteristics of the tests)
G2a	Complete the recommended vaccination schedule or have overcome the infection	Stimulating vaccination
		Promoting the recovery of rights for the infected
G2b	Have overcome an infection or have had a recent negative test result	Reduce or eliminate risks (depending on test characteristics or immunity gained from natural infection)
G2c	Completion of the recommended vaccination schedule or a recent negative test result	Reduce or eliminate risks (assuming natural infection does not provide immunity)
		Eliminate risk of voluntary infection (if infection provides immunity and no vaccines or tests are readily available)
G3	Complete the recommended vaccination schedule or have had a recent negative test result or have overcome an infection	Reduce or eliminate risks (depending on the characteristics of tests, vaccines or immunity gained from natural infection)
		Stimulating vaccination

In short, health certificates should not be considered as rigid tools, but quite the opposite. They are a very aseptic concept, which can be used for many different purposes and in many various ways. Table 2.1 shows, without being exhaustive, some diverse variants of certificates that can be considered. If we add to this the fact that the different types of certificates can be requested at various times or places, it is obvious that their degree of flexibility is superlative. For example, we could, in some epidemiological circumstances, ask for a G1c to enter an immunology ward, but a G2c to allow access to a nursing home and a G3 to get into a nightclub, or, in other scenarios, require only a G2b for access to a hospital ward (e.g. if no vaccines are available).

This table shows that the concept of health certificates is broad and their use could vary considerably. Therefore, it is absurd to conceive the debate on these tools as monolithic. There are likely to be people who are strongly opposed to some types of certificates and/or their possible uses while accepting others gladly. In fact, it will be rare to find positions of absolute acceptance or radical opposition to the use of each and every one of these tools. It is, therefore, necessary to be very scrupulous in the debates. To do otherwise is an invitation to confusion that will not allow consensus to be reached.

It is important to note that in this part of my work, as I have already mentioned, I will focus my attention exclusively on one particular type of health certificate, the certificate of sterilising immunity, which attests that its bearer has little chance of transmitting a pathogen. I am aware that in the case of SARS-CoV-2, this designation is used for G3s which, in reality, offer little guarantee of this immunity, as those vaccinated can also transmit the virus, especially in the aftermath of the Omicron variant. I believe that such confusion should be carefully avoided. Therefore, it must be kept in mind that when I refer to certificates of immunity in the following pages, I will not be talking about certificates that have been obtained in a certain way (e.g. a G3 or a G2b), but about tools that attest to a condition: the significant reduction of the transmission risk. Moreover, this is regardless of the means by which we can obtain them in order to ensure that this reduction occurs. In this sense, it will be easier to extrapolate the considerations I will include from now on to scenarios that may differ from the present or future ones.

2.2 Certificates of Immunity in the Absence of Vaccinations or Diagnostic Tests

Let us begin, therefore, by looking at the use of certificates of immunity in the particular circumstances that usually occur at the beginning of a pandemic. To do so, let us revise a bit of history. In March–April 2020, when most European countries had decreed a confinement of their populations due to the outbreak of SARS-CoV-2, the question arose as to what to do with those who had already recovered from the disease. That discussion was particularly interesting for the topic I now address, because it clearly showed the complexity of dictating balanced policies affecting populations with a different immune status: a large majority of the population highly vulnerable to a hitherto unknown virus and a minority that we could presume had already obtained substantial immunisation against it thanks to the mere fact of having overcome the disease.

A very interesting discussion arose at that time, with some other authors and I (Brown et al., 2021; de Miguel Beriain & Rueda, 2020) arguing that some groups should be treated differently from others, while others (Kofler & Baylis, 2020; Phelan, 2020) were strongly in favour of the opposite. From our position, it made sense to give those who had already passed the disease a certificate of immunity that would allow them to avoid the close confinement to which we were all subjected. From the opposing positions, this was clearly not the case. Then, the debate revolved around a series of arguments that reflect well the essential issues to be clarified. In this section, I critically discuss each of them, focusing preferably on those that are specific to a scenario in which vaccination or generalised access to diagnostic tests is not yet possible. It goes without saying that my reflections are hardly neutral, as I am part of one of the two trends. Nevertheless, I will try to be objective and to not hide the weaknesses of my own position.

2.2.1 The Question of Scientific Certainty

Firstly, it is clear that one can only treat people differently according to their immune status if it is possible to know exactly what status that is. This, unfortunately, is not easy. This is likely to require serological, or even more complex tests, which will not always be reliable or available (Kofler & Baylis, 2020; Phelan, 2020). The alternative, of course, is to trust the mere fact that having overcome the disease confers immunity. However, this would imply considering, first and foremost, that a diagnosis based on an examination of the symptomatology shown by a patient would be sufficient to certify that they have indeed suffered from the pathology in question and not another. This, of course, is more than debatable. On the other hand, we would have to assess to what extent it is appropriate to assume that overcoming the pathology does indeed provide immunity, or whether it should be sterilising or not. The situation is likely to change with each pathogen. Thus, each of these questions introduces a range of uncertainty that makes it hard to introduce any kind of public health policy that attempts to be respectful of the citizens' rights, which are based on their immunological status. Moreover, these kinds of considerations will often vary from the early stages of a crisis to later ones, when our knowledge and testing capabilities improve considerably.

This unavoidable uncertainty must be carefully weighed when approaching this debate. It must be borne in mind that an error in the consideration of a person's infectivity could lead to fatal consequences: if we grant him a certificate to leave confinement due to a failure to consider his immune status, we would be promoting a false security that could have lethal consequences for himself or for others. This does not seem acceptable from the perspective of public health policy or the need to ensure the patient's well-being. Hence, in principle, uncertainty makes it inadvisable to implement the initiatives we are contemplating. However, it is also true that, if we deviate from such a paternalistic view, it is reasonable to accept an interval of uncertainty, as long as both the person who may suffer the consequences of the error and third parties who come into close contact with them are informed of the risks they are taking. In addition, of course, at a time when the only ones who will not be confined will be those we presume to be immune (and surely also members of the essential professions), the risk of accidental contagion will be very small indeed. The objection due to lack of scientific knowledge is, in short, solid, but it does not need to be definitive in all circumstances. We should not forget, in case of doubt, the maxim *in dubio pro libertatis*, which advocates opting for the solution that is least invasive with the individual's sphere of freedom when the situation is unclear (Cierco Seira, 2018). In my opinion, we would do well to apply it in these cases.

2.2.2   The Privilege

One of the most repeated arguments against immunity certificates in circumstances such as those described above is that, if accepted, they would contribute to the creation of a community of the privileged. The latter would have rights and freedoms completely different from those of all other members of society on the basis of a (immunological) status that would not be the consequence of socially appreciable merit or effort, but merely of chance. Rewarding them with privileges potentially unattainable by the rest would be severely unjust. Moreover, it would promote the construction of a discriminatory social model. In this regard, a bad memory of historical precedent is often cited (Olivarius, 2019). In the nineteenth century, yellow fever was a lethal mosquito-borne virus that ravaged New Orleans in the USA. About half of those infected died. Over time, the population became accustomed to drawing distinctions between two large groups, immunised and non-immunised. Thus, white citizens were divided into "acclimatised citizens" at the top of the social pyramid and "unacclimatised outsiders". Between the two groups there were many differences in terms of where they lived, how much they earned, their ability to obtain credit and whom they could marry. Nor, of course, was the situation for taking out life insurance anywhere near similar. In the case of slaves, whether they had passed the disease or not made their market price fluctuate substantially.

Obviously, no one would like to rescue a society in which there was such a sharp social division between one another. However, it is difficult to draw any form of parallelism between the New Orleans case and what might give rise to a pandemic in our time. To begin with, most societies are no longer so strongly stratified into social classes, and slavery has been officially abolished in all countries. Neither is it true, moreover, that the kind of differentiation to which yellow fever gave rise can be extrapolated to that which would be generated by new pathologies with much more limited immunities. Nor was it possible at the time to think of this stratification as something temporary, which would surely disappear when a vaccine or a type of treatment became available to all those affected. Fortunately, our biomedical response capacity has improved greatly since the nineteenth century.

Let us imagine, however, that this were not the case, i.e. that there were reasons to believe that, unfortunately, the population would be divided into different social groups (in immunological terms) for a prolonged period of time. In such circumstances, should we not disregard any certificates to avoid privileges in favour of some of them? The answer, in my view, to this question must be no. There are good ethical and legal reasons for doing so. To begin with, it is profoundly wrong to think that, in a health crisis of the kind we are now suffering, extraordinary rights are being granted. What is being done, in the first instance, is to limit essential rights and, subsequently, to remove those limits. This is completely different from granting privileges. It is simply acting in accordance with what the circumstances require. At difficult times in a pandemic, fundamental citizens' rights are suspended or limited, introducing a confinement, as I have explained in the previous chapter of this book. Therefore, if there is a change in the scenario, and if there are purely immunological reasons why some people can still enjoy a curtailed form of their rights and freedoms, the logical path to follow is to repeal this constrictive measure on a selective basis. In doing so, we would not be granting rights to a few privileged, but we would be giving back to citizens who are no longer a danger to public health the ability to exercise rights that never ceased to be theirs.

In short, a devolution of fundamental rights cannot be conceived as a privilege in any case (De Miguel Beriain, 2021). Therefore, to speak of discrimination would make no sense, at least if we use it in the pejorative sense of the term. What would be discriminatory in any case is the opposite: treating people who are probably immunised as if they were not. As Hall and Studdert point out:

> Although certification discriminates by design, discrimination is not legally or ethically problematic unless it lacks good rationale. Indeed, when substantially different circumstances exist, it can be wrong not to differentiate. Only when differentiation is invidious (ie, unjustified, and thus imposing undeserved hardship) is it wrongly discriminatory (Hall & Studdert, 2020).

In this case, therefore, treating differently those who are presumably immune and those who are not immune at all would create an unjust situation. On the contrary, to do so would constitute a form of downward levelling that would be profoundly unfair under any reasonable conception of egalitarianism.

There are, moreover, legal reasons to argue that this form of discrimination against immunised persons would be inadmissible, at least within the EU. As I have written elsewhere (de Miguel Beriain & Rueda, 2020):

> It is necessary to refer to the Convention for the Protection of Human Rights and Fundamental Freedoms, signed in Rome on 4 November 1950. This is a fundamental legal tool that defends individual rights and freedoms in all signatory countries, including most European countries. According to article 5, "Everyone has the right to liberty and security of person. No one shall be deprived of his liberty save in the following cases and in accordance with a procedure prescribed by law: (...) (e) the lawful detention of persons for the

prevention of the spreading of infectious diseases, of persons of unsound mind, alcoholics or drug addicts or vagrants".

The Convention establishes a right to freedom of movement that cannot be restricted but 'for the prevention of the spreading of infectious diseases'. It is necessary to emphasise that the Convention does not even allow in principle to limit the freedom of movement to avoid a risk of collapse for the health system—one of the reasons given to justify the lockdowns, as Brown et al. pointed out. The question according to the Convention is simply whether or not a citizen poses a threat to public health. Moreover, the European Court of Human Rights determined in the case of Enhorn v. Sweden (application no. 56529/00 of 25 of January 2005) that the essential criteria when assessing the 'lawfulness' of the detention of a person 'for the prevention of the spreading of infectious diseases' are whether the spreading of the infectious disease is dangerous to public health or safety, and whether detention of the person infected is the last resort in order to prevent the spreading of the disease, because less severe measures have been considered and found to be insufficient to safeguard the public interest. When these criteria are no longer fulfilled, the basis for the deprivation of liberty ceases to exist.

This articulation of 'lawfulness' should be the key criterion in the entire process of awarding immunity passports: whether the deprivation of liberty is the only way to safeguard public interest.

It is true, of course, that the Convention itself states in Article 15 that "in the event of war or other public danger threatening the life of the nation, any High Contracting Party may take measures derogating from its obligations under this Convention to the extent strictly required by the exigencies of the situation". However, this possibility only empowers States to restrict the freedoms and rights recognised by the text if strictly necessary to safeguard fundamental public interests. Then, in principle, it will have to be up to them to justify why persons who are not likely to be a danger to public health are subject to the same restrictions as if they were. This will not always be straightforward, for all the reasons I have already explained.

The conclusion from all of the above is therefore simple: allowing immunised persons to exercise the rights suspended for those who are not immunised is not discriminatory. What would create such an unfair situation, however, would be to attribute the same rights, or rather the same restrictions, to all. If they do not share the same capacity to threaten the health of others, it is completely irrational to treat them in the same way. This would, in other words, be seriously discriminatory. Hence, the use of tools that allow distinctions to be made is not only legitimate, but can be considered an ethical and legal obligation.

2.2.3   The Promotion of Inappropriate Behaviour (Voluntary Contagion)

Another issue of particular importance in the discussion at hand concerns the impact that the introduction of such certificate might have on the behaviour of the population as a whole. Opponents of its introduction point out in this respect that "immunity passports could create perverse incentives. If access to certain social and economic liberties is given only to people who have recovered from COVID-19, then immunity passports could incentivize healthy, non-immune individuals to wilfully seek out infection—putting themselves and others at risk" (Kofler & Baylis, 2020).

This hypothesis is by no means implausible. In fact, it is more than likely that some people, especially in the lower social strata, would rather run the risk of voluntary infection than be deprived of their wages because they could not come to work (Phelan, 2020; Kates & Hastings Center, 2020). Therefore, in principle, it is reasonable to veto a tool that would cause equity and public health problems. However, there are powerful reasons that undermine these kinds of arguments when analysed in depth.

The main one is that it does not seem justified at all that part of the population has its rights and freedoms restricted simply because another part is going to behave inappropriately. I do not consider it reasonable to adapt our policies to the uncivil behaviour of one social group, but to try to prevent such behaviour from occurring by adapting our policies to the demands of those communities, if they are legitimate. If we do not want people to seek voluntary contagion in order to avoid poverty or job loss, it makes sense to introduce measures to protect them from such eventualities. Certainly not by unnecessarily restricting the freedoms and rights of other citizens who would assume unfair harm. These deleterious possibilities are, therefore, not a reason to maintain the unjust forced confinement of those who do not pose a threat to public health; rather, they are a reason to mitigate the overuse of resources and to reduce incentives for contagion.

What seems sensible, in short, is, on the one hand, to substantially limit the rights and freedoms from which the immunised could benefit, reducing them to the fundamental ones, such as mere freedom of movement, as suggested by José Luis Martí already at the beginning of the COVID pandemic. At a time when there may be confinement or a curfew, it would be reasonable for people who can prove that they are not capable of spreading the virus to be exempted from the obligation to remain at home. However, this exemption would not be necessarily extended to allowing them to attend social events or entertainment venues (which would probably not be open to the public in such circumstances either, by the way). On the other hand, it also seems reasonable to consider that we could ask them to perform some tasks with special public interest in the circumstances created by a pandemic, so that the final outcome in terms of rights and freedoms would be resolved more equitably among all members of society (Brown et al., 2021). This would also go a long way towards reducing incentives for voluntary contagion.

It must, however, be conceded that, despite these precautions, there are likely to be cases of willful self-infection. In such circumstances, one would have to think, as Hall and Studdert (2020) point out, that States "may need to tolerate some level of perverse behavior to realize the benefits of immunity, much as society tolerates but attempts to minimize destructive incentives that arise from other beneficial programs (e.g., fire insurance)". It does not seem, in any case, that this behaviour would turn out to be widespread. In fact, these policies of gradual devolution of freedoms and rights is what, in practice, was finally implemented when the vaccines began to be administered to part of the population. As soon as we found ourselves in such a scenario, which included population groups with various immune statuses, we completely forgot about the danger of negative stimuli. What we did was to give back to those already immunised rights such as the right to avoid close-contact confinement or to travel. It does not seem to have generated a huge social controversy or a wave of voluntary contagion. So the argument, in my opinion, is neither consistent from a theoretical point of view nor particularly unsettling from a pragmatic perspective.

2.2.4 Public Order Problems

Finally, it should be noted that accepting that some people could avoid confinement on the basis of their immune status might be fair in principle, but it would cause a considerable law and order problem. How could we be sure that many people would not try to take advantage of this situation to avoid confinement by pretending to be in possession of the certificate? The police could, of course, ensure that this scenario did not come to pass by asking for it at random, but this would increase their workload at a time when it would already be very high. However, this objection pales when we consider that, at least in the "weak" confinements we suffered in Western countries, people were allowed to go outside for ad hoc tasks, if not to work in essential jobs. There were no excesses that would suggest a scenario of massive fraud if the immunised were allowed to retain some of their rights. Probably because at the early stages of a pandemic, when fear is evident, it is unlikely that someone would put themselves at unnecessary risk. Then the overburden would probably not be as high as it might appear at first glance.

2.2.5 Concluding Remarks

Everything I have mentioned in the previous sections supports the strength of the arguments of those who advocate the introduction of certificates to avoid unjust restrictions of fundamental rights. While it is true that there are reasons to believe that they might have some side effects that are hard to control, it is difficult to consider that they would be such as to justify the sacrifice of the rights and freedoms mentioned. Liberal democracy is about respect for fundamental rights, which should only be sacrificed when there is no other feasible alternative. The moment this scenario is not fulfilled, we must opt for freedom.

2.3 Health Certificates When Vaccines and/or Screening Tests Are Already Available to the General Population

2.3.1 Introduction

Let us now look at a different scenario, in which one of these two circumstances apply: either vaccines that provide us with considerable sterilising immunity have been developed (and it is possible to distribute them to the entire population of a country) or, at least, we have tests capable of revealing a person's infectivity for a reasonable price at our disposal. In ethical and legal terms, the fundamental change implied by this scenario is that it is much more complicated to speak of incentives for self-infection. Since there are alternative possibilities to obtain a certificate of immunity, it is quite reasonable to dismiss that there are many people willing to take the risk of voluntarily infecting themselves.

Under these conditions, a new scenario emerges in which society is divided into several different strata, only this time it is even more intricate. There will be many groups with a different range of infectivity and/or vulnerability to the pathogen, such as (this list is not exhaustive) those who have natural immunity because they have had the disease; those who have been vaccinated against the disease; those who have been tested recently and know their degree of infectivity; and those who, not being in any of the other cases, pose a potential threat to the rest of society. In this complex framework, immunity certificates are useful tools, because they allow us to shift the focus of the response. It will no longer be essential to isolate the infectious person in a specific enclosure, as it will be sufficient to limit his or her access to defined areas by imposing the display of the immunity certificate as a condition to enter.

This, again, gives us much more flexibility in public health actions. It allows us to add variants to the traditional approach to pandemic control, based on home confinement or isolation of the infectious person, which, as I have already illustrated, is difficult to implement. The approach based on the use of immunity certificates complements this strategy, focusing on preventing an infectious person who is unaware of being infected or unwilling to act as expected from spreading the pathogenic agent in places particularly prone to its spread. This approach adds substantial advantages to one based solely on a more traditional strategy, such as the following:

- It improves our efficiency in preventing contagion by overcoming some of the limitations and difficulties implicit in the control of confinement/isolation. Ensuring that an affected person stays at home is much more complicated than preventing access to other bounded areas, as I have already explained.
- It is more respectful with the rights of those who are infectious or merely suspected of being infectious. It does not suspend their freedom of movement. It only limits their freedom of movement by preventing them from accessing certain areas.

- It allows the introduction of strategies to promote and encourage infectivity testing or vaccination, where available, without imposing it, unless the immunity certificate becomes a covert vaccination certificate.

In a sense, the use of this tool allows for something like a third way between the eradication and mitigation policies that I discussed in the previous chapter. It can be used to avoid confining people in their homes, but without allowing anyone to gain access anywhere. The construction of safe spaces is a middle ground that permits the most vulnerable to be protected without unduly harming the non-vulnerable. In this sense, it is a form of heightened mitigation, which can become extreme in certain circumstances (Romer et al., 2021).

Despite these advantages, however, some obstacles remain that could be a considerable stumbling block to the use of this kind of certificate. For a start, they can only be implemented effectively if we are able to accurately quantify infectivity. In the absence of sterilising vaccines (as in the case of SARS-CoV-2), this means using hundreds of millions of tests. This implies the development of an unprecedented industrial capacity and enormous economic costs. However, it will certainly be less than that of confinement, especially if it is only introduced when it is necessary, as some articles have proposed (Atkeson et al., 2020). This, however, is not the only problem. We would also need to have sufficient health professionals to test on an ongoing basis. We would probably need to involve pharmacies in the effort or even create new centres for this purpose. We could even think about how to do mass testing at work or educational settings, probably using techniques such as *pooled* saliva testing. However, these are technological and organisational health-care management problems that are beyond the scope of this book.

I will therefore focus on the ethical and legal issues involved by this tool, which are not minor. To begin with, we can mention (and have often done so) discrimination problems: is it not discrimination to treat people differently if they show no sign of being a danger to others' health? To this, it must be added the issue of invasion of privacy and/or violation of the right to informational self-determination. When a person uses an immunity certificate in order to be able to leave his/her home and avoid confinement, the conflicts related are rather tenuous (in principle, only the police would be entitled to ask for it). However, when it comes to a scenario in which the certificate may be required in order to access public premises, are we not illegitimately processing health data? To these two objections, it should be added, at the very least, that it is not clear that these measures satisfy the principle of proportionality, which we have already discussed in other chapters of this work. Finally, there are other reasons to oppose their introduction, such as the possibility of counterfeiting, or fraud in their use. I will now explore the consistency of these objections.

2.3.2   The Discrimination Argument

Do immunity certificates discriminate? At first glance, one may indeed consider that these tools clearly create a social reality of inequality, as they discriminate between those who have and those who do not have immunity, i.e. they are based on a criterion over which people have no control. For historical reasons, we tend to oppose discrimination based on biological criteria, reminiscent of eugenic tendencies (Ravitsky & Weinstock, 2020). It seems, in short, that there is a good reason to consider immunity certificates unjust, since they are discriminatory: they grant different rights and freedoms to individuals because of their immunological status, that is, on the basis of a health status that the subject has not chosen.

In reality, immunity certificates have no reason to discriminate unfairly against anyone, beyond the issues of fairness that I will discuss later. In fact, if we are talking about 3G certificates (the EU Digital Certificate is the archetypal example), it is difficult to understand why we should believe that there might be any form of unfair segregation a priori. There may not be, in fact, because where we differentiate in the treatment of people is not with respect to their health, but with respect to their ability to transmit a pathogen. This is an absolutely substantial difference from the previous scenario, where the question of devolution of rights was confined to the sphere of the person concerned. Now it is the health of third parties that is to be protected, ergo, public health.

From the logic of public health, it is not only permissible but also enforceable to draw treatment distinctions based on the different ability to transmit a contagious disease. If there is a measles outbreak at a school, for example, we quarantine all children in the class of the affected child. This is not only for their own health but also because of the suspicion that they might transmit it to others. It is therefore difficult to argue that we are discriminating against these children, who may be suspected of being a public health risk, by separating them from others. Even more clearly, if there is an Ebola outbreak, we will immediately confine all those suspected of having the disease, whether they like it or not. It will certainly not be only to protect their health, but undoubtedly that of others. In short, there is no doubt that differentiating access by means of a variable that is directly related to public health (contagiousness) is different to making a distinction, for example, based on factors such as race or religion.[2] It is therefore more than reasonable to treat people differently according to their infectious capacity, without violating the equality of all human beings in any way.

It is true that the case of an epidemic with community transmission is not similar to that of a localised outbreak. In this scenario, suspicion of infectivity is not limited to a group of people, but to the population as a whole. This, however, does not alter the logic of public health policies (separating the infectious from the non-infectious): it only makes them more complex to implement. When each member of the society is suspected of spreading the virus because of uncontrolled transmission, it is no

---

[2] Conseil Constitutionnel (2021) Décision n° 2021–824 DC du août 2021.

longer possible to isolate people selectively, in particular groups. It is necessary to consider everyone as a potential threat. It is in that situation, as I have already explained, that the complexity of identifying who has immunity, and who does not, ends up causing a downward equalisation: we assume that everyone is dangerous; therefore, we confine everyone.

This, of course, is unjust and discriminatory, as we would be curtailing the fundamental rights of people who pose no danger, simply due to a manifest inability of the authorities to discern who they are (Recchi et al., 2020). Resorting to immunity certificates is the best way out of this pernicious dynamic that is not compatible with the egalitarianism of a liberal society. Let us bear in mind, in this regard, that the fundamental aim of this form of organisation is that people, all of them—this nuance is essential—are, as far as possible, better off living in society than they would be acting as isolated entities, under any possible circumstances. Consequently, society tends to avoid policies that "level down" because it is counterproductive: bringing each person down to the least advantaged position punishes one party and does not solve the problem generated by the disadvantage (Persad & Emanuel, 2020). Worse still, this levelling is never equitable: there are many people for whom disenfranchisement means heart-breaking suffering, while others hardly notice its effects (Brown et al., 2021). It is precisely this discriminatory picture that could be avoided through the use of immunity certificates. Hence, not only is the use of this tool not discriminatory, it is actually discriminatory not to use it. Another issue is, as we will see below, that its implementation entails problems of equity.

2.3.3 The Equity Problem

Does an immunity certificate impose the same burdens on all members of a society? Can everyone get it with the same effort? This is a fundamental question in terms of fairness. I have already mentioned in the previous sections that a proper use of this tool is only possible if everyone has access to the means to obtain it. The reality is that this is not always the case. For a start, we will not all have the same options at certain times. If the vaccine starts to be distributed prioritising one population group (such as children, e.g. or the elderly) over others, it is clear that they will have more freedom in deciding how to acquire their certificate than others, at least temporarily.

More serious, however, are other factors. Authors such as Ganty (2021) or Kofler and Baylis (2020) have rightly emphasised that vulnerable populations are generally less able to obtain an immunity certificate. There are multiple reasons for this. First, it is well known that the most disadvantaged social strata, including undocumented migrants, have poorer access to health care. Hence, in the SARS-CoV-2 pandemic, many have not been officially diagnosed with COVID, even if they have suffered the disease. They are also less likely to be vaccinated, "not only because of practical and administrative obstacles, but also because of their higher vaccination hesitancy and their mistrust in the health system, which is partly explained by their experience of long-standing discrimination, as poor people usually belong to minorities and discriminated groups" (Ganty, 2021). This has led, for instance, to significantly lower COVID vaccination rates in some minority populations (Solaiman & Marette, 2021). Finally, it should not be forgotten that many countries do not provide free testing to their population. This entails an extraordinary outlay that the most vulnerable cannot afford, again leading to exclusion from the system. Not to mention those who cannot even benefit from a subsidy on the price of tests or vaccines because they are not included in any census.

There are, in short, considerably important obstacles that introduce serious doubts about the fairness of access to the means that immunity certificates provide. This being true, however, it must be said that this should not be a reason to renounce this tool. Instead, it would be more reasonable to do whatever is possible to alleviate or eliminate these inequity factors. Introducing popular test prices for people from disadvantaged groups (including those who do not even appear on the public health "radar") would be appropriated. More complex is the issue of low vaccination rates. While it is true that the less well off are less likely to be vaccinated due to social constraints, it is also true that this does not mean that they cannot access the vaccine or adequate information about it, if adequate policies are implemented (and this is perfectly doable if necessary resources are allocated). To deprive the whole of society of this tool because some communities suffer from a particular propensity not to vaccinate (probably as a consequence of an unfair discrimination) is excessive in my view. I know that there will be particularly vulnerable minorities (homeless, undocumented migrants) who will only be marginally affected by these solutions. For these it is necessary to provide creative solutions. However, it should be much easier in the EU than elsewhere, if the values of the European Charter of Rights were scrupulously applied. Unfortunately, this is not always the case (Wagenaar & Prainsack, 2021).

There are, however, problems that go beyond equity of access. As Ravitsky and Weinstock have highlighted:

> Far from being an advantage, the risk would be considerable that when a regime of immunity licenses is introduced into a context of structures of disadvantage, those holding them would find themselves subject to pressures to continue to occupy poorly remunerated and insecure jobs now deemed necessary, as those more advantaged now work comfortably from home. When cast against the backdrop of structural inequality, immunity licenses risk locking structural inequalities into place (Ravitsky & Weinstock, 2020).

We are therefore now referring to the lack of equity resulting from the effect of reinforcing social differences induced by the introduction of certificates, if we accept the thesis by the authors cited above. However, is this argument really sound? I think that it is not. It is more than doubtful that immunity certificates contribute to building or maintaining structures of inequality. Nonetheless, even if they did, not having this tool would aggravate the situation even more rather than solve it. Ravitsky and Weinstock's ideas would make more sense if the alternative to certificates were to be able to apply for a job with total safety. This is often not the case. It is precisely the less advantaged occupations that are least likely to offer workers acceptable protection. Of course, if there were other solutions, other than certificates, that would allow a return to normality, they would have to be used, although this is not the case. In fact, it is most likely that, in the absence of implementation of these measures, a total or partial confinement of the entire population will be unavoidable (see next section). Hence, it is easier to ask not whether the certificates are equitable or not, but if their possible alternatives would be more or less equitable. My suspicions in this regard are clear.

In a similar vein, the Nuffield Council noted that "positive tests may be used to require sections of the workforce to return to work, impacting unequally on those who are unable, through lack of wealth or power, to make the choice for themselves. Those with precarious incomes and working in low paying jobs, often in the service or industrial sector, are already more likely to experience social determinants of poorer health (unemployment, poor quality housing, less personal space, etc.), and worse outcomes of SARS-CoV-2 infection, than those in more privileged groups. Selective uses of certification are more likely to compound than redress these structural disadvantages and to add to the social stigmatisation of these groups" (Nuffield, 2020).

However, what this further argument misses is that, if certificates are used properly, they are likely to enable safer face-to-face working environments to be built. A factory floor, for instance, is less likely to become a source of infection if workers are tested for infectivity before being allowed on the premises. Therefore, in reality, certificates would be helping to protect precisely those in less skilled jobs, which do not make remote working feasible, a much-needed protection, to be honest, because, if there is a prolonged period of inactivity, the company could go bankrupt, which would eliminate the jobs of the vulnerable population concerned. Therefore, in reality, it is difficult to speak of unfairness, given all the circumstances.

On the other hand, it is more difficult to resolve the equity issues raised by immunity certificates in an international context (Osama et al., 2021). It is obvious that differences between countries in this context can be enormous. Some nations provide their citizens with the possibility of free vaccination or access to testing. Others are at the opposite angle. There are countries with an excellent administration, able to manage certificates efficiently and to enter into agreements with third countries. Others are unable to meet these challenges. Finally, there are considerable shortcomings in the mutual recognition of the validity of certificates issued by one country or another.

The consequence of these disparities is dire: human beings may have different rights and freedoms depending on where they live. Let me stress that the situation is particularly worrying if we bear in mind that unequal treatment will affect not only the ability to travel from one country to another but also the activities that one can carry out at the destination. Quarantine requirements will not be the same, nor will the recognition of the effectiveness of the certificates—and therefore the possibility of accessing the areas. Once again, we are facing a problem that is hard to solve. It seems reasonable to conclude that inequity should lead us to eliminate the use of certificates for international transit. However, it must be borne in mind that, if this were the case, what is likely is that in the context of a pandemic, we would once again experience the situation of spring 2020, i.e. a scenario marked by the paralysis of passenger transport, again, the famous issues with downward equalisation: third-country nationals will not benefit from the curtailment of the rights and freedoms of those from a particular Western country, as this scenario damages all parties to varying degrees. I do not think this is the best possible option. Working towards a progressive harmonisation of protocols and a fairer distribution of available health resources—vaccines or tests—are certainly the most promising alternatives. Obviously, I am not unaware that this is more a wish than a reality in many of the crises we will have to face.

In short, the conclusion of this section can only be one: health certificates entail equity problems, some of which are particularly serious. The question is whether we can consider alternatives that, while being less damaging to this value, are capable of achieving the intended objectives. In my opinion, this is very complicated. In summary, it would be logical to do everything possible to minimise the inequity inherent in the system and to limit the use of certificates to the time they are actually required. It does not make sense to me to prohibit the use of this tool for that reason.

2.3.4 The Proportionality of the Measure

An essential question as to whether or not immunity certificates are admissible in a given set of circumstances is the issue of the proportionality of the measure. Since this principle is essential in a liberal democracy, it is necessary to know whether any measure is capable of passing its filter before making a definitive judgement on it. I will therefore devote this section to examining this aspect.

As I have already expressed, this principle is composed of three parts: appropriateness, necessity and proportionality in the strict sense. The question of appropriateness is easy to test. The certificate will be suitable to reduce the risk of transmission of a pathogen in a given location if the conditions imposed to achieve it guarantee that result. If, for example, we have sufficiently sensitive and specific tests and we make the certificate conditional on a negative result, then, in principle, the suitability of the certificate can be assured. If, on the other hand, we link them to a vaccine that does not show the capacity to significantly reduce contagion, then the opposite is true (they will be suitable to encourage vaccination, of course, but that is a certificate of vaccination, and not of immunity that we are analysing now). Then, this first part is resolved by resorting to the best science available at any given time and the range of risk that we wish to assume (there are no absolute certainties, of course, so we have to gamble on a more or less variable amount).

The necessity of the measure is more complex to assess. In principle, we will assume a certain option to be necessary when we can consider it the least restrictive alternative, in terms of rights, of all the alternatives that will provide the same result. If, for example, we consider that risk reduction can be achieved by imposing hygiene measures on the whole population, or through the use of masks, or tracing and isolation systems, then the use of certificates is probably unjustified. If, on the other hand, the only reasonable alternative to achieve the same end is a total or partial confinement of a country's inhabitants, then the introduction of certificates is likely to be justified, because it is less harmful to fundamental rights such as freedom of movement or, in many cases, the right to work. Of course, there will be many scenarios in between, in which it is not easy to assess whether this condition is actually fulfilled or not.

Proportionality strictu sensu, in turn, depends on the balance between the goods to be preserved and those that will be violated if a certificate is imposed. Here one can think of many goods or rights at risk: obviously, freedom of movement, but also freedom of assembly and, in certain cases, even the right to work. Some authors even go a step further, as the following excerpt from Paris (2021, p. 296) shows:

> In the absence of adequate safeguards, creating this framework that would allow Member States to use EU COVID-19 Certificates in order to restrict access to certain places and activities could result in a disproportionate impact on the fundamental rights to privacy, data protection and non-discrimination, as well as other fundamental rights and freedoms. This could be an opportunity for some States to create a system in which fundamental rights are conditioned by health status, which would inevitably exacerbate existing inequalities and create further division and stratification based on immunological status.

However, this kind of slippery-slope argument is not easy to accept. It requires at least some proof that it can be so. For, as Burgess wrote long ago, "unfortunately, purveyors of the Great Argument rarely if ever work it into a detailed slippery-slope argument. They rest content with the sketchiest of formulations, leaving the detailed work to their opponents: we've shown you (sketchily) that it might happen; now show us (in detail) that it couldn't. But this is a fraud. The mere presentation of a slope does nothing to show that the onus of proof is on the reformer to demonstrate that a proposed change will not lead to disaster" (Burgess, 1993, p. 170).

This reflection is particularly pertinent in this case, because of the ease to create permanent firewalls. There is a huge difference between a measure adopted in a given context and one that remains permanent. Liberal democracies are built on a battery of checks and balances that would make everything that Paris suggests might hardly happen. As Greeley (2020, p. 19) puts it, "political pressures for watering down the certificate requirements, or for softening or removing the restrictions that the certificates could overcome, would soon prove irresistible. Whether ethical or not, I strongly suspect that the social and political effects of a substantial immunity certificate program would be sustainable for only a limited time". Moreover, if what he points out were true, we would already be lost, since these kinds of restrictions of fundamental rights have already taken place in many Western countries (read France, Italy, Germany, etc.). Therefore, the argument has its own reputation: if it is true, there is no point in appealing to it; and if the appeal is valid—because we avoid that slope—then the argument is false (de Miguel Beriain & Armaza, 2018).

It should also be borne in mind that the curtailment of fundamental rights is considerably reduced if the requirement for the certificate is limited to leisure areas and if assistance is allowed through a free or inexpensive negative test. In any case, the assets to be preserved are of considerable importance: public health or freedom of movement itself. I am aware that it seems counter-intuitive, but in reality, it can be argued that an immunity certificate defends, in certain circumstances, freedom of movement, as it avoids a much worse situation in terms of this right, namely, strict confinement. Of course, this judgement of proportionality will depend on the seriousness of the case. It is not the same, for example, to face pandemics at a time of low incidence as at one when it is very high. Hence, also, the assets at stake do not have the same weight in each scenario. The greater the threat, the more the balance will swing in favour of the certificates. The weaker the danger, the more difficult it will be to justify the proportionality of the measure.

In short, there is no real possibility to determine, in a general way, whether the adoption of immunity certificates will meet the requirements of the principle of proportionality. It will depend on the circumstances. What is certain, however, is that there is no reason to reject them outright based on this principle.

2.3.5   Other Considerations: The Possibility of Counterfeiting and Fraud

Another reason to oppose the introduction of immunity certificates is that they can be easily counterfeited, as there will be a clear demand for these documents. In the case of COVID-19, numerous fraudulent distribution channels for fake certificates have already been detected. Some articles already mention the possibility of buying them in most countries in the world (Georgoulias et al., 2021). Problems can also come from elsewhere, as Greeley (2020) rightly points out:

> Now assume the lab result document is authentic—but the applicant is not. He says he is Henry T. Greely. How hard do we make him prove it? A driver's license (which may not be authentic)? More? Less? Part of the answer to that will depend on the incentives of the person providing the certificate. Having a reputation for low standards could easily lead to more business—and, of course, frank bribery is possible. A newly established industry, or newly established government certifying offices, may well lack the kinds of controls and bureaucratic oversight that reduces fraud and corruption in more established contexts.

These objections have their own specific weight and should not be brushed aside as if they did not exist. There are, however, relatively simple ways to avoid these problems arising. In many countries, displaying a fraudulent certificate would be an offence of forgery of a public document, which can result in a prison sentence. Well-publicised, this scenario is already a serious incentive to stay on the right side of the law. If, in addition, the certificate is free of charge, there is unlikely to be a high demand for forgeries. Besides, if we have random checks to identify whoever uses a fake certificate, which would carry a heavy prison sentence, it would be even more irrational in terms of risk/benefit to enter these circuits. Of course, it will not be easy for every state to be able to put all these countermeasures in place at the same time.

A reasonable alternative or complement is to focus on issuance: the more professional the system for creating certificates, the easier it will be to implement measures to prevent forgery or fraud. Special care must be taken to keep a close watch on access to sensitive parts of the system, such as the keys that give authenticity to a certificate. Knowing who has had access to them is essential to identify possible leaks. It is also appropriate to establish a system of official tenders to establishments that can issue a certificate, so that it is more difficult for fraud to arise. However, there will be fraud, as with passports or driving licences. We are not abandoning these tools, but simply trying to reduce counterfeiting. That is probably the only way also in the case of certificates.

2.4 The Issue of Personal Data

One of the issues that has generated the greatest opposition to the creation and use of health certificates is related to the processing of personal data. It is undeniable that it is necessary for any system to work efficiently if such processing is to take place, at least at two different stages, on the one hand, when the certificate itself is being created, and on the other hand, when verifying the validity of a certificate in order to access a specific space. In the first case, it is necessary for the issuer to be able to access a database containing sensitive data on the person's health (such as whether he/she has been vaccinated or has passed the disease and, in both cases, when) or be able to verify his/her current health status by performing a test that will reveal whether the person is infected or not. In turn, whoever performs the test will have to enter the result in a database, so that whoever has to verify the accuracy of the document can do so. In a second step, it will be necessary, or at least possible, for someone to check the possession of a certificate and the adequacy of its contents to the conditions of access to an environment. This will again involve processing of sensitive personal data.

Such massive processing of data on citizens' health arouses great suspicion. In principle, our governments tend to ensure that the data processed will only be kept for a limited period of time and that it will be restricted to the purposes for which it was obtained. There are reasons to be wary. Certainly, some of the surveillance measures introduced since the 9/11 attacks in the USA are still fully in place, even if their introduction was justified on the basis of their temporariness (Gstrein, 2021a). It is therefore necessary to provide ourselves with the means and guarantees to ensure that both the introduction of the tool and the use of the data collected as a result do not end up generating a serious problem in terms of the fundamental rights and freedoms of citizens.

This is by no means impossible in the regulatory framework with which the EU has endowed itself, governed by the GDPR (Kędzior, 2021). This was pointed out in the Opinion prepared by the data protection agencies on the European Green Certificate (Digital Green Certificate).[3] This document made the processing of data conditional on the existence of a legal basis in Member State law that should at the very least include specific provisions clearly identifying the scope and extent of the

---

[3] EDPB-EDPS Joint Opinion 04/2021 on the Proposal for a Regulation of the European Parliament and of the Council on a framework for the issuance, verification and acceptance of interoperable certificates on vaccination, testing and recovery, 31 March 2021.

processing, the specific purpose involved, the categories of entities that could verify the certificate as well as the relevant safeguards to prevent abuse, taking into account the risks for the rights and freedoms of data subjects. However, the impact assessment did not take place in the case of the COVID certificate, and this is regrettable (Gstrein, 2021b).

On the other hand, the agencies established that the legal tool enabling the processing would necessarily include a regulatory development in the legislation of the Member States. This is appropriate, since, in the case of special category data, an exception to the general veto of Article 9.1 GDPR would have to be found before even proceeding to choose the basis for legitimising the processing. This probably implies the need to appeal to the circumstances included in Article 9.2 (g) or (i), which requires a regulatory development in the Member State. The tool in question should include, at a minimum, specific provisions clearly identifying the scope and extent of the processing, the specific purpose, the categories of entities serving to verify the certificate as well as the relevant safeguards to prevent abuse, taking into account the risks to the rights and freedoms of data subjects. In any case, and going one step further than the data protection agencies, I would like to introduce some questions about data protection and certificates that are particularly important.

First of all, it is complex to know why a certificate has to include precise information about the reason why a subject holds it. In reality, the person who has to control access to a safe space does not need to know this information in order to allow or prevent entry. The only relevant aspect is whether he/she can spread the pathology, not the reason why (if any). Consequently, it would be more reasonable for certificates not to contain this information, following the principle of data minimisation. I am aware that this would substantially complicate the technological challenge required for its implementation, but this should not be a reason to justify a breach of the data regulation.

Second, I consider that there is no reason to introduce a requirement to display these certificates for access to protected areas, except in truly exceptional cases (such as hospital facilities or old people's homes in the case of COVID). Forcing employees or business owners of different types of businesses to fulfil these security functions is an unnecessary operation and is against the principle of data processing. This is particularly disconcerting since those workers are not usually subject to confidentiality and secrecy regulations. It also places an excessive and unmanageable burden on them. If the authority (police) shows up at the premises, and if the customer denies having shown a certificate to enter (e.g. because it is a forgery), and the manager of the establishment subsequently receives a sanction, then we are committing a blatant injustice. The most efficient in terms of data protection and human resources savings would be to allow access by warning the customer of the need to have the certificate and to carry out random checks by agents authorised by the relevant authorities, capable of detecting forgeries. This is a system quite similar to the one in place in public transport in most EU countries, with considerable success in practice.

Third, it is essential to stress the importance of ensuring that all citizens have access to certificates, not only to the means to obtain them but also to the certificates themselves. In the case of COVID-19, many people with impaired digital capabilities had enormous difficulties in obtaining a paper copy of their certificate, despite the recommendations of the European authorities. On the other hand, there were obvious problems in adjusting the system to the medical situation of the citizens, which presented a greater variability than the regulations elaborated for obtaining the certificate included. Some people who could not be vaccinated for clinical reasons had problems obtaining the certificates. It was also complicated to deal with others who did not need to be vaccinated because they already had a diagnosis based on symptomatology attesting that they had passed the disease, but had not obtained confirmation through laboratory tests. These circumstances should not occur in the future, because they cause serious injustices that call into question the ethical consistency of the system as a whole.

Furthermore, we must consider that, as the EDPB-EDPS Opinion underlines, the introduction of these certificates entails a "risk for forgeries and therefore, it must be accompanied by the adoption of adequate technical and organisational measures safeguarding against manipulation and falsification of the certificates". Similarly, appropriate measures must be taken to prevent unauthorised access to data. This is not a minor problem. In the case of COVID-19, there were massive leaks. As Gstrein et al. (2021) point out, in the Netherlands:

> The rapid scaling of the COVID-19 test and trace system without appropriate governance and organisational safeguards has resulted in the leak of eight million datasets as of the end of January 2021, including highly sensitive personal data such as test results, names, addresses and social security numbers. That such data is increasingly at the centre of attention of cybercriminals is also demonstrated by a data leak of a health laboratory in France in February 2021, where information relating to approximately 500,000 persons was compromised.

When these situations arise, it is essential to have appropriate damage mitigation tools and transparency policies that provide for the communication of security breaches. Without these requirements, the security of citizens would be at serious risk.

2.5   Organic Disability: Privileges for the Vulnerable?

There is, finally, an issue that has hardly been addressed in the academic literature, but which I believe requires some attention. I have pointed out in these pages that any kind of pandemic divides the population into different groups, according to their characteristics in terms of immunity, contagiousness or vulnerability to the disease. The fact is that this differentiation may well persist once a pandemic has ended as such, and only an endemic disease that regularly causes contagion remains (obviously, if it does not, this section and its considerations are superfluous). In these circumstances, there will still be sectors of the population that are particularly vulnerable to the pathogen: people who have been unable to be immunised because they have no access to vaccines; people who have refused to be vaccinated and have not acquired natural immunity; people who have been vaccinated but have not generated an immune response; and so on.

A particularly interesting question is whether, once the pandemic is over, we should return to "normal" life, that is, a scenario in which we act as if nothing had happened, or whether, on the contrary, we should maintain some kind of measures to protect all these people. In my view, this second option is certainly more reasonable. At the end of the day, public health systems have to implement what they can to protect all their citizens, as long as this does not strain public resources disproportionately.

However, within all the groups I have listed in my description, a distinction should be made, at least, between those who have not been able to immunise themselves, those who have not had access to vaccines for social reasons linked to their vulnerability and those who have not wanted to make use of this resource. The response by a system to each of them needs to be different. In the case of those who have been left out of the allocation of vaccines, it seems obvious that the solution will be to provide them with an administrative channel that allows them to be immunised, providing all the necessary resources for this purpose. To do otherwise would be to perpetuate an injustice that should not have happened in the first place.

The situation of those who cannot be vaccinated for health reasons or those who never become immunised even though they are vaccinated is much more complicated. The impossibility of immunisation will place them in a particularly vulnerable situation from which they will not escape without determined support from the health authorities. This support is even a legal duty, at least for the signatory states of the Convention on the Rights of Persons with Disabilities of 13 December 2006 and probably also for all EU Member States. This idea is based on the fact that the lack of immunological capacity to cope successfully with an infection by a pathogenic agent constitutes a form of organic disability. This is a situation that encompasses many types of diseases: some localised in one organ, some systemic; some communicable/contagious and some not; and some hereditary and some caused by external or environmental factors. Nevertheless, all with a common component: a disability capable of eroding a person's health, where we understand the concept of health and disability from a broad perspective (Elliott et al., 2009), related to the difficulties experienced by the person to participate in social life.

This broad interpretation, which is the one required by my argument, has solid legal foundations. Indeed, it has been confirmed by the CJEU, inter alia in the judgement of 18 December 2014 (Case C-354/13), known as the Daouidi case,[4] when it stated that:

> (...) the concept of 'disability' must be understood as referring to a limitation, resulting in particular from long-term physical, mental or psychological impairment, which, in interaction with various barriers, may prevent the person concerned from participating fully and effectively in working life on an equal footing with other workers (...). This concept of 'disability' must be understood as covering not only the impossibility of carrying out an occupational activity, but also a difficulty in carrying out that activity.

---

[4] ECLI identifier: ECLI:EU:C:2014:2463.

With this legal framework in mind, persons unable to immunise themselves against a particular pathology of particular relevance for a clinical reason can be considered as suffering from a form of organic disability. Consequently, they are unable to develop full social lives if the state does not provide them with adequate means. These can range from research-related measures (encouraging the development of useful drugs or vaccines) to measures aimed at protecting them against contagion by building safe environments: underground or train carriages in which safety measures such as masks or air renewal are necessary, cinema sessions in which similar rules are imposed, freedom for bars or restaurants to introduce them into certain reserved areas, etc. It would also be important to provide them with priority access to such safe environments on presentation of an organic disability badge.

What about those who do not wish to be immunised even though they are able to do so? Would they also be considered organically disabled? Should the State also introduce measures adapted to their situation? Here the answer is simpler. It is obvious that there are limits to the State's obligation to care for its citizens. In fact, it is hard to argue that it should protect those who do not want to protect themselves. If a person does not want to take a vaccine that has been proven safe and effective and that the State makes available, it is perfectly legitimate to understand that this citizen is neglecting to protect himself. It is therefore excessive to understand that he has the right to expect the community to do something that he does not wish to do, namely, to take care of himself. Therefore, I do not believe that the recognition of this organic disability can be extended to those who freely choose not to be vaccinated.

References

Atkeson, A., Droste, M. C., Mina, M., & Stock, J. H. (2020). *Economic benefits of covid-19 screening tests* (No. w28031). National Bureau of Economic Research.

Brown, R. C., Kelly, D., Wilkinson, D., & Savulescu, J. (2021). The scientific and ethical feasibility of immunity passports. *The Lancet Infectious Diseases, 21*(3), e58–e63.

Burgess, J. A. (1993). The great slippery-slope argument. *Journal of Medical Ethics, 19*(3), 169–174.

Cierco Seira, C. (2018). *Vaccination, individual liberties and public law* (pp. 19–40). Marial Pons.

De Miguel Beriain, I. (2021). COVID-19 vaccinations without discrimination. *Spotlight, ELI Newsletter*, 2021, Issue 2, March–April 2021. Retrieved December 19, 2021, from https://europeanlawinstitute.eu/fileadmin/user_upload/p_eli/Newsletter/2021/Newsletter_March-April_2021.pdf

de Miguel Beriain, I., & Armaza, E. A. (2018). An ethical analysis of new gene editing technologies: CRISPR-Cas9 under debate. In *Anales de la Cátedra Francisco Suárez* (Vol. 52, pp. 179–200).

de Miguel Beriain, I., & Rueda, J. (2020). Immunity passports, fundamental rights and public health hazards: A reply to Brown et al. *Journal of Medical Ethics, 46*(10), 660–661.

Elliott, R., Utyasheva, L., & Zack, E. (2009). HIV, disability and discrimination: Making the links in international and domestic human rights law. *Journal of the International AIDS Society, 12*(1), 1–15.

Ganty, S. (2021, May 30). The veil of the COVID-19 vaccination certificates: Ignorance of poverty, injustice towards the poor (Vol. 12).

Georgoulias, D., Pedersen, J. M., Falch, M., & Vasilomanolakis, E. (2021). COVID-19 vaccination certificates in the Darkweb. *arXiv preprint arXiv:2111.12472.*

Greely, H. T. (2020). COVID-19 immunity certificates: Science, ethics, policy, and law. *Journal of Law and the Biosciences, 7*(1), lsaa035.

Gstrein, O. J. (2021a). *COVID-19 vaccine passports and their impact on privacy and autonomy.* Israel Public Policy Institute.

Gstrein, O. J. (2021b). The EU digital COVID certificate: A preliminary data protection impact assessment. *European Journal of Risk Regulation, 12*(2), 370–381.

Gstrein, O. J., Kochenov, D., & Zwitter, A. (2021). A terrible great idea? COVID-19 'vaccination passports' in the spotlight.

Hall, M. A., & Studdert, D. M. (2020). Privileges and immunity certification during the COVID-19 pandemic. *Journal of the American Medical Association, 323*(22), 2243–2244.

Kates, O. S., & Hastings Center. (2020). Show me your passport: Ethical concerns about Covid-19 antibody testing as key to reopening public life. In *Hastings bioethics forum.* The Hastings Center.

Kędzior, M. (2021, January). The right to data protection and the COVID-19 pandemic: The European approach. In *ERA forum* (Vol. 21, no. 4, pp. 533–543). Springer.

Kofler, N., & Baylis, F. (2020). Ten reasons why immunity passports are a bad idea. *Nature, 581*(7809), 379–381.

Nuffield Council on Bioethics. (2020). *Rapid policy briefing: Covid-19 antibody testing and "immunity certification".* Retrieved from www.nuffieldbioethics.org/publications/covid-19-antibody-testing-and-immunity-certification

Olivarius, K. (2019). Immunity, capital, and power in Antebellum new Orleans. *The American Historical Review, 124*(2), 425–455.

Osama, T., Razai, M. S., & Majeed, A. (2021). Covid-19 vaccine passports: Access, equity, and ethics. *British Medical Journal, 373*, n861.

Persad, G., & Emanuel, E. J. (2020). The ethics of COVID-19 immunity-based licenses ("immunity passports"). *Journal of the American Medical Association, 323*(22), 2241–2242.

Phelan, A. L. (2020). COVID-19 immunity passports and vaccination certificates: Scientific, equitable, and legal challenges. *The Lancet, 395*(10237), 1595–1598.

Ravitsky, V., & Weinstock, D. (2020). Are immunity licenses just?. *The American Journal of Bioethics, 20*(7), 172–174.

Recchi, E., Ferragina, E., Godechot, O., Helmeid, E., Pauly, S., Safi, M., Sauger, N., Schradie, J., Tittel, K., Zola, A. (2020). Living through lockdown: Social inequalities and transformations during the COVID-19 crisis in France.

Romer, P., Mina, M., Badger, D., & Fishpaw, M. (2021). *Rapid COVID tests: A cure for lockdowns, a complement to vaccines.* Heritage Foundation (Lecture 1319).

Schlagenhauf, P., Patel, D., Rodriguez-Morales, A., Gautret, P., Grobusch, M. P., & Leder, K. (2021). Variants, vaccines and vaccination passports: Challenges and chances for travel medicine in 2021. *Travel Medicine and Infectious Disease, 40*, 101996.

Solaiman, R. H., & Marette, S. (2021). COVID-19 vaccination inequity in the United States: An intersectional issue. *Journal of Health and Social Sciences, 6*(2), 167–174.

Wagenaar, H., & Prainsack, B. (2021). *The pandemic within: Policy making for a better world.* Policy Press.

Chapter 3
Vaccines (I): Creation and Distribution

3.1 Introduction

The development of COVID-19 vaccines and treatments in a surprisingly short time was one of the few positive pieces of news to come from the pandemic. It is curious, however, that this milestone has aroused considerable suspicion among much of Western society. In these circumstances, it is timely to include in a work such as this one a part aimed at analysing the many facets of such a thorny issue as vaccination policy. Of these, there are at least four major issues that require specific attention: how vaccines are developed, how they are distributed, how access to them is prioritised and whether they should be compulsory or not, for some social groups or for all. In this chapter, I will address the first three issues, leaving the one of mandatory vaccines for the next chapter. My comments will focus on a peculiar scenario, a moment marked by the outbreak of a public health crisis such as that produced by a pandemic caused by a highly contagious viral disease. Hence, only some of my considerations can be extrapolated to other times or other types of pathologies. The reason is obvious: in times of crisis, public health considerations carry a heavier weight than they do in other times. Moreover, an infectious-contagious pathology (such as tuberculosis) is certainly not the same as one in which these circumstances are not present (such as tetanus). In the latter, it is relevant to guarantee respect for an individual's autonomy, which should not necessarily be the case in the former.

I must also say in advance that I will only deal with vaccines, not with the reactive treatments that are administered when a person is already infected. The main reason for this is that vaccines tend to arouse greater suspicion because they are administered on a mass scale, to the whole population, and because the resistance they encounter is much greater. There are, of course, explanations for these differences: vaccines involve inoculating a pathogen into healthy patients. Treatments, on the other hand, attempt to cure those who are already suffering from a disease. Most people do not judge the two situations in the same way. Because of these

I. de Miguel Beriain, *The Ethical, Legal and Social Issues of Pandemics*,
https://doi.org/10.1007/978-3-031-03818-1_3

differences, almost everything that is stated about vaccines (their production, distribution and prioritisation) applies to medical treatments. However, the discussion on
vaccines also includes one aspect concerning whether vaccines should be compulsory, which is not usually raised in the case of treatments. In any case, the reader
should bear these caveats in mind if he or she wishes to extrapolate the reasoning
from one context to another.

3.2   Clinical Trials and Their Alternatives

3.2.1   Introduction: Clinical Trials in Times of Pandemic

If there is one issue that caused controversy in the development of the vaccines used
to tackle the SARS-CoV-2 pandemic, it was the extremely rapid pace of the clinical
trials phase. Critics were quick to claim that this was an attack on the fundamentals
of science and the methods of these biotechnologies. Are these criticisms sustainable? Clearly not. There are long-established guidelines that should be used to judge
the practices developed in the context of COVID-19, such as the guidelines developed by CIOMS (Council for International Organizations of Medical Sciences
2017, pp. 77 and 78), which already pointed out that:

> Disasters unfold quickly and study designs need to be chosen so that studies will yield
> meaningful data in a rapidly evolving situation. Study designs must be feasible in a disaster
> situation but still appropriate to ensure the study's scientific validity (...) researchers, spon-
> sors, research ethics committees and others must explore alternative trial designs that may
> increase trial efficiency and access to promising experimental interventions while still
> maintaining scientific validity. The methodological and ethical merits of alternative trial
> designs must be carefully assessed before these designs are used. For example, when testing
> experimental treatments or vaccines during an epidemic, the appropriate trial design will
> depend on the promise of the investigational agent, a variation in critical background fac-
> tors (for example mortality and infection rates), and measurement of outcomes,
> among others.

Can we state that in the SARS-CoV-2 pandemic these Guidelines were adequately followed? The general consensus is affirmative. As is well known, clinical
drug trials are usually divided into four phases. Each phase has different objectives
and must also meet different requirements, for instance, linked to the number of
participants or their population representativeness. These trials and their results are
carefully scrutinised by regulatory agencies, such as the European Medicines
Agency, which must approve their use before the product can be marketed. These
procedures are meticulous, so it is virtually impossible for a drug to be allowed onto
the market if there is something within the results that suggests that the trials have
not proven its safety or efficacy. Moreover, if at the drug surveillance stages there is
any reason to consider that the effects of the vaccine should be stopped, implementation is often ceased until the issue is clarified, or suspended, as happened with
AstraZeneca's compound, for example, in some countries. Knowing this, there is

little reason to be suspicious about the approval of vaccines or other drugs in times of pandemic. If the speed of the process is impressive, perhaps we should consider that in the circumstances of a pandemic the recruitment of volunteer numbers is much easier than in normal times. Adding to that the fact that there are many teams trying to develop vaccines at the same time, and that funding is assured, then it is not so surprising that the timescales are substantially shortened. In fact, the real novel problem generated by this high speed in the drug production process is how to proceed with placebo groups when one of the treatments is approved. This is what I will discuss in the next section.

3.2.2 Placebo Groups and Approved Vaccines

Once clinical trials eventually result in a safe and efficient vaccine, a conflicting scenario appears. As is well known, volunteers participating in drug development are separated into two groups, one of which receives only a placebo. In epidemiological terms, keeping them in this state is as much as depriving them, at least temporarily, of the vaccine, which obviously leaves them in a precarious situation. Worse still, we know that it is often the case that trial participants tend to relax their precautions, even if they do not know whether they have been inoculated with the vaccine and whether it is working properly. If, at a given moment, we are already confident that the vaccine is effective, preserving the anonymity of who has and who has not received the vaccine may pose an unnecessary risk to the latter. In fact, many will want to know if they were part of the placebo group and, if so, get vaccinated. This could have negative effects on the trial results, as it would prevent testing such important questions as the long-term safety of the vaccine, how long the immunity lasts or whether it protects all segments of the population equally. From this evidence, the question arises whether we are obliged to inform patients about their status, to disclose the composition of the placebo group or, moreover, to offer vaccination to participants, even if this might alter the conditions of the clinical trial.

The first of these issues is the easiest to be resolved. According to the Good Clinical Practice Guidelines, the head of a trial should inform participants of any circumstances that may affect their consent to continue in the trial (Dal-Ré et al., 2021). The emergence of a vaccine for the disease in question falls under this description. This, however, does not include the obligation to inform them whether they were part of the placebo group. Instead, it is necessary to explain in detail how the emergence of a new vaccine has altered the parameters under which the original consent was given. The information provided should explain the risks and benefits of remaining in the blind trial when placebo recipients would otherwise have access to the vaccine. In any case, it is difficult to think that the original consent is still informed (and therefore valid) when circumstances have changed so much. Hence, we might even consider the need to obtain a new consent (Dal-Ré et al., 2008). What is certain is that participants should at least be given an option to opt out of the trial with updated information to replace the previous one.

The question of whether there are ethical reasons to break the secrecy of group composition is more complicated. A committee formed by the UN to address this issue argued in 2020 that there are not necessarily (WHO Ad Hoc Expert Group, 2021), provided certain conditions are met:

> While vaccine supplies are limited, available vaccines are still investigational, or public health recommendations to use those vaccines have not been made, we believe it is ethically appropriate to continue blinded follow-up of placebo recipients in existing trials and to randomly assign new participants to vaccine or placebo. Moreover, under these conditions, we believe that trial sponsors are not ethically obligated to unblind treatment assignments for participants who desire to obtain a different investigational vaccine. People who enroll in clinical trials for altruistic reasons would probably understand the value of gathering data that will further elucidate the safety and efficacy of these vaccines and their appropriate use.

In practice, developers are likely to choose to disclose the composition of the placebo group. This was done, for instance, to the participants in their clinical trials in 2021 by Pfizer and Moderna (Herper, 2021). Moreover, both companies offered the members of their placebo groups the possibility to administer their compounds, which certainly altered the trial conditions. Surely the explanation for this course of action is that, in a situation of complex resolution, the companies consider that, since the vaccines have already been proven effective, the safety of the participants, as well as the need to reward them for their behaviour rather than penalise them for contributing to the development of science, must take precedence over the potential usefulness of the data to be collected.

There are some possibilities that could serve to maintain the viability of clinical trials in such scenarios. First, participants could be unblinded only when, according to national vaccination plans, they are eligible to be vaccinated. In this way, only participants with priority access to a vaccine would be disclosed. If they were not going to be able to access the vaccine anyway, it would not be unfair to keep them uninformed. In addition, if vaccine administration was slow, this could give researchers ample scope for analysis, although they would likely lose heterogeneity in the sample, as the most at-risk participants would be the first ones to have access to the drug (e.g. unless the allocation criterion was interruption of transmission). There is also an alternative option proposed by authors such as Dal-Ré, Orenstein and Caplan (2021), which consists of giving the vaccine to all those who received the placebo and giving the placebo to those who were vaccinated ("crossover double-blind design"). None of the trial participants would know which of the two groups they belonged to, so the trial would remain blinded. In this way, the researchers could compare the groups to see whether the efficacy of the vaccines faded over time.

Of course, we could also consider recruiting new participants, who would be randomly assigned to the placebo group, replacing those who dropped out of the trial. In principle, the new participants would be particularly aware of the circumstances involved, so they should be more likely to continue to the end, although they would be under no obligation to do so. Obviously, this possibility is always more complicated when the product is already available to the entire population. A useful tactic would be to include people with a firm decision not to be vaccinated in the placebo group, as proposed by Stoehr et al. (2021). While it is true that this would break some of the principles governing the formation of the groups, such as randomisation, or even blindness in their composition, the data obtained could still be useful. However, it would be unusual if it were precisely those who rejected an approved vaccine who would agree to participate in a clinical trial for the development of the same or an alternative vaccine.

If these options are discarded, there is only one feasible, though not uncontroversial, alternative: to take advantage of the inequities that accompany the distribution of vaccines between countries. This would involve moving trials to places where the drug is not yet sufficiently accessible, so that it would be possible to find volunteers willing to enrol. The problem with accepting this option is that it would further exacerbate global health inequity, given pre-existing inequalities in access to vaccines between high-income and low-income countries.

If all these options are discarded, only the vaccinated group could be compared with data from the general population. Despite the shortcomings of this methodology—the biases produced by the lack of randomisation, the unreliability of data from observational studies (WHO Ad Hoc Expert Group, 2021; Collins et al., 2020)—it would surely be better than doing nothing at all. Of course, one could opt for an exposure or *challenge study*, a particularly challenging concept that I will discuss below.

3.2.3   Challenge Studies or Exposure Studies

A *challenge study* is the deliberate administration of a pathogen to healthy volunteers who have been previously vaccinated, to test the efficacy and safety of vaccines, to increase the likelihood that the vaccines ultimately used will be the most effective and to accelerate their development (Eyal et al., 2020). If we are in a time of pandemic when there are hardly any cases in the population, using these techniques may be particularly interesting, as clinical phase III trials need many participants. Over the past 50 years, such studies have been conducted to accelerate the development of typhoid and cholera vaccines and to determine correlates of immune protection against influenza (WHO, 2020). In periods that do not require such urgency for vaccine development, however, these tactics are not used, because deliberately infecting a human being without knowing what the end result of the trial will be is considered unethical, if we do not have an effective treatment for the disease that the vaccines are intended to prevent. In fact, history shows many examples of research in which subjects were deliberately infected in a completely unethical manner (Jamrozik et al., 2021).

However, when there is a need to shorten timeframes, provocative trials are legitimate, provided they meet a set of standards, such as those set by the WHO, which include the following eight criteria: scientific justification; assessment of risks and potential benefits; consultation and engagement; coordination between researchers, funders, policy makers and regulators; site selection; participant selection; expert review; and informed consent (WHO, 2020). There are three ideas related to these criteria that I find particularly interesting.

Firstly, we must take particular care to do what we can to reduce the risks involved, by introducing a number of measures, regardless of the cost they may entail. These include particularly careful selection of trial participants, including only those we consider to be at low risk of developing a severe form of the disease. Also, of course, careful monitoring of participants' health outcomes, so that any problems can be detected early and appropriately. Isolating them from third parties would also help to avoid negative consequences from accidental transmissions of the agent. In addition, special care must be taken in the preparation of the biological agent to be inoculated to ensure that the dose is not excessive. A level of risk that goes beyond what is strictly necessary should not be allowed, and it is advisable that it does not exceed what is acceptable in other types of clinical trials (Hope & McMillan, 2004). Finally, an efficient and appropriate compensation system for the harm caused must be guaranteed for the characteristics of this type of study (Bambery et al., 2016).

Secondly, it must be borne in mind that, when we talk about minimising risks, we must think of each participant. It is worth remembering that, according to Article 2 of the Oviedo Convention, the welfare of the participants in biomedical research must take precedence over the interest of society as a whole. Or, in the wording of the Declaration of Helsinki (point 8), "while the primary purpose of medical research is to generate new knowledge, this goal can never take precedence over the rights and interests of individual research subjects". This is likely to involve a careful analysis of *each* participant's health circumstances, excluding those who are a priori prone to a harmful outcome. Finally, it should be considered that, as far as possible, essential workers should not be recruited for exposure studies when this would unduly compromise the public health response to the pandemic. It makes little sense to expose health professionals—despite the fact that they are traditionally the most likely to be exposed—to such studies when they will be the main contributors in a situation such as the one described. To do otherwise, in fact, it would be to introduce an unnecessarily high-risk factor for the population.

Thirdly, we must emphasise the extraordinary importance of proper oversight of both the design and conduct of these studies (Bambery et al., 2016). Given their particular risk, as well as the importance of maintaining trust in the conduct of scientific research, we must ensure that errors are not made due to poor monitoring. The involvement of ethics committees, as well as the participation of external experts, is highly recommended. Transparency policies must be followed particularly strictly, and, of course, the information provided to both participants and the public must be especially accurate. Scrupulous compliance with data protection regulations is another essential requirement. It is not clear that, in these cases, we should avoid the use of consent as a basis for legitimising data processing (which is recommended in other clinical trials due to the asymmetry of power between patient and researcher). However, if this finally is what we are going to use, we must ensure that the participant is fully aware of what he or she is giving their consent to.

3.3 Patents and Other Intellectual Property Rights (Data Rights/Industrial Secrecy)

3.3.1 Introduction

One of the most heated discussions during the COVID-19 pandemic was how to increase global vaccine production in a short period of time. Some countries took early initiatives to achieve this goal. On 2 October 2020, South Africa and India asked the World Trade Organization, as the international organisation that administers trade rules among its 164 member countries, to support their initiative to suspend patent protection on medicines, medical devices and technologies related to the fight against COVID-19 in general (Usher, 2020). NGOs such as Médecins Sans Frontières quickly joined this initiative through a social media campaign (Gonsalves & Yamey, 2021). Their proposal was widely debated within the WTO. As a result, on 21 May 2021, a revised version calling for a suspension of intellectual property rights on "health products and technologies including diagnostics, therapeutics, vaccines, medical devices, personal protective equipment, their materials or components, and their methods and means of manufacture for the prevention, treatment or containment of COVID-19" was presented.

To date, this initiative has garnered the support of more than 100 countries, as well as international organisations such as the World Health Organization and the UN AIDS charity UNAIDS. Of these endorsements, some are particularly significant, such as those by the USA and China (although in both cases limited to COVID vaccines, not including other technologies for treatment, prevention and containment of the virus). However, several WTO members, such as the European Union, Norway, the UK and Switzerland, opposed this exemption. Their argument was that current TRIPS flexibilities, such as compulsory licensing, are sufficient to address these difficulties (MSF Access Campaign, 2021; Nature, 2021). On this basis, the proposal put forward by the European Commission to the other WTO member countries was to arrive as soon as possible at "a global trade initiative for equitable access to vaccines and therapies from COVID-19, encompassing the following three components (1) trade facilitation and export restriction regulations; (2) expansion of production, including through commitments by vaccine producers and developers; and (3) clarification and facilitation of TRIPS flexibilities on compulsory licensing" (EU Commission, 2021).

The question to be asked in the light of these debates is whether we can speak of a moral obligation to relax intellectual property protection on relative medical devices when faced with a health emergency, and whether this would allow a more efficient response to the problem, or whether to focus on other initiatives. I will devote the following sections to these issues.

3.3.2   The Legal Regime of Intellectual Property: An Overview

The general intellectual property protection regime developed in the West revolves around a fundamental concept: the patent. A patent can be defined as a pact or contract between an inventor and a particular state, whereby the inventor reveals the intricacies of his invention, and the state guarantees him a counterpart in the form of a monopoly: the inventor is granted an *ius prohibendi*, i.e. the possibility of preventing a third party without his consent (licence) from manufacturing, offering, introducing into commerce or using a patented product or importing or possessing it for any of the aforementioned purposes. In this way, the aim is both to promote the public interest (thanks to the possibility of access to information that would not otherwise be in the public domain) and to encourage private initiative in technological innovation.

International intellectual property law is framed by the Agreements on Trade-Related Aspects of Intellectual Property Rights (TRIPS), which were signed within the framework of the General Agreement on Tariffs and Trade (GATT). Through these agreements, the patent-based regime was given a global scope. However, the agreements introduced a mechanism that sought to introduce some exceptions to the general framework, the *compulsory licence*. This is understood as the possibility granted to a state to authorise the use in its territory of a patented invention without the consent of the patent holder. Over the last 30 years, this figure has caused a great deal of conflict in the pharmaceutical industry, including a heated debate on the scope of patent rights and their relationship with other rights (De Miguel Beriain, 2013).

The Declaration on the TRIPS Agreement and Public Health at the Fourth WTO Ministerial Conference in Doha (Qatar) on 14 November 2001, usually referred to as the Doha Declaration, is fundamental to understand the correct interpretation of compulsory licensing. This declaration established a criterion according to which, when interpreting TRIPS, access to existing medicines should be allowed to underdeveloped countries for public health reasons, without any negotiation with the patent holder. In addition, the Doha Declaration allowed producing member countries to adopt a compulsory licence for the production of pharmaceuticals for export, which was essential to overcome the production problems faced by many nations, especially on the African continent (Son & Lee, 2018). However, according to Article 31(h) of TRIPS, the patent rights holder is entitled to receive adequate remuneration.

Current intellectual property law, in short, allows WTO member countries to apply for compulsory licences on patents in cases of health emergencies. During the COVID-19 crisis, Hungary and Russia used compulsory licensing for government use of remdesivir; Israel did so for lopinavir/ritonavir (Gurgula & Lee, 2021).

Moreover, Bolivia requested permission from the WTO to activate this process and manufacture Johnson & Johnson's COVID vaccine. The problem is that, in practice, compulsory licensing is unlikely to be the response that many countries need to a pandemic situation that cannot be delayed, for several reasons. First, they only extend to patents that already exist, but not to patents that are in the pipeline. These would therefore fall outside the umbrella of the clause. Moreover, each licence must be processed separately for each product. Worse still, vaccines often comprise not one but several patents, belonging to different inventors, with different legal statuses. For example, "plastic, single-use bioreactor bags have been scarce due to the global dependency on a few suppliers for these materials; crucially, there are currently 2800 patents that cover them, making entering the market as a new supplier onerous" (Thambisetty, 2021). This situation ends up leading to a time-consuming process that is ill suited to the needs of a pandemic. In the case of mRNA vaccine manufacture, there is also a global shortage of essential components, especially nucleotides, enzymes and lipids. This is because relatively few companies manufacture these products, and there is not enough for the global supply. Moreover, these companies are reluctant to license manufacturing so that others can do so. For example, each strand of RNA requires a "plug" that prevents the human body from rejecting it as foreign material. This is the most expensive component of the entire vaccine, and the intellectual property rights to this component are held by only a few companies. The same is true for at least one of the four lipid nanoparticles that form the RNA envelope (Irwin & Nkengasong, 2021).

A further complication is that, as I have already explained, patents are agreements between inventors and specific countries. Their scope of application is therefore limited to a specific nation. Consequently, a compulsory licence would only cover a specific territory, the one in which the patent is in force. This means that each country would have to grant them separately, with no such thing as a compulsory licence with regional or worldwide coverage being possible. Finally, it should not be forgotten that Article 31 of TRIPS states the following:

> when the law of a Member permits other uses of the subject matter of a patent without the authorization of the right holder, including use by the government or by third parties authorized by the government, the following provisions shall be observed (...) (f) such uses shall be authorized primarily to supply the domestic market of the Member authorizing such uses.

It is true that the Doha Declaration put a stop to this limitation, resulting in an amendment to TRIPS, in the form of article 31bis, which allows at present the export of medical devices produced under the umbrella of a compulsory licence to third countries, with some exceptions. Thus, interestingly, the European Union and its Member States opted not to apply this clause, so they cannot import medicines produced under compulsory licences. However, in practice this system is extremely difficult to enforce, as it introduces difficulties "through requirements that range from adding unnecessary steps (i.e. mandatory differential packaging and colouring of products under the compulsory license), to actively impeding the flexibility needed in an evolving public health crisis (i.e. requiring importing countries to specify the quantity needed for each product in each compulsory license used under the notification made to the WTO)" (Médecins Sans Frontières, 2020). In short, the patent regime does not offer many advantages in terms of dealing with a pandemic, despite its flexibilities.

3.3.3 Other Forms of Industrial Property Protection: Data and the 8 + 2 + 1 Rule

Patents are not the only form of industrial property protection. A proper approach to this issue must take into account the role that the confidentiality of data pertaining to innovative medicines plays in creating barriers to compulsory licensing. As such, they fall outside the scope of TRIPS. Data have their own regulatory framework, often referred to as the regulated data protection regime, which exists in more than 40 countries, according to a report on the subject by the International Federation of Pharmaceutical Manufacturers Associations in 2011 (IFPMA, 2011).

The case of the EU is paradigmatic in this regard, as established by Regulation (EC) No 726/2004 of the European Parliament and of the Council of 31 March 2004 laying down Community procedures for the authorisation and supervision of medicinal products for human and veterinary use and establishing a European Medicines[1] Agency. As Carla Schoonderbeek et al. explain, "under European pharmaceutical law innovator pharmaceutical companies are granted a period of regulatory data exclusivity in which a generic applicant cannot refer to the innovator's data to obtain a marketing authorisation. The European legislation was amended in 2004 and currently contains a period of eight plus two (plus one) years of regulatory data protection (RDP)".

We therefore find that the regulated data protection (RDP) framework in the EU establishes a period of time during which the applicant for a generic patent cannot use the data entered by the original inventor in his application. This is commonly referred to as *data exclusivity* protection. Moreover, the product cannot be introduced on the market until at least 10 years after the initial marketing authorisation of the original product. This is called *market exclusivity*. In some circumstances (such as when the originator company receives a marketing authorisation for a significant new indication), the deadline can be extended for an additional year, and therefore the whole system is known as the 8 + 2 + 1 year rule (FM 't Hoen et al., 2017).

This regulatory situation (which does not stem from TRIPS, it must be stressed) places the different market players, de facto, in a very unequal position and makes it difficult for the producer of a generic product to gain rapid access to the market. This is because in order to commercialise a medical device, its developer must first obtain a marketing authorisation. In order to do so, it must demonstrate that the

---

[1] Regulation (EC) No. 726/2004 on the authorisation and supervision of medicinal products and establishing a European Medicines Agency (EMA Regulation).

medicinal product is safe and effective for use, which requires a huge amount of data to be provided. This data is of course only in the possession of the developer of the original product. It is part of their industrial capital, and it is rare that the holder would wish to share it with third parties. However, this general industrial property protection regime, which may make sense under normal conditions, becomes a definite obstacle to the rapid development of generic products when the occasion arises. As FM't et al. say, since the European pharmaceutical industry regulation knows no exceptions to these rules, this implies that "They cannot register a generic product during the data/market exclusivity period, even when the medicine is needed for compelling public health reasons or emergencies or when a compulsory or government use license has been issued on a medicine patent" (FM 't Hoen et al., 2017).

The most reasonable approach would be to address this obstacle by including in our regulations mandatory suspensions to data exclusivity, as already proposed by some authors (FM 't Hoen, 2022). Unfortunately, this currently exists only in a relatively small number of countries such as Chile, Malaysia or Colombia. This would not necessarily mean giving up all forms of data protection, but rather introducing a data compensation regime in which the original producer of the data would receive some form of compensation for its use. In addition, we should limit such uses by third parties to scenarios where it is strictly necessary and urgent in the general interest. FM't Hoen et al. proposed the introduction of such a clause in EU law, which seems to me to be a reasonable proposal:

> The protection periods set out in article 14 (11) of Regulation 726/2004 shall not apply in cases where it is necessary to allow access to and the use of pharmaceutical test data to register a generic of a reference medicinal product, which is or has been authorised under article 6 of Directive 2001/83/EC, for reasons of public interest including public health, in case of compulsory licensing of patents, including for public non-commercial use, and in situations of national emergency or extreme urgency (FM 't Hoen et al., 2017).

3.3.4 The Introduction of Waivers on Intellectual Property-Related Rights

If I had to summarise what I have shown in the previous section, it would probably be that the compulsory licensing regime is not efficient in enabling the production of vaccines or other products in a quick and agile manner. If we add to this the fact that the protection of data enabling the approval of drugs creates additional hurdles, it seems obvious that new forms of regulation in the field of intellectual property on medical devices and drugs need to be introduced. We have already discussed the possibility of introducing a concept such as suspensions in the field of data ownership. The initiative undertaken by India or South Africa seeks to extend this concept to patents. Nevertheless, what exactly does a waiver consist of?

As I have already mentioned, the international regime for the protection of industrial property is based on agreements (TRIPS) that can be modified if those who have concluded them decide so. In this case, the proponents of the waiver seek to have TRIPS member countries temporarily waive the right that these agreements give them to sanction those who violate their protocols under certain circumstances. According to the model proposed by India and South Africa in 2020, this would include times when we are in a health emergency and only for a limited period of time. This suspension of intellectual property rights could be very broad, covering, of course, the right to block, but also those that complement it. Other aspects, such as whether this would give rise to compensation, could even be considered (Gurgula, 2021).

If such changes to TRIPS were achieved, the benefits could be many. For a start, rights could be suspended on multiple products including different patents, without having to go on a case-by-case basis (Sengupta, 2021). It would also avoid resorting to the procedure established by Article 31bis of TRIPS for the export of vaccines or medicines to third countries with no or limited manufacturing capacity. Above all, the suspension would allow companies and research institutions to develop and produce vaccines and other health technologies in the fight against COVID-19 without fear of litigation (Thambisetty, 2021).

3.3.5 Licences and Suspensions: The Arguments

What are the chances that these suspensions will succeed? It is difficult to say, because there is strong reluctance on the part of some WTO members, such as Australia, Japan, Norway, Singapore, South Korea, Switzerland and Taiwan, for example. The position of EU Member States and their institutions on this issue has been mixed. Some of them, such as Germany, Portugal, Estonia and Belgium, have shown strong reservations, while Greece, France and Italy seem a priori in favour of introducing these suspensions. As for the Commission, it is worth noting that on 4 June 2021, it issued a communication to the WTO on TRIPS and COVID-19, reiterating an alternative health policy proposal that focuses on compulsory licencing, limiting export restrictions and expanding production, rather than waiving patent rights. On 18 June, the Council adopted its own conclusions on the role of intellectual property in the fight against the COVID-19 pandemic, underlining the EU's commitment in the WTO and its readiness to find pragmatic approaches. It cited patent pooling, licensing and knowledge-sharing platforms as acceptable solutions. It also showed its readiness to discuss further flexibilities in the TRIPS agreement. The Parliament finally adopted a resolution on this subject in June 2021[2] calling for the opening of negotiations on temporary TRIPS suspensions in order to improve global access to COVID-19-related medical products.

Countries that oppose suspensions argue that such a system could lead to the manufacture of low-quality health products, although this belief has been clearly

---

[2] European Parliament resolution of 10 June 2021 on meeting the global COVID-19 challenge: effects of the waiver of the WTO TRIPS Agreement on COVID-19 vaccines, treatment, equipment and increasing production and manufacturing capacity in developing countries.

disproved in the past (Okereke & Essar, 2021). The fact that countries such as India, Egypt and Thailand are manufacturing vaccines based on viral vectors or mRNA should, in fact, dismiss this objection (Erfani et al., 2021).

There is another argument that is often made in this regard: that the incentive to innovate would be drastically reduced if we weakened intellectual property rights, setting a precedent that could deter firms from investing in innovation in the future. However, this classic critique does not seem to be strong in practice, based on the evidence (Thambisetty et al., 2021). Strange as it may seem, innovation does not stop just because specific rights are temporarily suspended. Furthermore, the argument loses much of its force if we think of products, such as the SARS-CoV-2 vaccines, whose research was largely paid for by states (Sariola, 2021), which bore the costs of possible failure. The context of a pandemic, in which a further $18 billion in public funding has been allocated to support the development of COVID-19 vaccines, provides a strong argument against patent protection at this time (Katz et al., 2021).

More robust are the criticisms made by the biotech industry, which has generally questioned the breadth, vagueness and feasibility of implementing the exemption in national laws around the world. It is quite probable that acceptance of the derogations would lead to a slow change of regulations in multiple countries, resulting in a melting pot of legal situations. This would probably make it impossible for IPR holders to understand which products or services would lose IPR protection in each country, or for how long, and this does not facilitate the development of innovation in any way. Although it has been said that the suspension would be temporary, there are certain categories that do not allow for this. Trade secret information, manufacturing know-how, clinical data packages, etc. that are proposed for sharing cannot be hidden again once disclosed (Sauer, 2021; Gurgula & Hull, 2021). This, of course, complicates the picture, although this hurdle could be cleared by introducing confidentiality clauses in licences or suspensions imposing strict obligations on the parties to maintain secrecy, including the obligation to enter and observe the security of information transferred under the licence or suspension. However, it must be acknowledged that some important questions have not been adequately addressed. As Gurgula and Hull put it:

> Even if we start from the premise that trade secrets should be shared, another challenging question is how should 'trade secret sharing' or their compulsory licensing be carried out? More specifically, how might this be achieved in a way that balances the needs of the public and fairness to trade secret rights holders whose fragile rights are to be put into the hands of third-party licensees? In this respect, most of the proponents of the IP waiver, compulsory licensing or enforced technology transfer are notably silent (Gurgula & Hull, 2021).

There are, at last, doubts as to whether a suspension would really be able to increase our production quickly and efficiently. Unfortunately, it does not seem easy, due to a lack of industrial capacity. It is difficult to know how many manufacturers are capable of producing COVID-19 vaccines. Industry routinely reports that there are not many (or, rather, that all capacity has been absorbed (Kuchler, 2021)), but there are companies based in different countries—such as Canada (Biolyse), Israel (Teva), Denmark (Bavarian Nordic) and Bangladesh (Incepta)—that have offered their manufacturing capacity to the big vaccine producers and have been turned down (Thambisetty et al., 2021). What is certain, however, is that it is not easy to extend manufacturing lines to those who usually produce traditional vaccines with conventional manufacturing technology. It is simply not possible to make such an industrial leap in a nimble way. Different facilities would be needed, and building, certifying and commissioning them would take time, money and valuable expertise. In addition, it is not easy to say who will pay for all this effort (Burki, 2021). It is also true, on the other hand, that if this argument is as strong as it seems at first glance, it is hard to understand the opposition to suspensions of intellectual property rights, which would in any case be merely futile.

Finally, some argue that the suspension of the industrial property regime would not in itself make it possible to multiply the available raw materials or ensure the continuity of supply chains (Sauer, 2021). Recall that in the case of SARS-CoV-2, countries have blocked international trade in vaccine components (Nature, 2021). It is obvious that this can happen in any pandemic and is not easy to solve. Any kind of miracle cure can lead to deep mistrust. If the accelerated production of drugs in a pandemic already generates enormous suspicion among a large part of the population, incorporating lines created at high speed with a precarious knowledge of the necessary technology in the process could be counterproductive. Fortunately or unfortunately, in the world of the biotech industry, complex problems are often more easily solved through cooperation than imposition (Pitts et al., 2021).

3.3.6 Concluding Remarks: Pros and Cons of the Different Options and Difficulties Underlying Any of Them

In my view, there is little moral reason to oppose the introduction of policies aimed at maximising the production in the shortest possible time of vaccines and other essential drugs to protect human life or health in circumstances such as those presented by a pandemic. In such cases, public health considerations must take precedence over all other considerations. However, there are many pragmatic reasons why this theoretical conviction does not necessarily mean opting for licencing or intellectual property rights suspensions.

In reality, it is likely that these tools would not be sufficient to ensure improved production of pharmaceuticals involving the use of complex biotechnologies. To produce such products reliably, it would require adequate data and access to trade secrets whose legal regime is not part of TRIPS. Getting pharmaceutical companies to agree to disclose their know-how, with all that this implies, is extremely complex. Moreover, forcing them to do so is probably unfair. It is part of their wealth and I doubt very much that, if we deprive them of it against their will, we will not end up suffering the consequences in the future. As Katz et al. (2021) put it, "even with patent waivers, we may simply lack sufficiently consistent manufacturing capacity globally to develop and produce the current generation of vaccines. Long-term investment strategies are critical if we are to withstand the current pandemic and be prepared for future ones".

However, even if we were to reach such a milestone, we should not be so naïve as to think that an increase in production capacity will be instantaneous and allow us to produce sufficient doses of the required drugs at a reasonable price. There is no real reason to believe that this will be the case. Even if we were able to multiply lines, while ensuring sufficient quality (which is not easy), it is not easy to ensure sufficient supplies. In addition, what is even more complex is to finance the process, of course. Many countries do not have the capacity to set up their own pharmaceutical industry, both because of lack of financial resources and lack of trained personnel. Nor would they be able to import what is produced by third parties in the quantities required, for example, in the case of COVID. Even if the exporting country were to lower its price to the cost of production and transport, it would still be prohibitively expensive in the quantities of doses required.

My conclusion, in short, is that a liberalisation of intellectual property is ethically desirable, certainly, but I doubt that it will solve many problems. The crux of the matter is not in this part of the process, but in the distribution of what is produced. There is little point in multiplying the lines if the final prices are unaffordable for many people or if developed countries hoard all new shipments to protect their own population. The bottom line, therefore, is to understand that someone has to give up the economic or social benefit of vaccines so that others can have access to them. If we do not accept this simple principle, the ethical discussion is completely meaningless.

3.4 The Question of Distribution: Vulnerability and Imminence of the Risk

Beyond the problems related to its production, if there is one thing that the COVID-19 pandemic has brought to the table, it has been the enormous difficulty in ensuring a fair distribution of available resources. While there is almost absolute consensus that equitable distribution is a major ethical requirement, in practice this has been of little consequence. The question of vaccine allocation can in fact be raised at two different levels. Firstly, from a purely governmental point of view, national governments need to ask themselves whom they will vaccinate first and subsequently develop guidelines. From a global perspective, the relevant question is how the distribution of vaccines between countries should be carried out. The first of these issues is very much related to emergency triage, so I will refer here to the chapter where I deal with this issue and look at the global perspective of the problem.

3.4.1   The Distribution of Vaccines Between Countries: Equity and Utility

How should we allocate a scarce resource between countries? This question has, in principle, a simple answer: it would be appropriate to direct the vaccines to the people who need them most, irrespective of their nationality. There are two fundamental reasons for this. The first stems from considerations of equity. What the postulates of justice require is that an essential resource should be distributed among human beings according to the degree of protection it offers to different people. Nonetheless, this is exactly what the principle of utility demands: the fight against a pandemic is only efficient if we distribute vaccines in such a way as to minimise the chances of proliferation of a pathogen. Therefore, there is a second reason related to the efficiency of the response: a drastic reduction of infection only in some countries while infections persist in others leads to the emergence of new variants that may not be sensitive to existing vaccines (Fontanet et al., 2021).

Unfortunately, the immediate impulse of any politician is usually to take the decision that serves his electoral interests best. Given that their voters are generally more appreciative of self-serving policies, their temptation will be to grab all the resources available to their country, in a feverish exercise of vaccine nationalism. In the context of COVID-19, WHO, the Coalition for Epidemic Preparedness Innovations and Gavi, the Vaccine Alliance, launched the COVID-19 Vaccines Global Access (COVAX) programme, which aimed at improving equity in access to vaccines across countries. COVAX aimed at purchasing enough doses to vaccinate at least 20% of the population in 92 of the poorest countries by the end of 2021. The initiative was certainly commendable. The problem is that many of the rich countries signed individual contracts with vaccine manufacturers, allowing them to corner the global market. In fact, COVAX went straight to the bottom of the buyers' queue. At the same time, these same countries introduced restrictions on exports of both vaccines and the components needed to manufacture them (Hassan et al., 2021).

The result was devastating in terms of equity. By mid-November 2020, rich countries, comprising 14% of the world's population, had already reserved 51% of vaccine doses, leaving low- and middle-income countries with very few options to access them (So & Woo, 2020). By October 2021, more than six billion doses had been administered worldwide. However, more than 80% of these doses were administered in high- and upper-middle-income countries, and only 2.5% of people in low-income countries received at least one dose (Gurgula, 2021). In fact, COVAX was only able to access 163 million doses, rather than the billions needed (Hassan et al., 2021). Thus, we reached a point where many countries introduced booster doses or vaccinated non-vulnerable segments of the population (including children), while others were unable to provide the product to those among their citizens who needed it most. Worse, COVAX "has been criticised for an absence of transparency and accountability and for ignoring need in COVID-19 vaccine distribution" (Emanuel et al., 2021). Other authors have also pointed at failures related to its governance structure (Storeng et al., 2021). Moreover, some have even pointed out that its mission—to provide low- and middle-income countries with vaccines—should in fact be to equip countries with the infrastructure and means to produce their own vaccines. Some even consider COVAX to be part of the problem, not the solution (Ley Ravelo, 2021).

What is certain, in any case, is that the final distribution of vaccines has not only been a mistake but also a gross immorality. The underlying problem is probably that we consider vaccines and essential medicines as market commodities rather than public goods (Ho, 2021). This reinforces widespread inequalities in access and exacerbates wide disparities in health and economic well-being between different countries. These erratic policies, however, are difficult to rectify, because doing so entails a high degree of political risk in nation-state terms (Katz et al., 2021).

The question that arises in this situation is not so much a moral one—there is no doubt about the lack of ethics in the behaviour of rich countries—but a health policy question: how to prevent it from continuing. Moreover, this question is extremely complex. Probably the strongest answers are those that reflect past successes. An example might be, in the US context, the President's Emergency Plan for AIDS Relief (PEPFAR), launched by President Bush in 2003. This programme was successful in improving access to antiretroviral therapies for previously underserved populations and was instrumental in improving our response to HIV. Besides, the programme also helped to create the critical personnel, organisational and physical infrastructure needed to address other challenges—such as malaria, tuberculosis, maternal and child health, immunisations and unplanned outbreaks of infectious diseases. Specifically, the programme contributed to the sustainability of the health system in host countries by investing in critical laboratory infrastructure and training more than 220,000 health workers (Fauci & Eisinger, 2018).

Such state-driven cooperation schemes can be much more useful in the face of the COVID-19 pandemic and others that may come in the future, at least as far as vaccine production is concerned. Equity in collaborative research is both a global value and a strategy to diversify global health investments in ways that expand global R&D capacity by mobilising more efficiently the extraordinary intellectual, social and economic capacity of lower middle-income countries. These countries need to embrace and invest in science with the support of global R&D funds, building on the lessons of the past (Ijsselmuiden et al., 2021). Unlike other medicines, where production is much simpler, a vaccine requires a transfer of know-how, which in turn involves much more than a patent licence, as I have said. The transfer of this type of knowledge is probably more feasible under a cooperation scheme than under a compulsory licensing scheme.

Fortunately, new initiatives are already emerging, and they can serve to optimise the global distribution of vaccines by creating the right incentives to do so. Recently, a group of 65 institutional investors, including asset managers Nomura, BMO and GAM, have written to major pharmaceutical companies urging them to "make the global availability of vaccines part of the remuneration policy of managers and directors" (Financial Times, 2022). The signatories represent more than $3.5 trillion in assets under management. Such encouragement (or pressure) is likely to be effective in getting pharmaceutical company leaders to find ways to ensure greater production and better distribution of vaccines around the world.

3.4.2   The Distribution of Vaccines Between Countries: Where Are They Most Needed First?

The discussion on whether vaccines should be allocated preferentially to rich countries or to poor countries should not make us forget that there are other criteria that should also be relevant and that have not found much resonance. The preference of the virus for vulnerable human beings opens up an interesting discussion on whether those countries that manage to implement efficient policies to prevent contagion should be left out of the prioritisation in the allocation of resources. I will try to explain. In the case of SARS-CoV-2, there were several countries, such as Australia, New Zealand, China or Taiwan, that managed to eradicate the virus through their zero-COVID policies. The inevitable question, in such circumstances, is whether it would not be advisable to delay the vaccination of their vulnerable populations until those of other countries—that is, those countries with uncontrolled transmission—were protected. On the one hand, it seems reasonable to include the imminence of risk as an important factor in allocating scarce resources. On the other hand, however, these policies would punish those countries that cope best with the crisis, forcing them to prolong mass containment measures.

While this is true, it is also true that delaying vaccination has advantages. Countries that move slowly on vaccination have other conveniences. Health authorities will have more time to organise the logistics of transporting vaccines, sometimes through hostile terrain. Technology can be put in place to track doses through the supply chain and monitor wastage. There will be longer to train staff to administer the vaccine and to conduct education and safety campaigns to ensure public confidence. All in all, it is difficult to give an even-handed answer to this complex dilemma.

References

Bambery, B., Selgelid, M., Weijer, C., Savulescu, J., & Pollard, A. J. (2016). Ethical criteria for human challenge studies in infectious diseases. *Public Health Ethics, 9*(1), 92–103. https://doi.org/10.1093/phe/phv026

Burki, T. K. (2021). Ensuring fair distribution of COVID-19 vaccines: Is an intellectual waiver the answer? *The Lancet Respiratory Medicine, 9*(7), e64.

Collins, R., Bowman, L., Landray, M., & Peto, R. (2020). The magic of randomization versus the myth of real-world evidence. *New England Journal of Medicine, 382*, 674–678.

Council for International Organizations of Medical Sciences. (2017). *International ethical guidelines for health-related research involving humans.* Retrieved from https://cioms.ch/wp-content/uploads/2017/01/WEB-CIOMS-EthicalGuidelines.pdf

Dal-Ré, R., Avendaño, C., Gil-Aguado, A., Gracia, D., & Caplan, A. L. (2008). When should re-consent of subjects participating in a clinical trial be requested? A case-oriented algorithm to assist in the decision-making process. *Clinical Pharmacology & Therapeutics, 83*(5), 788–793.

Dal-Ré, R., Orenstein, W., & Caplan, A. L. (2021). Trial participants' rights after authorisation of COVID-19 vaccines. *The Lancet Respiratory Medicine, 9*(4), e30–e31. https://doi.org/10.1016/S2213-2600(21)00044-8. Retrieved December 19, 2021.

de Miguel Beriain, I. (2013). *Patentes y VIH/SIDA: la crónica de un cambio del que congratular-nos* (pp. 119–130).

Emanuel, E. J., Buchanan, A., Chan, S. Y., Fabre, C., Halliday, D., Heath, J., Herzog, L., Leland, R. J., McCoy, M. S., Norheim, O. F., Saenz, C., Schaefer, G. O., Tan, K.-C., Wellman, C. H., Wolff, J., & Persad, G. (2021). What are the obligations of pharmaceutical companies in a global health emergency? *The Lancet, 398*(10304), 1015–1020.

Erfani, P., Binagwaho, A., Jalloh, M. J., Yunus, M., Farmer, P., & Kerry, V. (2021). Intellectual property waiver for covid-19 vaccines will advance global health equity. *Britich Medical Journal, 374*, n1837.

EU Commission. (2021). *Urgent trade policy responses to the covid-19 crisis: Intellectual property. Communication from the European Union to the Council for TRIPS, Brussels, 4 June 2021*. Retrieved December 19, 2021 https://trade.ec.europa.eu/doclib/docs/2021/june/tradoc_159606.pdf

Eyal, N., Lipsitch, M., & Smith, P. G. (2020). Human challenge studies to accelerate coronavirus vaccine licensure. *The Journal of Infectious Diseases, 221*(11), 1752–1756. https://doi.org/10.1093/infdis/jiaa152

Fauci, A. S., & Eisinger, R. W. (2018). PEPFAR-15 years and counting the lives saved. *New England Journal of Medicine, 378*(4), 314–316.

Financial Times. (2022, January 6). *Covid vaccine makers face investor pressure over global access*. Retrieved December 19, 2021, from https://www.ft.com/content/948196b8-27c7-4dec-996b-c5a1587c6676

FM 't Hoen, E., Boulet, P., & Baker, B. K. (2017). Data exclusivity exceptions and compulsory licensing to promote generic medicines in the European Union: A proposal for greater coherence in European pharmaceutical legislation. *Journal of Pharmaceutical Policy and practice, 10*(1), 1–9.

Fontanet, A., Autran, B., Lina, B., Kieny, M. P., Karim, S. S. A., & Sridhar, D. (2021). SARS-CoV-2 variants and ending the COVID-19 pandemic. *The Lancet, 397*(10278), 952–954.

Gonsalves, G., & Yamey, G. (2021). The covid-19 vaccine patent waiver: A crucial step towards a "people's vaccine". *British Medical Journal, 373*, n1249.

Gurgula, O. (2021). Compulsory licensing V the IP waiver: What is the best way to end the COVID-19 pandemic? *Policy brief, 104*.

Gurgula, O., & Hull, J. (2021). *Compulsory licensing of trade secrets: Ensuring access to COVID-19 vaccines via involuntary technology transfer* (Queen Mary Law Research Paper, 363).

Gurgula, O., & Lee, W. H. (2021). COVID-19, IP and access: Will the current system of medical innovation and access to medicines meet global expectations? *Journal of Generic Medicines, 17*(2), 61–70.

Hassan, F., Yamey, G., & Abbasi, K. (2021). Profiteering from vaccine inequity: A crime against humanity?. *British Medical Journal, 374*, n2027. https://doi.org/10.1136/bmj.n2027

Herper, M. (2021). *Pfizer and BioNTech speed up timeline for offering Covid-19 vaccine to placebo volunteers*. STAT. Retrieved December 19, 2021, from https://www.statnews.com/2021/01/01/pfizer-and-biontech-speed-up-timeline-foroffering-covid-19-to-placebo-volunteers/

Ho, C. M. (2021). IP nationalism: Addressing the COVID crisis and beyond. SSRN 3910806.

Hoen, E. (2022). Protection of clinical test data and public health: A proposal to end the stronghold of data exclusivity. In C. M. Correa & R. M. Hilty (Eds.), *Access to medicines and vaccines*. Springer. https://doi.org/10.1007/978-3-030-83114-1_7. Retrieved December 19, 2021.

Hope, T., & McMillan, J. (2004). Challenge studies of human volunteers: Ethical issues. *Journal of Medical Ethics, 30*(1), 110–116.

IFPMA. (2011). *Data exclusivity: Encouraging development of new medicines*. White paper, International Federation of Pharmaceutical Manufacturers and Associations. Retrieved November 2021, from https://www.ifpma.org/resource-centre/data-exclusivity-encouraging-development-of-new-medicines/

IJsselmuiden, C., Ntoumi, F., Lavery, J. V., Montoya, J., Karim, S. A., & Kaiser, K. (2021). Should global financing be the main priority for pandemic preparedness? *The Lancet, 398*(10298), 388.

Irwin, A., & Nkengasong, J. (2021). What it will take to vaccinate the world against COVID-19. *Nature, 592*(7853), 176–178.

Jamrozik, E., Littler, K., Bull, S., Emerson, C., Kang, G., Kapulu, M., Rey, E., Saenz, C., Shah, S., Smith, P. G., Upshur, R., Weijer, C., & Selgelid, M. J. (2021). Key criteria for the ethical acceptability of COVID-19 human challenge studies: Report of a WHO Working Group. *Vaccine, 39*(4), 633–640.

Katz, I. T., Weintraub, R., Bekker, L. G., & Brandt, A. M. (2021). From vaccine nationalism to vaccine equity—Finding a path forward. *New England Journal of Medicine, 384*(14), 1281–1283.

Kuchler, H. (2021, May 6). Will a suspension of Covid vaccine patents lead to more jabs? *Financial Times*. Retrieved December 19, 2021, from https://www.ft.com/content/b0f42409-6fdf-43eb-96c7-d166e090ab99

Ley Ravelo, J. (2021, March 11). *Is COVAX part of the problem or the solution, Devex*. Retrieved December 19, 2021, from https://www.devex.com/news/is-covax-part-of-the-problem-or-the-solution-99334

Médecins Sans Frontières. (2020). WTO COVID-19 TRIPS Waiver. Doctors without borders Canada briefing note.

MSF Access Campaign. (2021, July 26). *Opposing countries must stop filibustering negotiations on 'TRIPS Waiver' at WTO*. Press Release. Retrieved from https://msfaccess.org/opposing-countries-must-stopfilibustering-negotiations-trips-waiver-wto

Nature. (2021). A patent waiver on COVID vaccines is right and fair. *Editorial, 593*, 478.

Okereke, M., & Essar, M. Y. (2021). Time to boost COVID-19 vaccine manufacturing: The need for intellectual property waiver by big pharma. *Ethics, Medicine, and Public Health, 19*, 100710.

Pitts, P. J., Popovian, R., & Weingarden, W. (2021). Waiving COVID-19 vaccine patents: A bad idea and a dangerous precedent. *Journal of Commercial Biotechnology, 26*(2).

Sariola, S. (2021). Intellectual property rights need to be subverted to ensure global vaccine access. *BMJ Global Health, 6*(4), e005656.

Sauer, H. (2021, April 9). Waiving IP rights during times of COVID: A "false good idea," IP WATCH DOG.

Sengupta, D. (2021, May 11). Pat(i)ent rights: Will waiver of IP rights on Covid vaccines, drugs help developing nations like India? *Economic Times*. Retrieved December 14, 2021, from https://economictimes.indiatimes.com/news/morning-briefpodcast/morning-brief-patient-rights-will-waiver-of-ip-rights-on-covid-vaccines-drugs-help-developingnations-likeindia/podcast/82539966.cms?utm_source%3Dwhatsapp_web%26utm_medium%3Dsocial%26utm_campaign%3Dsocialsharebuttons247SOddi'TRIPS–Natural

So, A. D., & Woo, J. (2020). Reserving coronavirus disease 2019 vaccines for global access: Cross sectional analysis. *British Medical Journal, 371*, m4750. https://doi.org/10.1136/bmj.m4750

Son, K. B., & Lee, T. J. (2018). Compulsory licensing of pharmaceuticals reconsidered: Current situation and implications for access to medicines. *Global Public Health, 13*(10), 1430–1440.

Stoehr, J. R., Hamidian Jahromi, A., & Thomason, C. (2021). Ethical considerations for unblinding and vaccinating COVID-19 vaccine trial placebo group participants. *Frontiers in Public Health, 9*, 702960.

Storeng, K. T., de Bengy Puyvallée, A., & Stein, F. (2021), COVAX and the rise of the 'super public private partnership' for global health. *Global Public Health*, 1–17. https://doi.org/10.1080/17441692.2021.1987502

Thambisetty, S. (2021). *It's not just about patents on COVID vaccines: Why I am not celebrating World Intellectual Property Day*. LSE COVID-19 Blog. Retrieved from https://blogs.lse.ac.uk/covid19/2021/04/26/its-not-just-about-patents-on-covid-vaccines-why-i-am-notcelebrating-world-intellectual-property-day/

Thambisetty, S., McMahon, A., McDonagh, L., Kang, H. Y., & Dutfield, G. (2021). The TRIPS intellectual property waiver proposal: Creating the right incentives in patent law and politics to end the COVID-19 pandemic.

Usher, A. D. (2020). South Africa and India push for COVID-19 patents ban. *The Lancet, 396*(10265), 1790–1791.

WHO Ad Hoc Expert Group on the Next Steps for Covid-19 Vaccine Evaluation. (2021). Placebo-controlled trials of Covid-19 vaccines—Why we still need them. *New England Journal of Medicine, 384*(2), e2.

World Health Organization. (2020). *Key criteria for the ethical acceptability of COVID-19 human challenge studies*. World Health Organization. Retrieved from https://apps.who.int/iris/handle/10665/331976. Licence: CC BY-NC-SA 3.0 IGO.

Chapter 4
Vaccination (II): Vaccination Policies

4.1 Introduction

The controversy surrounding vaccines was, even before the appearance of SARS-CoV-2, one of the great headaches for public health authorities in our time. The strength of the anti-vaccine movement was already such that the World Health Organization identified it as one of the ten threats that humanity faces. In fact, the rejection of vaccination was already causing devastating effects in terms of the fight against pathologies already practically eradicated, such as measles, which had quadrupled its incidence in developed countries in recent years (Rechel et al., 2019). The reaction of the Member States to this situation was not long in coming. At least 12 countries of the European Union (Belgium, Bulgaria, Croatia, Czech Republic, France, Hungary, Italy, Latvia, Malta, Poland, Slovakia, Slovenia and the Czech Republic) have been introducing a compulsory vaccination schedule (García Ruiz, 2014, p. 269). In the world, in general, the trend is the same. A comprehensive study produced in 2020 identified that 105 (54%) out of a total of 193 countries had evidence of a national immunisation mandate requiring at least one vaccine in December 2018: 35 in Asia, 29 in the Americas, 23 in Europe, 11 in Africa and 7 in Oceania (Gravagna et al., 2020).

It is obvious that the situation created by the emergence of SARS-CoV-2 intensified the debate on compulsory vaccination. As much as one might believe a priori that the creation of vaccines capable of offering a high degree of efficiency against such a formidable threat would be a strong argument to reinforce our faith in this resource, the truth is that what happened was, to a large extent, the opposite. At the time of writing these lines, the anti-vaccine movement is firmly entrenched in Western societies, and the conflict between those who do not wish to be vaccinated and the rest of the society is becoming increasingly bitter. The fact that some countries, such as Austria, have already announced their intention to opt for compulsory vaccination, or that others, such as Singapore, are going to force those who have not

I. de Miguel Beriain, *The Ethical, Legal and Social Issues of Pandemics*,
https://doi.org/10.1007/978-3-031-03818-1_4

been vaccinated against the virus to finance the costs of their own COVID-19 treatments, does not seem to do much to relax the atmosphere.

Unfortunately, it is not easy to give an answer to the question of whether we should introduce measures to force vaccination on the whole population. The choice usually depends, first of all, on the point at which we initiate the discussion. If we are talking about a moral obligation, it is likely that the answer will be positive, at least in certain circumstances, such as saturation of the health-care service.

This, however, should not necessarily mean the introduction of a legal obligation. Not everything that is morally required should become legally sanctionable. This transition will be justified (or not) depending on different considerations related to crisis management policies. It may be that the intervention of the law is counterproductive in terms of achieving the intended objective, or it may be possible to achieve the objective without resorting to this measure because there are alternatives, more respectful of individual freedom, that allow it (which, by the way, would eliminate from the equation the requirement of the necessity of the rule, with all that this entails). On the other hand, it is likely that there are substantial differences between vaccines depending on the type of pathology we are facing or the characteristics of each vaccine, that is to say, the way in which they protect the people to whom they are administered, or third parties.

In the scope of this book, I will focus exclusively on vaccines that treat diseases that are transmitted via human to human, such as the different types of influenza viruses or coronaviruses, leaving aside those that do not use these vehicles, such as tetanus. The reason is simple: it is extremely complicated (if not impossible) to have a pandemic without a vector of transmission from one living being to another. Finally, it must be said that there are different compulsory vaccination systems, from those that impose fines on those who are not vaccinated or prevent them from accessing certain places or institutions to those that introduce criminal sanctions or, directly, allow the vaccine to be inoculated by force. Each of them has its own characteristics, both in terms of efficiency in achieving its objective and in terms of the degree of intrusion in the privacy of each person or even in their bodily integrity. It is, therefore, worth introducing some considerations in this regard (as I will do in the following section).

4.2   Compulsory (or Not) Nature of Vaccines: Questions of Morality

If we want to address the problem of whether vaccines are compulsory, the first aspect that we have to explore is that related to their morality. This is for a simple reason: if we consider that there are no solid moral reasons to impose this measure, we will hardly be able to defend its legality. In addition, if we determine that forcing people to be vaccinated is neither ethically justifiable nor legally sustainable, then it is obvious that health policies will have to opt for alternative routes to the imposition of compulsory vaccination.

Let us begin, then, by analysing this question: are there any ethical obligations to enforced vaccination? Would it be ethically justified if public policies imposed vaccination on all citizens? There are several reasons that support this, at least a priori. Some have to do with equity and others with solidarity. In principle, we can group them into three main arguments: those that consider that we must protect people against a pathology "for their own good", those that base the obligation on the need to interrupt the transmission of a pathogen and those that seek to justify these measures with the preservation of public resources (always scarce) involved in the fight against the pathogen. I will explore each of them below.

4.2.1   Compulsory Nature "For Your Own Good": The Seat Belt Analogy

Vaccines, in general, are primarily intended to prevent a person who is exposed to a pathogen from developing the most severe forms of the relevant disease. With this in mind, the question that arises is whether people should be forced to be vaccinated on this basis alone. That is, whether it would be ethically acceptable to force people to be immunised even if the vaccines only protect them, but not others (as in the case of tetanus). The strongest theory in favour of this option is the one that considers this to be a scenario similar to the obligation to wear a helmet on a motorbike, or a seat belt in a car, when one occupies the front seats (in the back seats there is a component of protection from those in the front that I will leave aside for the moment). As Giubilini and Savulescu (2019) put it, the argument starts from the fact that seat belts laws have reduced the risk of death by 45% and the risk of serious injury by 50% or even more (US Department of Transportation, 2010).

We can therefore assume that, in general, the policies that require us to wear seat belts have saved thousands of lives around the world. This does not mean, however, that they are always beneficial. There is no doubt that their use can cause direct injury to the wearer, such as skin abrasions in the neck or chest, or perforation of the ileum and other internal organ damage that requires surgery to be repaired (the so-called seat belt syndrome) (Al-Ozaibi et al., 2016). In some cases, they might block a person's escape from a burning car. In others, they prevent one from being able to get out of the vehicle to call for help to other drivers. However, the risk of these side effects (let us label them so for the sake of analogy) is definitely small. Therefore, all generic risk/benefit assessments are clearly in favour of seat belt policies, regardless of the individual physical condition of those who wear them.

What does all this have to do with the issue of compulsory vaccination? A lot, in principle. In these cases, as in the case of a motorist's seat belt or helmet, it makes sense to ask whether the driver should be forced to protect himself, even if he himself seems unwilling to do so. Giubilini and Savulescu (2019) seem to think so, because they assume two facts. First, that the case of vaccines and this of helmets or seat belts are similar. Secondly, because they believe that the imposition of those means was undoubtedly right. In their own words:

We can think of seat belts as a metaphor for vaccination: a vaccine protecting individuals against an infectious disease is like a seat belt protecting individuals in car accidents (...) Wearing a seat belt significantly reduces the risk that the car accident results in serious injury or death; in the same way, in the case of infectious diseases, vaccines significantly reduce the risk that exposure results in serious injury or even death.

I must confess that, as I have already stated in a recent article (De Miguel Beriain, 2021), I do not agree with these arguments, despite their apparent solvency. Hence, in general, I do not accept their conclusion about the compulsory nature of vaccines that are only imposed "for our own good", for two reasons: the first is that I do not believe that the paternalistic mentality that allowed the seat belt to be imposed so many years ago still prevails nowadays (or that we should return to it); the second is that there are many differences between the variability of individual risk involved in the seat belt (a mechanical element) and that involved in a vaccine (a biological agent).

Let us start by questioning the morality of compulsory seat belts. As is well known, the policies imposing these measures are based on the assumption that we must protect drivers and passengers, even against their will. However, circumstances have changed a great deal since that time. The paternalistic mentality that inspired them, still present in the 1980s, no longer retains its former vigour (Flanigan, 2017). Although we still accept these practices in the case of driving, the scenario has changed substantially in the field of health care. These days, the paradigm governing doctor-patient relations is the informed consent: treatments are no longer imposed on the patient on the basis of his or her perceived best interests, but it is now the patient who makes the decision to be treated or not, to the point that he or she can perfectly well refuse, for example, an amputation, even if such a decision results in his or her death.

This development in the social framework cannot be ignored when drawing analogies between seat belts and vaccines. Otherwise, we run the risk of falling into unacceptable paradoxes. Take, for example, the treatments for COVID-19 that are being announced as I am writing these lines. No matter how effective they prove to be, it will not be possible to administer them to a patient *for his or her own good*. Moreover, it would not be possible for the same reason in the case of any other drug or treatment: because from the moment we use the autonomy of the patient or their integrity as the fundamental criteria in health care, it is not possible to sacrifice this value for the sake of the protection of the patients themselves.

One could respond to this argument by saying that this case is different and that vaccination could be coercively imposed to avoid risks to third parties. However, this would not weaken my thesis at all, since the only thing that this reply would demonstrate is that the justification of the mandate would not be related to considerations linked to paternalism, but to the need to protect the health of a third party, that is, a person other than the one being vaccinated. I will go into this later, but I can already venture that it is a completely different matter, since it involves the incorporation of public health considerations into the analysis, not clinical care. Therefore, these variables are completely irrelevant when we think in terms of protecting a patient *for his or her own good.*

On the other hand, an alternative rejoinder can also be used. It can be argued that a return to paternalism might be acceptable in this exceptional case, given the circumstances. However, this would be unreasonable, because it would create an unjustifiable dissonance with other spheres of biomedical practice. Moreover, from a pragmatic point of view, I do not think it is a good idea either. If we accept the permissiveness of vaccine mandates for the sake of the vaccinated, we could set in motion a dangerous dynamic, which could end up eroding the paradigm of autonomy, reintroducing a paternalism that we had a hard time banishing. As Joel Feinberg once said in the context of these debates, "the trick is to stop dead in our tracks once we start down this road, unless we want to ban whiskey, cigarettes and fried food" (Feinberg, 1971).

We must therefore conclude that the argument in favour of mandatory vaccines for the sake of the vaccinated is not solid. Moreover, we should not assume that extrapolating the paternalism inherent in the use of seat belts in cars, or helmets while riding motorcycles or bicycles to the field of biomedicine, is a good idea. The argument in favour of making it compulsory is further weakened when we see that the analogy of risk between vaccines and seat belts does not hold water. While it is undeniable that in both cases—vaccination and seat belts—the risks are often outweighed by the benefits (Pierik, 2018), in the case of seat belts, this is true not only at the population level but also for each specific individual. With vaccines, it is not possible to state so.

I will explain what I mean. A priori, anyone and everyone who wears a seat belt in a car, or helmet on a motorcycle, is more likely to benefit from these tools than to be harmed by them in the event of an accident. This is true regardless of their particular characteristics. In the case of vaccines, on the other hand, we depart from the belief that their imposition will improve the situation in terms of population (in the sense that fewer people will die or suffer serious aftermaths as a result of the disease in question). Nonetheless, this will not necessarily be true for every individual. In fact, there will be some people for whom, in terms of risk/benefit, it is preferable not to be vaccinated. This is for a simple reason: unlike seat belts, vaccines are biological tools that interact differently with each person's body. Therefore, the variability of outcomes grows exponentially. Most people benefit equally from seat belts (people with obesity may benefit slightly less than others (Reed et al., 2012)).

The side effects of vaccination, however, vary greatly depending on the circumstances of a particular individual. In addition, the scenario to be avoided is also much more varied. The severity of a traffic accident does not depend much on the individual characteristics of the driver or passengers, but the severity of an illness does. It is therefore important to know what the chances of developing a severe form of a pathology are for each individual in order to indicate whether or not to be vaccinated. Another essential difference is that both the possible effects of vaccines and the course of a disease in a particular patient can be intuited, at least a priori, something that does not apply to traffic accidents. If we think of COVID-19, for example, a person who is diabetic, elderly or severely obese does not have the same level of risk as someone who has none of these characteristics (Fagard et al., 2021). Similarly, with some vaccines, at least, it does not appear that the side effects are the same if the patient is a 70-year-old man or a young woman in her 30s (Ledford, 2021), nor, of course, are the risk levels the same between a patient who is allergic to some of the excipients in the vaccine and one who is not. Moreover, in the case of some viruses, such as SARS-CoV-2, the different vaccines, in turn, offer different levels of protection. It goes without saying that in the case of seat belts, on the other hand, it does not seem that the brand that manufactures them implies substantial differences in their performance.

This means that the analogy between seat belts and vaccines is not valid, if we focus on the risk/benefit analysis for each patient. Such considerations are much more complicated for vaccines than for seat belts. Hence, the assessment should be individualised, as far as is reasonably possible. The conditions of the individual play a key role, which is not at all the case for seat belts. Therefore, the argument that we should impose vaccination for the same reason of risk reduction as forcing people to wear seat belts is not as valid as it might appear at first. On the contrary, we must consider the circumstances of each individual person. In some cases, if we really want to protect the person for their own sake, we should actually *prevent them* from being vaccinated. We would hardly state the same in the case of seat belts. This makes a dramatic difference to the design of public health policy. In this respect, the consideration introduced by Judge Wojtyczek in the Vavricka case, which refers to child vaccination, but which can be extended, with nuances, to the case of any adult, is particularly commendable:[1]

> *The central question around the best interests of the children is not whether the general health policy of the respondent State promotes the best interests of children as a group, but instead how to assess in respect of each and every specific child of the applicant parents, with the child's specific health background, whether the different benefits from vaccination will indeed be greater than the specific risk inherent in it.*

The conclusion we reach in this section is that, in short, it is not easy to defend mandatory vaccination based on the patient's own benefit. Despite its apparent strength, a deeper analysis of the analogy with the policies of imposing seat belts in cars, or helmets on bicycles or motorcycles, reveals that the two scenarios are very different. Hence, the conclusions are different. This leads us, in short, to conclude that vaccination should not be imposed solely for the benefit caused to the patient, unless (1) the patient is someone without autonomy (a child, for instance) whose interest must be protected (and the risk/benefit analysis recommends his or her vaccination) or (2) we admit that protecting oneself is a moral duty—which is at odds with the principle of autonomy and the possibility that it is up to each individual to decide what is in his or her own interest. Another issue would be the possibility of

---

[1] ECtHR Judgment of 8 April 2021, Vavricka et autres v. Republique Tchèque, EC:ECHR:2021: 0408JUD004762113. Dissenting Opinion of Judge Wojtyczek, p. 13.

protecting third parties or to reduce the health cost bill or to alleviate the weight carried by an overwhelmed health-care system. However, these are different reasons, which we will analyse in the next sections.

4.2.2 Compulsory Nature as a Way of Breaking the Chains of Contagion

When analysing the obligatory nature of vaccines, we must always keep in mind that not all vaccines allow us to achieve the same objectives, nor are all pathologies the same. Some vaccines manage to provide us with a high degree of capacity that prevents us from transmitting the pathogenic agent. As previously stated (see Chap. 1), this quality is called sterilising immunity (Dutta et al., 2016). For a long time, we have not been able to understand well how it works. Historically, it was considered, for instance, that the measles vaccine was able to provide the inoculated with almost absolute protection, preventing them from infecting others. More recent studies have shown that this is not really the case, however (Wu, 2021). In the case of COVID-19 Delta variant, what we came to understand as we analysed the available data was that, although the viral load is similar in vaccinated and unvaccinated individuals (Singanayagam et al., 2021), the transmission capacity of the former is substantially lower, because they are less likely to become infected, they take less time to shed the virus and also these high viral load peaks last fewer days (Feehan & Apostolopoulos, 2021; Elliott et al., 2021; NSW, 2021; Mallapaty, 2021). In the case of omicron, it is not yet clear, but preliminary available data suggest that vaccines may also provide some sterilising immunity (Wald, 2022).

These preliminary thoughts serve perfectly well to illustrate an essential message: most vaccines do not offer absolute sterilisation, although they usually reduce our ability to act as transmitting agents. The greater the sterilising immunity of a vaccine, the more sense it makes to contemplate its use as a way to prevent a pandemic from thriving, not just as a tool for personal protection. This has implications within our ethical duties framework. If a vaccine has a reasonable ability to prevent contagion, it becomes much more obvious that we have a moral obligation to vaccinate ourselves, since in doing so we would not only be protecting ourselves but also preventing us from unintentionally transmitting the disease to others. This is particularly important because while it is tenable, as I have just argued, that one does not have to protect oneself if one does not want to, what is no longer tenable at all is that one would not do one's best to protect others. We are not forbidden to drink before driving just to protect ourselves, but because other drivers and pedestrians could be injured or killed due to a lapse in a driver's concentration caused by the effects of alcohol.

Thus, there should not be much discussion about whether, in general, we have a moral duty to be vaccinated if a vaccine reduces the risk of transmission of a pathogen. Clearly we do, even if our contribution is only significant in a relatively small way (Dawson, 2007, p. 170). However, it may sometimes happen that there is a circumstance that complicates such an apparently simple moral judgement: that the risk/benefit ratio of a vaccine may not be homogeneous across social groups. In other words, the problem arises when there are population groups that are unlikely to suffer severe forms of a pathology but can, however, transmit it to others who will develop it. A typical example of this is rubella, which is caused by a virus that is spread through the air or by close contact. In general, the virus causes a mild illness in children. However, it can affect foetuses seriously if pregnant women are infected. Since, in addition, a person with rubella can transmit the disease to others as early as 1 week before the onset of the characteristic rash, it is difficult to prevent transmission. With these facts on the table, our vaccination policies have opted to include the rubella vaccine in the MMR immunisation. Its purpose is not so much to protect children (the degree of protection is minimal, given the normal mildness of the pathology), but to safeguard pregnant women's health. The fact that serious side effects produced by this vaccine in children are extremely rare has undoubtedly been a key factor in sustaining these policies. The question, however, is whether this reasoning—to vaccinate some people who do not suffer from serious diseases in order to protect others—would be valid in the event that a vaccine could produce serious side effects on a significant segment of the individuals to be vaccinated.

In the case of COVID-19, Giubilini, Savulescu and Wilkinson made an argument in 2020 in favour of vaccinating children against the virus even if this would not only be of little benefit to them but might, in some cases, even cause harm (Giubilini et al., 2020). In general, they considered that this would be morally acceptable if four circumstances were present, namely, (1) vaccines work better in children than in the elderly; (2) children are a vector of contagion for the elderly, who are not adequately protected by the vaccine; (3) they involve little harm to children; and (4) this proves to be the most effective strategy to save the greatest number of people. If all these conditions were met, we should, in his view, vaccinate children rather than the elderly, even if this was considered to be using children as mere means. It should be noted that later, in 2021, with the data on incidence and risk/benefit ratio, Giubilini expressed a position against child vaccination (Giubilini et al., 2021).

This final stance, however, is not based on a change of opinion about the reasoning put forward, but on specific data. In addition, as I have expressed at other times, I do not agree with that reasoning (De Miguel Beriain, 2021), so my criticism is still valid and, I think, particularly pertinent. In fact, I find it difficult to accept that sometimes "treating people as means in a way that is harmful or disrespectful to them and without their consent may be considered permissible" (Giubilini et al., 2020). The well-known Kantian formula against treating people as mere means ("[s]o act that you treat humanity, whether in your own person or in the person of any other, always at the same time as an end, never merely as a means") still seems to me to be a necessary barrier against the worst ghosts of the past. I do not think it is appropriate or convenient to introduce exceptions now, which may become the rule in the future. Moreover, I do not think it is necessary to break this principle in order to justify that we can subject anyone to a small harm in exchange for safeguarding the interests of the group.

In fact, this is precisely what we do when we institute duties such as those of assistance to third parties in the event of accidents. Consider in this regard that the introduction in our criminal codes of the offence of failure to render assistance is, after all, nothing more than a way of forcing us to suffer minor inconvenience or even harm (one may get a bump or injury while assisting an injured person) for the sake of common good. I know that this is not the case in some US states, for example, so this reasoning will not be as tenable there, but it is clearly valid in the EU context, which is the scope of this book.

It is, therefore, far from nonsensical to argue that we can force people to accept small risks and inconveniences in order to protect the interests of the human group to which they belong without calling into question the Kantian maxim above. The problem is that it is often the case that the distribution of risk related to the side effects of vaccines is not uniform. Let us imagine, for example, that a life-threatening disease arises in women but with minor effects on men. Let us also think that we are able to develop a vaccine capable of preventing contagion efficiently, but with a risk, even if it is low (say 1/50,000), of causing profoundly serious side effects, even death for all those who are inoculated, regardless of their gender. This would open up a complex scenario from an ethical point of view. If we know that this probability exists, we can assume that in a country where there are 10 million people, 5 million of whom are male, and we vaccinate all of them, 100 men will die. Since the disease does not cause such consequences in healthy men, this means that we would be assuming the death of those men in exchange for saving the lives of thousands of women, certainly.

From a utilitarian perspective, this should not be problematic. As Giubilini et al. have written, "A utilitarian approach supports a moral obligation to be vaccinated, *unless the individual cost of being vaccinated would be so great as to outweigh the expected negative contribution of non-vaccination to the aggregate wellbeing of others*" (Giubilini et al., 2018). Conversely, therefore, to force one person to be vaccinated even if this could cause serious harm would be legitimate as long as that harm did not outweigh the expected benefit to all others.

In my opinion (obviously, I am not a utilitarian), this would be ethically unacceptable. In fact, this discussion reminds me very much of the survival lottery posed by one of the most important bioethicists of our time, John Harris (1975). For those unfamiliar with his provocative thought experiment, it suggests that, since organ donation saves lives and donors are always in short supply, we should draw lots in a lottery every time donations are needed. Those selected would give up their lives to allow several people to live. In both Harris's proposal and the fictional case of coercive vaccination of men against the disease described above, some people are sacrificed for the good of society. In both, the ex ante cost is also small (given the very low probability of being selected to donate organs or die from the vaccine), but there is a large post facto cost to be faced, and this seems unacceptable. Therefore, I think we should be clear that when we talk about "small risk", we are considering mild consequences for everyone, although this may include a large percentage of those vaccinated, but not serious side effects, even though this may only occur in a small number of cases (De Miguel Beriain, 2021).

There is, finally, an argument to be introduced into the debate: compulsory vaccination to break the chains of contagion should not be considered if there were other means capable of achieving the same result. This does not seem theoretically impossible. After all, we must not forget that the only person who cannot really transmit an agent is the one who is not infected or, in other words, that only those who are infected are contagious. Therefore, if we were able to develop efficient mechanisms to identify those who are infectious and separate them from the rest of the population, vaccination would be unnecessary. Of course, I am thinking of the introduction of health certificates, mass testing (including also cellular immunity testing), the necessary ventilations and proper epidemiological surveillance.

4.2.3   Mandatory Nature as a Way to Save Public Resources

In previous sections, I have analysed two of the fundamental reasons why vaccines should be imposed: paternalistic policies that aim at protecting citizens, even if they themselves do not want to, and public health considerations aimed at ending an epidemic by hindering the chains of transmission of the pathogenic agent. There is, however, a third scenario that lies between the two. I refer to the one in which a pandemic causes an alarming shortfall in available health resources or simply pushes the health-care bill to unbearable limits. In such circumstances, it may be ethically acceptable to introduce mandatory vaccination to prevent a drain on health resources. Obviously, this argument will be stronger as the bill for the excess expenditure produced by the population group refusing to be vaccinated increases or the lack of available resources becomes dramatic.

The ultimate basis of this argument is that in circumstances such as those that characterise a pandemic, it must be remembered that the foundation of any public health system is an individual responsibility. Based on this conception, it is necessary to adhere to the Principle of Group Beneficence, according to Otsuka's (1991) denomination, which was already used by the lucid mind of Derek Parfit (1984). By virtue of this principle, each member of a group has the moral obligation to contribute as much as possible so that the group can benefit from a desirable effect. A principle of utility maximisation underlies this mentality, since the best outcome of an action is the one in which people benefit the most and, according to Parfit, individuals should do what produces the best outcome for all.

Against this reasoning, one might object that such an obligation would be excessive, a disproportionate infringement of individual autonomy. If we accept that people can develop unhealthy lifestyle habits (eating processed foods, smoking, drinking alcohol, etc.), or engage in high-risk activities that may cause an avoidable health cost, why can we not accept that someone can choose not to be vaccinated, even though this might deprive others of health care? However, this kind of objection implies several flaws. The fundamental one is that no one is actually saying that those who smoke or drink are not doing something that they should, in principle, avoid doing out of social responsibility. Nor is it true that the conduct of those who unnecessarily expose themselves to hospitalisation (e.g. by extreme skiing) at a time when all resources are needed is not ethically reprehensible. On the other hand, it should be borne in mind that this kind of objection seems more sustainable from the point of view of introducing a specific health policy than judging the morality of an act. To this must be added, finally, that comparing a habit or way of life, such as a sedentary lifestyle, with a specific act is always complex. I will return to these points when discussing health policies. In any case, what I can point out now is that, from a strictly ethical point of view, every citizen should indeed do his or her best to contribute to the collective effort by avoiding unnecessary risks or causing superfluous expenses to a health system that is already limited in its resources. This, of course, becomes particularly important in times of pandemic, where such constraints can reach unbearable limits.

4.2.4   Moral Consideration of the Obligatory Nature of Vaccines: Concluding Remarks

In the light of all that has been discussed in this section, it must be concluded that there are indeed reasons to justify vaccination as a moral duty, provided that vaccines are capable of adequately addressing their essential objective, that is, to protect people efficiently. Indeed, the obligation becomes much stronger if vaccines provide some sort of sterilising immunity. It is not a question of the need to protect oneself, which is not necessarily a moral duty, but more of an obligation that living in society imposes on us vis-à-vis third parties. Both the need to break the chains of contagion and to alleviate the burdens on the health system, especially at certain times, dictate it so.

There can be exceptions to this general rule, of course, depending on the circumstances that accompany each vaccine and each person. The risk/benefit criteria should not be considered from a population point of view, but in each specific case. On the other hand, it must be taken into account that the moral duty to be vaccinated can be conditioned by facts such as inaccurate or negative information about the products leading to an insurmountable fear of inoculating one's own body with a pathogenic agent or a general lack of confidence in the health authorities. Hence, it is possible to apply many nuances to this abstract and generalised obligatory nature that make it necessary to adequately address these scenarios.

4.3   The Obligatory (or Not) Nature of Vaccines: Legal Issues

In the previous section I concluded that, in general, there is a moral obligation to be vaccinated. This, however, should not necessarily mean the introduction of a similar legal obligation. Not everything that is morally enforceable should become legally punishable. This transition will be justified (or not) depending on different considerations related both to the system of fundamental rights and freedoms and to the health crisis management policies. It may be that the intervention of .the law is counterproductive to achieve the intended objective or that it is possible to reach it without resorting to this measure, because alternatives exist that are more respectful of individual freedom. This, by the way, eliminates from the equation the requirement of the necessity of the rule, with all that this entails. On the other hand, it should be remembered that there are different systems of compulsory vaccination. Each of them has its own characteristics, both in terms of efficiency in achieving its objective and the degree of intrusion into the privacy of each individual or, indeed, their bodily integrity (Cierco Seira, 2018). Hence, it is worth introducing some considerations in this regard when we talk about the legal acceptability of these measures.

No EU-wide vaccination policy exists, with vaccination programmes falling under the competence of the Members States (Utrilla, 2021). Thus, in the context of the European Union, any answer to the questions merely asked has to be constructed within the framework of the European Convention on Human Rights of 4 November 1950 (hereafter "ECHR"), which is applicable in all its member countries. As is commonly known, this treaty includes some articles that are applicable in the context of compulsory vaccination policies. Particularly relevant is Article 8, entitled "Right to respect for private and family life", which states that:

> 1. *Everyone has the right to respect for his private and family life, his home and his correspondence.*
> 2. *There shall be no interference by a public authority with the exercise of this right except such as is in accordance with the law and is necessary in a democratic society in the interests of national security, public safety or the economic well-being of the country, for the prevention of disorder or crime, for the protection of health or morals, or for the protection of the rights and freedoms of others.*

The question that arises in the light of this wording is whether compulsory vaccination policies are legitimised by the exceptions introduced in the second point of the aforementioned article. The case law of the European Court of Human Rights (hereinafter "ECHR") has repeatedly ruled on these issues. The last of these rulings was in 2021, when it had the opportunity to set out in detail its doctrine in this regard due to COVID-19. This time it was a response to the cases brought by a group of Czech citizens who were opposed to vaccination or, rather, to satisfying the sanctions provided for those not vaccinated by the regulations of the Czech Republic (Vavřička and Others v. the Czech Republic).[2]

What was the ECHR's position on the issue? In short, that compulsory vaccination is indeed admissible in this context. In fact, this is not surprising if we take into account that the possibility of establishing this measure in a state governed by the rule of law has a long tradition. As César Cierco wrote (Cierco, 2021, p. 52):

---

[2] Judgment of the ECtHR of 8 April 2021, Vavricka et autres v. Republique Tchèque, EC:ECHR:2021:0408JUD004762113.

Compulsory vaccination has behind it, as far as its legal framework is concerned, a solid and long-standing endorsement. The admissibility of a duty to be vaccinated has passed through the sieve of many constitutional guarantors and continues to do so nowadays. There is, therefore, a well-established body of jurisprudence that supports the legitimacy of the restriction of individual rights for the benefit of systematic vaccination programmes. This body of jurisprudence has, in fact, deep roots. The landmark cases of Jacobson v. Massachusetts (1905) and Zucht v. King (1922) of the US Supreme Court are often cited in this regard. I insist, however, that the constitutionality of the duty to be vaccinated has been endorsed in many States and not only in the past, but also in recent times. Thus, going back to the European continent and to our days, one can refer to the decisions by the Constitutional Courts of the Czech Republic (27 January 2015); France (20 March 2015); Serbia (26 October 2017); Italy (18 January 2018); or Moldova (30 October 2018) a.

The admissibility of compulsory vaccination is, therefore, clear within the framework of the legal tradition to which the ECHR belongs, but only if certain conditions are met that the ECHR took care to make explicit. To begin with, it must be clear that, according to the Convention, the general rule is that the acceptance or refusal of medical treatment or the choice of a form of alternative treatment is vital to the principles of self-determination and personal autonomy. However, there are precise limits to this right under Article 8(2). From its wording, it can be inferred that it is possible to restrict the fundamental right in circumstances of particular importance, such as the protection of public health, provided that the restriction of rights is necessary and supported by a law. This law will have to be sufficiently accessible so that everyone can be aware of its existence, as well as understand it, and its clauses must be formulated with the necessary precision so that its addressees can foresee the legal consequences that derive from a hypothetical non-compliance with them (Sánchez Patrón, 2021).

The judgement in the Vavricka case reiterated—as the ECHR had already pointed out on other occasions[3]—that this restriction of rights includes the imposition of vaccines (not only but above all) when a public health emergency requires it so. The reason is that these tools are intended to protect against diseases likely to generate a serious health risk both to "those who receive the vaccinations concerned as well as those who cannot be vaccinated and are thus in a state of vulnerability, relying on the attainment of a high level of vaccination within society at large for protection against the contagious diseases in question".[4]

This, in the court's view, creates a bond of solidarity among all members of a society, whereby a majority (suitable for vaccination) can protect a few (incapable of being vaccinated) by exposing themselves to minimal risk. It is on this basis that the court develops its doctrine. However, and here begins the most complex part of the judgement, any state wishing to impose this form of vaccination must be able to demonstrate that the compulsory nature of the measure is necessary to achieve the intended purpose (that there is an "imperative social need", according to

---

[3] ECtHR Judgment of 10 June 2010, Case of Jehovah's witnesses of Moscow and others v. Russia, EC:ECHR:2010:0610JUD000030202, para. 136.

[4] ECtHR Judgment of 8 April 2021, Vavricka et autres v. Republique Tchèque, EC:ECHR:2021:0408JUD004762113, para. 272.

section 114) or that "social pressure" justifies it (section 115). This is where the principle of proportionality, already explored in the previous chapters, comes into play. For, if vaccines are accepted as a suitable means to reduce the importance of a public health crisis caused by a pandemic, the key issue will be to demonstrate that, in addition, their compulsory imposition constitutes an essential measure to that end. This is as good as attesting that it is far more efficient in achieving that goal than any possible alternative that is less restrictive of rights, or better still, that it is the only policy that will ensure that the goal is effectively achieved.

Who is to judge whether such a need is present? About this question, "The Court starts with the general point that matters of health-care policy are in principle within the margin of appreciation of the domestic authorities, who are best placed to assess priorities, use of resources and social needs".[5] It is up to those authorities to decide what health measures are essential.[6] The question of whether or not to establish compulsory vaccination policies is, therefore, in the hands of the states, which are the ones that have to prove the concurrence of the requirement of necessity of the measure, although the ECHR reserves the power to judge, in the end, if this necessity was as unavoidable as a public authority could manifest. In practice, it is difficult for this court to correct the policies implemented by a state in a situation such as the one caused by a pandemic, because its doctrine has traditionally left the verification of compliance with this requirement in the hands of the states (Rainey et al., 2020). In any case, if the reader wishes to know when the requirement of the need for vaccination should be considered fulfilled, I recommend that they read the following sections, dedicated to public health policies.

Before concluding this legal analysis, it remains for me to introduce a question of undoubted relevance: whether the compulsory nature of vaccination has, as a counterpart, the imposition of measures of reparation for the damage caused to the states. On this question, the ECHR has been somewhat lukewarm. What it has made clear is that the side effects of voluntary vaccination do not give rise to any obligation by the states to provide compensation on the basis of the Convention.[7] It is, of course, possible that the claim by a victim against the pharmaceutical companies producing the vaccine may be successful or the state may assume the cost of these reparations, but the individual cannot demand them on the basis of the ECHR as they fall outside its scope of protection (Sánchez Patrón, 2021). However, this position does not provide definitive guidelines on whether the side effects produced by compulsory vaccination confer rights on the affected person or not. In fact, this is a question that the court did not wish to address in the Vavricka case, limiting itself to pointing out that, given that the Czech regulations did not impose vaccination on

---

[5] ECtHR Judgment of 13 November 2012, Hristozov et autres v. Bulgaria, EC:ECHR:2012: 1113JUD004703911, para 119.

[6] ECtHR Judgment of 3 November 2011, S.H. et autres v. Austria, EC:ECHR:2011: 1103JUD005781300, para. 92; 6 ECtHR Judgment of 5 July 1999, Matter v. Slovakia, EC:ECHR: 1999:0705 JUD003153496, para. 66.

[7] ECtHR decision of 12 March 2013, Baytüre et autres v. Turkey, EC:ECHR: 2003: 0722JUD002420994, para. 30.

any of the appellants, it was not relevant to resolve it.[8] However, as Sánchez Patrón eloquently points out, the ECHR:

> Palliates its silence on the question of the liability that would arise from the harmful effects of compulsory vaccination by recalling the pronouncements adopted by several constitutional courts, in particular the Czech, the Italian and the Slovak Courts145. The case law of these special courts can be summarized in the following key principles. Firstly, the choice of a compulsory vaccination model must be complemented by the establishment of a liability regime covering the harmful effects caused by such vaccination146. Secondly, these harmful effects would justify the recognition of reparation to the individual without the need to prove medical error, whether negligent or voluntary147. Thirdly, the State must pay such reparation (Cristol, 2009, p. 565)148. And, finally, fourthly, the receipt of such reparation is not incompatible with that which may be demanded to other persons in the case of medical error, whether intentional or negligent (Cristol, 2009, p. 565).

I would like to end this section introducing a final point. The acceptance, in general, of individual rights restrictive policies, such as those that are necessary in the cases we are dealing with, does not mean that the guarantees provided for this purpose must be the same in all circumstances. A system based on economic sanctions, for example, erodes individual autonomy, but does not affect bodily integrity. This violation of the right to avoid actions against one's own body is precisely what is implied by any system that provides coercive vaccination of those affected since, in this case, it is simply a matter of being inoculated with the health product by using "brute-force". Given that this range of interference of fundamental rights is of a necessarily higher nature, a measure of this type can only be accepted in very specific circumstances and under higher legal guarantees. In many countries (such as Spain), prior judicial intervention authorising such an intervention would be necessary. Moreover, interventions should be differentiated according to the characteristics of each person. It is necessary to keep all this in mind when we talk about whether compulsory vaccination is legal in a given country. The nuance is essential, because not all the different options entail the same cuts in fundamental rights. In addition, the ECHR has defended the idea that any compulsory vaccination policy cannot be carried out at the cost of undermining the health of the individual. This, at least, seems to be deduced from point 36 of the Solomakhin judgement,[9] which states the following:

> In the Court's opinion the interference with the applicant's physical integrity could be said to be justified by the public health considerations and necessity to control the spreading of infectious diseases in the region. Furthermore, according to the domestic court's findings, the medical staff had checked his suitability for vaccination prior to carrying out the vac-

---

[8] ECtHR of 8 April 2021, Vavricka et autres v. Republique Tchèque, EC:ECHR:2021:0408JUD004762113, para. 302.

[9] Case *Solomakhin v. Ukraine* (no. 24429/03, § 33, 15 March 2012, at https://hudoc.echr.coe.int/eng#{%22itemid%22:[%22001-109565%22]}   https://hudoc.echr.coe.int/eng#{%22itemid%22:[%22001-109565%22]}.

cination, which suggest that necessary precautions had been taken to ensure that the medical intervention would not be to the applicant's detriment to the extent that would upset the balance of interests between the applicant's personal integrity and the public interest of protection health of the population.

In my opinion, it is obvious that the court would have condemned Ukraine if the vaccination had been imposed without considering the risk/benefit balance for the plaintiff or, even worse, if that ratio had resulted in a detrimental outcome for him (Utrilla, 2021). This is the only plausible conclusion if we bear in mind that the dignity of the human being constitutes an insurmountable barrier for our legal systems when it comes to coercive measures (Cierco Seira, 2005).

4.4   Health Policies: An Analysis of the Different Options Available

Now that it is clear that there is a moral obligation to be vaccinated and that it is possible to introduce this obligation in law without violating our liberal systems (at least in the EU context), it is time to consider whether these measures are also desirable from a health policy point of view. This is a different approach, because not everything that meets the requirements of ethics, and is legally possible, is also politically desirable. For example, a general ban on the sale and consumption of alcohol might make sense from an ethical perspective, and a legal initiative to that effect could be introduced without infringing fundamental rights. As a health policy, however, it would probably be a huge failure, as historical experience shows. The question we must now ask ourselves, in short, is which vaccination-related policies are likely to make more sense, that is, which will achieve the intended objectives in terms of increasing the rate of immunisation without causing excessive social tension. I dare say that this will surely be much more complicated to analyse than anything to do with ethics or rights.

To this end, I will begin by presenting the policies that are most readily acceptable by the population, that is, those based on incentives to be vaccinated, which can be of very different kinds, as I will show. I will then analyse policies that impose some kind of harm to those who do not wish to be vaccinated, including both the classical modalities (access restrictions, fines, coercion) and those that have been appearing in the context of COVID-19, such as the health-care cost pass-through announced by Singapore or the selective restriction of movements proposed by Austria (and almost by Germany).

4.4.1 Proactive Measures to Increase Vaccination: Persuasion, Manipulation and Incentives

Often the best way to have some people vaccinated is simply to persuade them. This is not surprising when you consider the reasons why many people do not get vaccinated. Not everyone is a denier, in the sense that they deny the usefulness of vaccines in general (for the meanings of the term, see Navin, 2015, p. 2). Nor does everyone base his or her opposition on beliefs that are difficult to counter through evidence. Many people are simply unable to make rational risk/benefit calculations, do not understand the importance of being vaccinated or do not know when and how to do so. Policies that rely on persuasion simply attempt to fill these gaps by providing people with the kind of information or arguments that would encourage them to get vaccinated (Rossi & Yudell, 2012). To this end, it is feasible to resort to different techniques. In this sense, it is important to distinguish between persuasion and manipulation. Unlike the former, the latter uses subliminal messages or seeks the complicity of people endowed with power to achieve its goal. As conceptualised by Giubilini (2019), based on the work by Faden and Faden (1978), the difference is that persuasion appeals to reason and manipulation to impulses. It is not that manipulation is necessarily immoral when it comes to overcoming irrational resistance to vaccination, but it is convenient, at least, to distinguish them. In any case, it is complex to appeal to feelings, because people do not always react as one expects. For example, there are studies that show that providing frightening information about diseases does not convince those who are already inclined to refuse vaccines (Nyhan et al., 2014).

Some authors consider that nudges (Thaler & Sunstein, 2009) are, to a large extent, a form of manipulation, since they do not try to convince through reason, but to motivate to action by taking advantage of our biases and our automated cognitive processes (Blumenthal-Barby & Burroughs, 2012, p. 5; Ploug & Holm, 2015). What is important, in any case, is that they may diminish our autonomy (Giubilini, 2019), but by no means do they completely override it. As long as they are used to addressing situations where opposition to a perfectly reasonable public health policy lies in a belief that defies any scientific demonstration, or for attitudes that have no motivation other than pure apathy, their use is admissible, as long as the information is transparent. A fairly obvious example is policies that allow schools to vaccinate children if parents do not object. Since refusal is an active intervention, which as such involves more effort than simply not signing a paper authorising vaccination, it ends up raising the numbers of children immunised. In principle, one could argue that since these strategies are really trying to "lull" us into not exercising our autonomy in a direction contrary to the public interest, there is something immoral about them. However, and bearing in mind that in a particularly delicate situation such as a pandemic, public health considerations take precedence over individual autonomy, the objection is undoubtedly weak. Even more so if, as Giubilini points out, this autonomy is in no case significantly curtailed.

Financial or material incentives, finally, are those that simply try to increase vaccination by offering citizens a quick reward, in the form of money or other goods, in exchange for immunisation. Here we can think of multiple modalities, from a cash payment or tax cut to gifts in the form of household goods or invitations to drinks. There are no fixed limits or boundaries. In some countries, we have seen creative offers, some with some success. Such actions, however, have significant moral problems. For a start, it is not very flattering to think that we have to pay people to do the right thing. In a sense, it is a bribe that ends up rewarding those who have been unwilling to do the right thing out of pure altruism. The lower the amount, the less significance this effect is likely to have, but also the lower the resulting stimulus. If the sum is somewhat higher, we will improve the achievement but will increase the problems related to equity. In a sense, we will be forcing the poor, which is somewhat suspect in terms of social justice (Voigt, 2017). Moreover, the introduction of this kind of incentive may have some counterproductive effects: some people who are willing to be vaccinated for essentially altruistic reasons might not do so if they think that someone might interpret that they have done so for financial reasons. Finally, it should be noted that payment is particularly controversial when it comes to motivating parents to vaccinate their children (Savulescu, 2021).

However, the most powerful type of incentive for vaccination, without being strictly a form of compulsory vaccination, is of another type. I am referring to non-financial incentives, such as the possibility of not wearing masks, not keeping safety distances or not needing to obtain health certificates. As I pointed out in the previous chapter, these allow the holder access to certain places that would otherwise be off limits. In their less restrictive forms (3G), they are not models that introduce a strict obligation (one can live a quite normal life without being vaccinated, just by getting tested periodically). What they will do, however, is make life much easier for those who decide to get immunised, avoiding the need for continuous testing. For this reason, we could consider them as incentives to vaccinate, rather than as a means of coercively imposing vaccination (Savulescu, 2021).

I would not want to close this section without highlighting one final point of particular importance: payment in kind has an advantage over cash, in the sense that it is unlikely to send the signal that vaccination is unsafe. "A cash payment may paradoxically undermine vaccination uptake by introducing unwarranted suspicion (though this is an intuition that may need to be tested). Benefits in kind are less susceptible to this concern because they are directly linked to the benefit provided by the vaccine itself: the vaccinated person is no longer a threat to others" (Savulescu, 2021). This should be taken into account in the formulation of relevant health policies.

4.4.2   Classical Compulsory Measures: Vaccination Policies Based on Sanctions (Mandatory Vaccination)

Having analysed the policies based on positive incentives, it is time to focus on those that involve sanctions, in one way or another, for those who do not get vaccinated. I will start with the two most commonly applied policies in practice, those that impose a fine or other type of financial penalty on citizens who refuse to be vaccinated or those that limit their access to certain places. The first, fines or the infliction of some other type of economic damage, is frequently used in EU member countries and other geographical areas. For example, Australia introduced years ago measures that deprived parents who did not comply with the recommended child vaccination schedule of the right to receive state childcare benefits (Wigham et al., 2014). This is what has been termed the "no jab, no pay" policies. The evidence, however, does not speak highly in favour of these policies, which can disproportionately affect disadvantaged groups. In Australia, both economically disadvantaged and immigrant families reported being negatively affected by the measures imposed, with vaccination-linked payments and inability to access childcare having a greater impact on them (MacDonald et al., 2018; Gravagna et al., 2020).

In other cases, it is simply a matter of imposing a penalty on those who are not vaccinated. For example, in the case of COVID-19, the Czech Republic imposed fines of up to 10,000 Czech korunas (CZK) (about 400 euros) on those who did not get vaccinated,[10] and Austria considered for some time penalties of about 2800 euros. This, in principle, seems to be considered more coercive than the deprivation of state subsidies. However, Cierco (2020, p. 52) has lucidly argued that this may not be the case: determining if the ineligibility for a grant of x euros is softer than the payment of a penalty of y euros depends on the amounts behind the x and y.

The harm can also be derived from a specific tax or an extraordinary levy on a common tax. The philosophy behind this modality is surely very similar to the one behind Pigovian-type taxes: it is about "forcing people to internalize the negative externalities, that is, the costs to society, of certain behaviours (e.g. drinking or smoking)" (Giubilini, 2019, p. 85). Evidently, the degree of this system's coerciveness will hinge fundamentally on the sanction amounts. Depending on what it is, it may be more efficient in terms of achieving its objective (increasing the percentage of vaccinated people) than the modality based on the restriction of the right of access. It is important, in any case, to bear in mind that the amount of taxes or penalties may have particularly serious legal consequences. Thus, for example, in the case of Italy, when the compulsory vaccination schedule was introduced, the Constitutional Court warned that the amount of the sanction could jeopardise proportionality. Hence, during the parliamentary procedure, it was considerably reduced.

---

[10] Section 29(1)(f) and (2) of the Minor Offences Act (*Zákon o přestupcích*) (Law no. 200/1990 Coll., "the MO Act").

In short, we find ourselves with systems that, in their different modalities, try to force the will of those who do not wish to be vaccinated by harming their economic interests. They may be efficient, but they will always suffer from equity problems, unless the legislator introduces parameters that relate the amount of the penalty to the income or wealth of the offender. Moreover, they will probably be extremely ineffective with the population at the extremes of the economic spectrum: the very rich will surely avoid it by paying affordable amounts, and the very poor will be immune to a sanction that threatens to take away what they do not have, an undoubtedly important weakness of the system.

The most common alternative to the economic injury model is the movement limitation model. By virtue of it, one cannot access certain spaces, services or institutions if one is not vaccinated. The classic examples of compulsory vaccination systems of this type are those that make attendance at day-care centres conditional on the presentation of a vaccination certificate. In some countries, such as Spain, this may or may not be implemented by the places themselves. In other countries, such as Italy, it is a government-imposed policy that schools must scrupulously comply with. In the extreme cases, such measures would extend not only to physical locations but also to jobs or professions, for example. This is the case when there is a requirement to be vaccinated to serve in the military or work in health professions (Navin & Attwell, 2019).

Currently, these are policies that the population has already internalised, because of their similarity to the use of the health certificate in the case of COVID-19. This certificate, as I explained in Chap. 2, could be considered a tool for the introduction of compulsory vaccination or an incentive to get vaccinated depending on the degree of difficulty to lead a minimally bearable life that it entails. A similar case to the day-care centres is the policies implemented in some parts of Germany from mid-November 2021, when the country was facing the fourth COVID wave. At that time, the 2G certificate was imposed on leisure, i.e. the type of certificate that makes access only possible for those who are vaccinated or those who have passed the disease. Since leisure is not the most essential life activity, one might think that we are talking about an incentive to be vaccinated and not—strictly speaking—an obligation (I concede that this statement probably depends of the extension of the concept of "leisure". It is not the same to be deprived of football matches and cinema than to restrict the access to restaurants and bars). However, if it were required for access to workplaces or for public transport, it would be a formidable coercive tool. Compared to the system of fines, these policies have the advantage that they affect people equally regardless of their purchasing power, which is clearly better in terms of equity.

4.4.3   Reimbursement of Health-Care Costs: The Singapore Proposal

A new variant of sanctions policy for the unvaccinated is the one introduced by Singapore on 8 November 2021: persons not vaccinated by choice would not have their care costs borne by the public health system (Berger, 2021). The justification for the measure, in the words by the Minister of Health of that country, was that "unvaccinated persons make up a sizable majority of those who require intensive inpatient care, and disproportionately contribute to the strain on our health care resources". In short, it would be a matter of imposing on the voluntarily unvacci-nated, who consume expensive resources, the obligation to meet these expenses. In principle, this proposal is similar to the paradigm of the economic sanction that I have already explained, in fact, at least secondarily, to impose vaccination coer-cively, since most of us would prefer to avoid facing a cost that can be very high. However, it differs from the mere sanction in its spirit of compensation. Here it is not just a matter of causing harm to those who are not vaccinated but of introducing a new factor, the need to meet the cost of the resources that have had to be consumed by their irresponsible behaviour of not being vaccinated by choice. It is therefore a different, novel and interesting scenario that requires special attention.

Nonetheless, is it reasonable to introduce this new variant into our arsenal of health policies? On the face of it, it might seem so. The idea is that if we can directly identify those who have caused the waste of a valuable public resource, justice demands that they take responsibility and compensate the rest of us for it. In this sense, Davies and Savulescu have stressed that it is logical to conclude that public health policy makers have, in the context of health emergency, "the right to penalise some users who are responsible for their poor health. This derives from the fact that solidary systems involve both rights and obligations and, in some cases, those who avoidably incur health burdens violate obligations of solidarity" (Davies & Savulescu, 2019).

However, I consider that the system designed by Singapore is a mistake, although my conclusion might be different if we were to make some substantive changes to the distribution of burdens. I will try to explain why. To put it simply, Singapore's proposed design focuses only on the voluntarily unvaccinated who get sick. This seems to me to be a poor choice. Since they will have to bear the costs of treatment, it can have pernicious effects on disease containment strategies. Many of those who become infected while unvaccinated by choice will go out of their way to avoid going to a clinic in order to save the expense, at least until it becomes absolutely necessary for them. This, of course, will increase the number of infections. For this reason alone, I find it difficult to accept such a health policy. However, that is neither the only reason nor the main one why I think it is a bad idea. The main reason for my opposition is that I do not see this system as being any fairer or more efficient than the one that penalises all those who are not vaccinated by choice. It is not fairer because, in reality, it suffers from the same problem that the system of fines has. Either the amounts are linked to the income or wealth of the sanctioned person or the sanction will not be fair. It will not be efficient in encouraging vaccination, or, at most, it will be no more efficient than a sanction for all those who have opted not to be vaccinated. After all, many of these people do not vaccinate because they under-estimate the risk to themselves, so a sanction that will only be applied if they need health care will hardly motivate them much. If the intention is really to defray the material costs of a use of resources that could have been avoided if we had all been vaccinated, this is not a reasonable measure either. Just think that, in such a case, the only ones who will pay will be those voluntarily unvaccinated who are unlucky enough to contract a severe form of the disease that requires hospitalisation.

The latter, in my opinion, is particularly unfair. Although it is true that the level of risk is not zero and the measure of irresponsibility differs substantially when we talk about a healthy 30-year-old person or a 70-year-old one with several previous pathologies, it is also true that the reasons why each of them is not vaccinated can be quite different. It is not the same for those who do not get vaccinated out of panic than for those who do not do so out of mere laziness. It is also true that the unvac-cinated by choice, in general, share a basic responsibility. In both cases, the risk has arisen as a consequence of their reckless decisions taken freely. Therefore, leaving only some of them—those who have had the misfortune to become seriously ill—to face the consequences of a reckless act is far less equitable than opting for the oppo-site, imposing compensation for the excess expense caused by the lack of vaccina-tion on all those who decide not to get vaccinated, directly.

In short, I believe that focusing on the voluntarily unvaccinated as a whole is much more reasonable than focusing only on those who have required the use of valuable public resources, because what it does is to mutualise responsibility and compensation to others for the excess resources consumed (Cappelen & Norheim, 2005). Thus, what we would be doing is to pass these costs on to a collective that has not done all they could to prevent them from arising, regardless of its particular fortune. The tax, of course, should be linked to each citizen's economic status, so that it would be as equitable as possible. The approach, unlike the one suggested by Savulescu and Davies, would be based on compensation, not sanction, which I think is more appropriate. If these conditions were met, the system would be more effi-cient and equitable than any other alternative.

In the face of this argument, it is perfectly possible to introduce several counter-arguments. To begin with, we should not forget that, among those vaccinated, there are also people with a high predisposition to end up hospitalised, who should adopt additional protective measures at times of high incidence. However, some do not do so, which ends up causing serious damage to the system. Would it not be unfair to put the focus of the extra cost exclusively on some for the mere fact of not being vaccinated and not on others, although all of them are largely responsible for their situation? In my opinion, the answer to this question should indeed be positive. It would certainly be somewhat discriminatory to force some to pay the costs of their care and not others when both had engaged in irresponsible behaviour by choice (Daniels, 1985). However, in the case of the imprudent vaccinated person, it would be necessary to demonstrate that these factors (the possibility of foreseeing a serious course of the disease, voluntary undertaking of risky activities, etc.) have concurred and that they have been decisive in explaining this unnecessary consumption of public resources. In the case of a voluntarily unvaccinated person, on the other hand, we would have to speak of a presumption of irresponsibility for the fact of not being vaccinated by choice. Then, the question would not be so much of avoiding this measure as of extending it to people other than the unvaccinated, that is, the vaccinated who have needed assistance because of their imprudence, given their particular circumstances. The problem would certainly be evidentiary in the case of the latter. Therefore, if we decided to introduce this system, my recommendation would be, ultimately, to avoid their participation in the mutualisation fund, replacing this effort by the payment of a penalty linked to irresponsible behaviour, regardless of its result (the danger produced would be penalised, not the result caused). I understand that this, without being the fairest to do, would certainly be the most feasible.

The second objection to this reasoning has a lot to do with the fact that, in general, we do not usually introduce distinctions in free public health care based on people's behaviour or habits (De Lora et al., 2009). We do not force smokers to pay the costs of treating lung cancer or alcoholics for cirrhosis, nor do we charge insulin costs to people who suffer from diabetes because of their sedentary lifestyle, for example. Why should we act differently in the case of people who decide not to get vaccinated? This reasoning is, at first glance, clearly seductive. However, it should be noted that the differences between the two situations are striking. To begin with, the vaccination data is easy to verify objectively. It does not, therefore, imply that a thorough investigation of the circumstances of the case is necessary. This, in turn, prevents the health professional from becoming a sort of "behavioural police" of the patient or anything of the sort, which is essential in terms of respecting the relationship of trust between the two. Beyond that, the rebuttal I have presented makes the mistake of equating lifestyle habits with concrete acts. Getting vaccinated is a simple act, which can be done in a moment and without much effort. Quitting smoking or drinking, avoiding being overweight, giving up a sedentary life, etc., these are issues that involve changing habits that have been ingrained over many years. In addition, some of them have to do with addictions that the subject cannot easily get rid of, which, moreover, have often been socially promoted. Hence, if we adopt the perspective of egalitarian liberalism, which considers that "society should eliminate inequalities in health that arise from factors outside individual control, but not inequalities in health that arise from differences in choice" (Cappelen & Norheim, 2006, p. 313), both cases are different. It is easier to think in terms of freedom of choice when we talk about the decision not to get vaccinated than when we think about lifestyle habits developed in an uncritical social environment, so the consequences may be different.

In addition, we must not forget that to draw a link between lifestyle habits and specific pathologies is not as easy as between an act such as non-vaccination and the development of a disease such as COVID-19. The parallelism that we are trying to draw works much better, in fact, when we compare the refusal to be vaccinated with the behaviour of the person who carries out a specific action when the occasion demands them to avoid it in order not to use up a scarce resource. Let us think, for example, of a cyclist who goes out on the road without a helmet when there is a state of hospital saturation. Is he not being enormously imprudent? And if so, why not extend mutualisation of costs to his case? Again, I agree: when it comes to clear breaches of guidelines that call for responsible behaviour, some form of liability should be extended to these people. It is just that it would be much more practical to use the mechanism of administrative sanction, rather than to include them in the mutualisation of the cost of unnecessary care by COVID-19. In fact, that is what we usually do when a person puts himself or herself at risk if they ignore all the guidelines around avoiding a risky situation, causing costly intervention by the emergency and rescue services, for example. We make them pay a penalty for irresponsible behaviour that has caused a cost, but we do not include health care in it. It does not seem absurd to me a priori to draw a parallel in this respect.

Finally, one must consider that our common beliefs, based on a scrupulous respect for life choices and the individual's autonomy, are not applicable to exceptional situations, such as those in which a pandemic places health systems at their limits. In these scenarios, as I have reiterated throughout this work, it is necessary to give much greater weight to public health considerations. Hence, the comparison between lifestyle habits and an isolated act loses much of its weight. To this must be added that, at least in the case of tobacco or alcohol, we impose de facto a compensation to the system for the costs incurred through the taxes that those who smoke or drink have to pay (Persaud, 1995). Restoration of excess resource use then comes as a matter of course. This, obviously, does not happen in the case of non-vaccination against a particular pathology in the midst of a pandemic.

In short, I believe that the option of passing on the costs of excess health expenditure as a result of a refusal to be vaccinated may be reasonable, which by no means implies that it should necessarily be introduced, of course (indeed, I do not support it myself). However, if the legislator finally decides to implement this measure, it is necessary that some conditions are met. Among them, one that stands out is that it would have to announce its intention to pass on the cost caused by the pathology to those who engage in irresponsible behaviour and allow time for those who are not vaccinated by choice to change their status. This would prevent them from being defenceless in the face of new legislation. I also understand that this compensation should be extended to the whole group of the voluntarily unvaccinated, although I know that there may be a greater or lesser degree of irresponsibility among them. However, I consider that what would enable the satisfaction of a proportional part of the costs is the mere fact of not being vaccinated by choice. This is an injustice, since vaccinated people behave differently. Some of them are careful about getting infected or infecting others. Others are not. Treating all of them in the same way is unfair, of course, but health policy knows limits. Introducing similar penalties for irresponsible behaviour by vaccinated people, irrespective of the result, might be the best way to avoid such injustices as far as possible.

4.4.4   Coercive Systems or Forced Vaccination Systems

There are, finally, systems for implementing compulsory vaccination that use tools whose capacity for coercion is much greater. First of all, "brute force" could be used to inoculate the agent into the body of those who refuse to do so voluntarily. This blatant violation of the right to bodily integrity (as well as autonomy) would be difficult to justify in a state governed by the rule of law, except in truly exceptional circumstances. Beyond this scenario, it is even possible to think about the intervention of criminal law, through the criminalisation of the refusal of vaccination. A custodial sentence could be assigned to this conduct, but it would be clearly excessive and unrealistic in practice, given the available places in the prisons in most of our countries, although there are at least 12 States in the world that contemplate it in their regulations, including Monaco in Europe (Gravagna et al., 2020). A fine penalty would probably be a more appropriate penal intervention. Although there is the possibility of implementing a similar sanction through administrative law, the psychological factor would make a notable difference. The nature of the measure—turning the offender into a criminal—could influence the degree of unconscious coercion. Against this criminalisation, on the other hand, it should be noted that "it may lose much of its ethical charge if the consequences are minor or easily avoidable, such as a small one-time fine" (Navin & Attwell, 2019, p. 1047).

In either of the two cases I have just described, judicial intervention would be inexcusable. In practice, this makes it almost impossible for these alternatives to be introduced in the context of resistance to vaccination by a significant percentage of the population. It is difficult, if not impossible, to force millions of people to get vaccinated, and the option of imprisonment is clearly unfeasible. Therefore, and beyond the disproportion that such measures would imply, they should be discarded because of their material impossibility.

4.4.5   Different Systems for Different Collectives?

One of the most controversial issues related to COVID-19 was probably the issue of mandatory vaccination for those in certain professions. These typically include health professionals and caregivers. The rationale behind these proposals is that these groups have greater responsibility than others towards third parties, as they usually deal with people belonging to vulnerable groups. Furthermore, one of the main mandates that a caregiver must follow, according to traditional medical ethics, is to *do no harm*. Therefore, the caring professions have an enhanced obligation to be vaccinated to protect their patients (Bowen, 2020). From a completely different angle, it has been pointed out that "a mandatory COVID-19 vaccination programme could be seen as discriminatory and may cause stigmatisation, further loss of trust and overall widen the inequalities already seen during the pandemic" (Khunti et al., 2021, p. 236).

The truth, in my opinion, is that there are several inconsistencies in the arguments that support the compulsory nature of a vaccine that fails to fully prevent the transmission of a pathogen. I cannot understand why, when it comes to protecting third parties, we consider this the optimal tool. I am aware that there are some apparently convincing reasons for this. Quite simply, the sterilising immunity that, to one degree or another, vaccines confer mean that in any pandemic the vaccinated group will show fewer infected people as a percentage. However, this fact is not essential when it comes to sustaining the imposition of compulsory vaccination on the unvaccinated. Let us keep in mind that the individual who does not really disseminate a pathogenic agent is the one who is not infected, and this is not necessarily the one who is vaccinated. In other words, the fact that a worker is vaccinated does not mean that he or she does not spread the disease. Therefore, in order to guarantee the health of third parties, we are more interested in knowing a person's state of contagiousness, not their vaccination status. This is achieved through testing, not through vaccines (unless they are sterilising, which is unlikely). Hence, if we want to prevent contagion, in the strictest sense of the word, it is more logical to require workers to undergo periodic testing (and isolation if necessary), not vaccination. I am aware that if we were purists, this would lead us to require such tests even for those who are vaccinated. This is particularly advisable at complicated times in epidemiological terms. In other calmer scenarios, we could relax this requirement for vaccinated people, trusting in their lower probability of being infected and, consequently, infecting third parties, although this will always depend on the sterilisation power of each vaccine and on the individual.

The problem with this alternative probably lies in the cost that would have to be assumed for carrying out the necessary tests and in the logistical difficulties involved in implementing it. I am aware that this is a headache for those in charge of companies or institutions, where forcing their workers to be vaccinated is a much simpler option. However, if it is the one that is finally adopted in a pandemic, we will have to be honest and say that we have chosen the simplest alternative, even though it is not the one that best contributes to guaranteeing the health of the vulnerable. Nor is it the one that best responds to the respect required for the fundamental rights of employees who do not want to be vaccinated. If an employee agrees to be routinely tested, it is hard to justify making vaccination compulsory on the grounds of protecting third parties. Hence, the principle of proportionality clearly plays in his or her favour: there will simply be an alternative for the intended purpose that is much less restrictive of his or her rights. In this case, the requirement of the necessity for vaccination would not be met. Therefore, we should not impose mandatory vaccination, since other alternatives, less harmful to protecting the interests of the vulnerable, would be as good or better (Blank et al., 2020; Gur-Arie et al., 2021). Another issue will be to determine who should bear the costs of such routine testing (in my view, clearly the worker who can be vaccinated and refuses to do so).

To all of the above must be added a pragmatic argument, which was highlighted during the COVID-19 crisis and which a UN report has very aptly expressed (World Health Organization, 2021):

Given current rates (and concerns) of health worker "burn-out" as a result of the pandemic and the potential consequence of an inadequately resourced health workforce (18), mandatory vaccination policies that require unvaccinated health workers to stay at home or require vaccination as a condition of employment or hospital privileges might have significant negative consequences for already overburdened health systems. Policies that require unvaccinated health workers to be transferred to settings where the risk is lower might have similar consequences, as they might remove critical health workers from settings that badly need health human resources, such as congregate living settings where care is provided to older adults.

4.5 Concluding Remarks: What Vaccination Policies Are Relevant in a Public Health Crisis?

All that has been said in the previous sections has been aimed at determining the appropriate answer to the big question: would it be legitimate to establish obligatory vaccination when we are facing a serious health emergency, such as that created by a pandemic? There are no definitive conclusions. Everything will depend on the scenario in which we find ourselves on each occasion. This was clearly described by Judge Wojtyczek in his dissenting opinion in the Vavricka case:[11]

A rational assessment of whether the obligation to vaccinate complies with the Convention requires that the case be examined separately for each disease, proceeding on a disease-by-disease basis. For each and every disease, it is necessary to establish:

- the manner and speed of its transmission;
- the risks for infected persons;
- the average cost of individual treatment for the disease in the case of non-vaccinated patients, and the prospects of success of such treatment;
- the precise effectiveness of the available vaccines;
- the average cost of a vaccination;
- the risk of side effects of vaccination;
- the average costs of treating the undesirable effects of the vaccination;
- the minimum percentage of vaccinated persons which would prevent the disease from spreading (if applicable) and the prospects of achieving such an objective.

All the factors cited by Wojticzek—and probably some more—can change considerably from one pandemic to another, so it is difficult to make general judgements. However, there are some ideas that seem reasonable in all circumstances. In principle, we should always opt for those policies that entail the least curtailment of fundamental rights and freedoms. Therefore, it makes sense to prefer policies that are based on encouragement to those that introduce a sanction. However, those that are limited to punishing us with fines or limitations of access, in turn, will be preferable to those that involve the use of coercive force, because if the former involve a limitation of freedom, the latter involve, in addition, an attack on bodily integrity.

---

[11]ECtHR Judgment of 8 April 2021, Vavricka et autres v. Republique Tchèque, EC:ECHR:2021: 0408JUD004762113. Dissenting Opinion of Judge Wojtyczek, p. 9.

Hence, in compliance with the principle of the least restrictive alternative, implicit in the requirement of the necessity for a solution, we should prefer them. The distinguished Australian bioethicist Julian Savulescu has designed some algorithms based on the reliability of vaccines, the importance of the risk, the possible alternatives, etc. that might serve us well to decide on the implementation of some policies over others (Savulescu, 2021, p. 82; Savulescu et al., 2021). It is useful to keep them in mind when formulating these policies, without, of course, strictly adhering to them, if the occasion demands otherwise. What we must consider, in any case, is that, as an expert as impressively thorough as César Cierco points out (Cierco Seira, 2020, p. 51):

> The dichotomy between obligation and recommendation constitutes, therefore, and it must be stressed as many times as necessary, an instrumental choice about the best way to achieve the same end. What changes is the strategy: while for some it is better that generalization is ensured through the establishment of a legal duty that weighs on all citizens equally; for others, instead, it is preferable to rely on the voluntary participation of the same on the basis of good education and information able to convince of the advantages, individual, social and solidarity, of vaccination.

In short, there are no exact formulas; rather, the assessment of the state of necessity or the proportionality of the measures should depend on each specific scenario. In times of uncertainty, following the paradigm of staggered intervention proposed by the British Nuffield Council seems reasonable (Nuffield Council on Bioethics, 2007). Furthermore, any kind of restriction of rights, in addition to being proportionate, should try to distribute the burdens as equitably as possible, without leaving aside considerations of efficiency, of course. This is in line with the fact that sometimes "The use of penalties for non-compliance may be counter-productive in cases where they further prevent access to vaccination, especially among groups already facing barriers to vaccine access" (Gravagna et al., 2020, p. 7872). This inequitable and clearly inefficient effect should be avoided at all costs.

4.6   Addenda: Vaccination as a Factor to be Included in Triage Protocols

I would like to end this chapter by introducing the question of the relevance of vaccinated or voluntarily unvaccinated status when emergency health services collapse. This, for example, clearly happened in the case of SARS-CoV-2, which not only made triage necessary due to the lack of emergency resources but also caused considerable deficiencies in health care for patients with other pathologies. The fight against the virus absorbed human and material resources that would otherwise have been used to attend other pathologies in a timely manner. This probably caused damage to many more people than those who now appear as direct victims of the pandemic. That said, the question that inevitably arises, and that I will address briefly here, is the following: in that scenario, would it make sense to differentiate in the way we treat the vaccinated and the voluntarily unvaccinated in terms of allocation of resources? Here we enter a different terrain, not necessarily darker, than the one we have explored before. In the chapter on triage, I argue that an equity-based structure may be the most appropriate for allocating scarce health resources in an emergency. I do not think it is unreasonable to consider that the fact of not being vaccinated may influence the final outcome of the allocation. If we accept that socioeconomic criteria should play a role in giving preponderance to some patients over others, introducing this other variable is, to a large extent, its logical consequence. It seems fair to differentiate between those who have done their best not to monopolise scarce health goods and those who have not acted in the same way.

Moreover, there is also a fact that characterises emergency triage situations: the consequence of one person being attended is, inevitably, that another is not. The question is that if we consider a group of candidates trying to access a scarce resource, and some are vaccinated and others are not (because they refused), the truth is that not all of them have done their best to avoid needing it. At least some of the voluntarily unvaccinated could have avoided the severe form of the disease by getting vaccinated. This means that if we allocate the resources to them, and other vaccinated (or involuntarily unvaccinated) people die as a result, there is a certain relationship between the two facts. This inevitably brings us back to Jeff McMahan's argument that responsibility should affect the final outcome of the allocation of scarce resources (McMahan, 2007), or, more to the point, to the principle of restitution. This says that if a patient is at fault for the scarcity of a resource, the principle of restitution requires that he or she gives priority to those who are not at fault. Or, in Smart's version, it is morally defensible to "give people lower priority in priority-setting contexts if the individuals are responsible for their ill health and if the behavior that caused the ill health has no (or a low) social value" (Smart, 1994). The conditions under which this would apply were splendidly synthesised by Wilkinson in 1999 (Wilkinson, 1999).

If all these conditions are met, it seems reasonable to think of introducing the fact of voluntary non-vaccination as a compensatory factor of equity in a triage. Against this opinion, I have to say that authors such as Wilkinson himself or John Harris have opposed the application of this principle on different grounds. Harris, for example, believes that to let a person's health worsen, or even die, because of some moral defect in his or her personal traits is to let decision-makers punish immorality with capital punishment (Harris, 2006, p. 105). However, this argument only implies, in my view, that failing to care for a person suffering from a disease for which treatment exists merely because he or she has not been vaccinated is unacceptable (with which I agree). It does not mean, however, that it is immoral to consider that, if we are to choose between two people to whom we allocate a scarce resource, the question of responsibility should not be taken into account at all. Wilkinson, on the other hand, thinks that accepting the principle would be as much as allowing the state to moralise individual choices about our lifestyle, as well as assuming that it is possible to determine which of them are more or less acceptable (Wilkinson, 1999). The problem in this case is that there are big differences between life habits and exceptional acts, such as vaccination, as I have expressed previously in other sections of this chapter.

The conclusion, in short, is that, if we must choose a patient to which we allocate a scarce resource, when there are not enough resources for all, the fact that some patients are voluntarily unvaccinated should at least serve to break a tie between them. By this, I mean that if there is no overriding criterion, we should allow a factor associated with social responsibility, such as voluntary refuse to vaccination, to decide the situation. Obviously, this should be announced sufficiently in advance, so that everyone can understand why this criterion has been invoked and cannot cry out about its unfairness (justifiably, by the way). Finally, may I point out that, in a scenario of a dramatic lack of health resources, these considerations should extend beyond the voluntarily unvaccinated to those who subject themselves to unnecessary risks by illegally engaging in activities that are currently prohibited. It does not seem fair to use chance to allocate necessary goods when one of the two people who need it has put themselves at risk by failing to comply with a mandate. The rule of giving priority in access to the resource to those who do their best to protect themselves when this also involves maximising the protection of others would extend to these cases. It will be, of course, another matter to prove it, as I have indicated above.

References

Al-Ozaibi, L., Adnan, J., Hassan, B., Al-Mazroui, A., & Al-Badri, F. (2016). Seat belt syndrome: Delayed or missed intestinal injuries, a case report and review of literature. *International Journal of Surgery Case Reports, 20*, 74–76.

Berger, M. (2021, November 8). People 'unvaccinated by choice' in Singapore can no longer receive free covid-19 treatment. *The Washington Post.* Retrieved November 19, 2021, from https://www.washingtonpost.com/world/2021/11/08/singapore-unvaccinated-medical-costs-health-care-covid-19/

Blank, C., Gemeinhart, N., Dunagan, W. C., & Babcock, H. M. (2020). Mandatory employee vaccination as a strategy for early and comprehensive health care personnel immunization coverage: Experience from 10 influenza seasons. *American Journal of Infection Control, 48*(10), 1133–1138.

Blumenthal-Barby, J. S., & Burroughs, H. (2012). Seeking better health care outcomes: The ethics of using the "nudge". *The American Journal of Bioethics: AJOB, 12*(2), 1–10.

Bowen, R. A. (2020). Ethical and organizational considerations for mandatory COVID-19 vaccination of health care workers: A clinical laboratorian's perspective. *Clinica Chimica Acta; International Journal of Clinical Chemistry, 510*, 421.

Cappelen, A. W., & Norheim, O. F. (2005). Responsibility in health care: A liberal egalitarian approach. *Journal of Medical Ethics, 31*(8), 476–480.

Cappelen, A. W., & Norheim, O. F. (2006). Responsibility, fairness and rationing in health care. *Health Policy, 76*(3), 312–319.

Cierco Seira, C. (2005). Epidemics and administrative law. The possible responses of the administration in situations of serious health risk for the population. *DS, 13*(2), 201–256.

Cierco Seira, C. (2018). *Vaccination, individual liberties and public law* (pp. 19–40). Marial Pons.

Cierco Seira, C. (2020). Compulsory or recommended vaccination: Annotations from the law. *Vacunas, 21*(1), 50–56.

Cierco Seira, C. (2021). La vacuna-condición o el pasaporte de vacunación y su eventual encaje en un marco general de vacunación recomendada contra la COVID-19 [The vaccine-condition or vaccination passport and its eventual fit into a broad recommended vaccination framework against COVID-19]. *Vaccine, 22*(2), 82–88. https://doi.org/10.1016/j.vacun.2021.02.001. Retrieved November 19, 2021.

Cristol, D. (2009). Vaccination obligatoire. Responsabilité de l'Etat. Préjudice et réparation. *Revue de Droit Sanitaire et Social, 3*, 565–575.

Daniels, N. (1985). *Just health care*. Cambridge University Press.

Davies, B., & Savulescu, J. (2019). Solidarity and responsibility in health care. *Public Health Ethics, 12*(2), 133–144.

Dawson, A. (2007). Herd protection as a public good: Vaccination and our obligations to others. *Ethics, Prevention, and Public Health, 160*, 163.

De Lora, P., Fajuri, A. Z., & Machado, S. M. (2009). *El derecho a la asistencia sanitaria: Un análisis desde las teorías de la justicia distributiva*. Iustel.

De Miguel Beriain, I. (2021). We should not vaccinate the young to protect the old: A response to Giubilini, Savulescu, and Wilkinson. *Journal of Law and the Biosciences, 8*(1), lsab015.

Dutta, A., Huang, C. T., Lin, C. Y., Chen, T. C., Lin, Y. C., Chang, C. S., & He, Y. C. (2016). Sterilizing immunity to influenza virus infection requires local antigen-specific T cell response in the lungs. *Scientific Reports, 6*(1), 1–14.

Elliott, P., Haw, D., Wang, H., Eales, O., Walters, C. E., Ainslie, K. E., Atchison, C., Fronterre, C., Diggle, P. J., Page, A. J., Trotter, A. J., Prosolek, S. J., The COVID-19 Genomics UK (COG-UK) Consortium, Ashby, D., Donnelly, C. A., Barclay, W., Taylor, G., Cooke, G., Ward, H., Darzi, A., & Riley, S. (2021). REACT-1 round 13 final report: Exponential growth, high prevalence of SARS-CoV-2 and vaccine effectiveness associated with delta variant in England during May to July 2021. *medRxiv*.

Faden, R. R., & Faden, A. I. (1978). The ethics of health education as public health policy. *Health Education Monographs, 6*(2), 180–197.

Fagard, K., Gielen, E., Deschodt, M., Devriendt, E., & Flamaing, J. (2021). Risk factors for severe COVID-19 disease and death in patients aged 70 and over: A retrospective observational cohort study. *Acta Clinica Belgica*, 1–8.

Feehan, J., & Apostolopoulos, V. (2021). No, vaccinated people are not 'just as infectious' as unvaccinated people if they get COVID. *The Conversation*. Retrieved November 9, 2021, from https://theconversation.com/no-vaccinated-people-are-not-just-as-infectious-as-unvaccinated-people-if-they-get-covid-171302

Feinberg, J. (1971). Legal paternalism. *Canadian Journal of Philosophy, 1*(1), 105–124.

Flanigan, J. (2017). Seat belt mandates and paternalism. *Journal of Moral Philosophy, 14*(3), 291–314.

García Ruiz, Y. (2014). Public health and multiculturalism: Population immunization and food security. *Anuario de la Facultad de Derecho de la Universidad Autónoma de Madrid, 18*, 269–288.

Giubilini, A. (2019). *The ethics of vaccination*. Springer Nature.

Giubilini, A., Douglas, T., & Savulescu, J. (2018). The moral obligation to be vaccinated: Utilitarianism, contractualism, and collective easy rescue. *Medicine, Health Care and Philosophy, 21*(4), 547–560.

Giubilini, A., Gupta, S., & Heneghan, C. (2021). A focused protection vaccination strategy: Why we should not target children with COVID-19 vaccination policies. *Journal of Medical Ethics, 47*(8), 565–566.

Giubilini, A., & Savulescu, J. (2019). Vaccination, risks, and freedom: The seat belt analogy. *Public Health Ethics, 12*(3), 237–249.

Giubilini, A., Savulescu, J., & Wilkinson, D. (2020a). COVID-19 vaccine: Vaccinate the young to protect the old? *Journal of Law and the Biosciences, 7*(1), lsaa050.

Gravagna, K., Becker, A., Valeris-Chacin, R., Mohammed, I., Tambe, S., Awan, F. A., Toomey, T. L., & Basta, N. E. (2020). Global assessment of national mandatory vaccination policies and consequences of non-compliance. *Vaccine, 38*(49), 7865–7873.

Gur-Arie, R., Jamrozik, E., & Kingori, P. (2021). No jab, no job? Ethical issues in mandatory COVID-19 vaccination of healthcare personnel. *BMJ Global Health, 6*(2), e004877.

Harris, J. (1975). The survival lottery. *Philosophy, 50*(191), 81–87.

Harris, J. (2006). *The value of life: An introduction to medical ethics*. Routledge.

Khunti, K., Kamal, A., Pareek, M., & Griffiths, A. (2021). Should vaccination for healthcare workers be mandatory? *Journal of the Royal Society of Medicine, 114*(5), 235–236.

Ledford, H. (2021). COVID vaccines and blood clots: Five key questions. *Nature, 592*(7855), 495–496.

MacDonald, N. E., Harmon, S., Dube, E., Steenbeek, A., Crowcroft, N., Opel, D. J., Faour, D., Leask, J., & Butler, R. (2018). Mandatory infant & childhood immunization: Rationales, issues and knowledge gaps. *Vaccine, 36*(39), 5811–5818.

Mallapaty, S. (2021). COVID vaccines cut the risk of transmitting Delta-but not for long. *Nature News, 5*.

McMahan, J. (2007). Justice and liability in organ allocation. *Social Research, 74*(1), 101–124.

Navin, M. (2015). *Values and vaccine refusal: Hard questions in ethics, epistemology, and health care*. Routledge.

Navin, M. C., & Attwell, K. (2019). Vaccine mandates value pluralism and policy diversity. *Bioethics, 33*(9), 1042–1049. https://doi.org/10.1111/bioe.12645

NSW Health. (2021). *Vaccination among COVID-19 cases in the NSW Delta outbreak reporting period: 16 June to 7 October 2021*. Report. Retrieved November 19, 2021, from https://www.health.nsw.gov.au/Infectious/covid-19/Documents/in-focus/covid-19-vaccination-case-surveillance-051121.pdf

Nuffield Council on Bioethics (Great Britain). (2007). *Public health: Ethical issues*. Nuffield Council on Bioethics.

Nyhan, B., Reifler, J., Richey, S., & Freed, G. L. (2014). Effective messages in vaccine promotion: A randomized trial. *Pediatrics, 133*(4), e835–e842.

Otsuka, M. (1991). The paradox of group beneficence. *Philosophy & Public Affairs, 20*(2), 132–149.

Parfit, D. (1984). *Reasons and persons*. Oxford University Press.

Persaud, R. (1995). Smokers' rights to health care. *Journal of Medical Ethics, 21*(5), 281–287.

Pierik, R. (2018). Mandatory vaccination: An unqualified defence. *Journal of Applied Philosophy, 35*(2), 381–398.

Ploug, T., & Holm, S. (2015). Doctors, patients, and nudging in the clinical context-four views on nudging and informed consent. *The American Journal of Bioethics: AJOB, 15*(10), 28–38.

Rainey, B., McCormick, P., & Ovey, C. (2020). *Jacobs, white, and Ovey: The European convention on human rights*. Oxford University Press.

Rechel, B., Priaulx, J., Richardson, E., & McKee, M. (2019). The organization and delivery of vaccination services in the European Union. *European Journal of Public Health, 29*(Suppl 4), ckz185-375.

Reed, M. P., Ebert-Hamilton, S. M., & Rupp, J. D. (2012). Effects of obesity on seat belt fit. *Traffic Injury Prevention, 13*(4), 364–372.

Rossi, J., & Yudell, M. (2012). The use of persuasion in public health communication: An ethical critique. *Public Health Ethics, 5*(2), 192–205.

Sánchez Patrón, J. M. (2021). Vaccination in European jurisprudence. *European Community Law Review, 69*, 511–553.

Savulescu, J. (2021). Good reasons to vaccinate: Mandatory or payment for risk? *Journal of Medical Ethics, 47*(2), 78–85.

Savulescu, J., Pugh, J., & Wilkinson, D. (2021). Balancing incentives and disincentives for vaccination in a pandemic. *Nature Medicine, 27*(9), 1500–1503.

Singanayagam, A., Hakki, S., Dunning, J., Madon, K. J., Crone, M. A., Koycheva, A., Derqui-Fernandez, N., Barnett, J. L., Whitfield, M. G., Varro, R., Charlett, A., Kundu, R., Fenn, J., Cutajar, J., Quinn, V., Conibear, E., Barclay, W., Freemont, P. S., Taylor, G. P., … ATACCC Study Investigators. (2021). Community transmission and viral load kinetics of the SARS-CoV-2 delta (B. 1.617. 2) variant in vaccinated and unvaccinated individuals in the UK: A prospective, longitudinal, cohort study. *The Lancet Infectious Diseases, 22*(2), 183–195.

Smart, B. (1994). Fault and the allocation of spare organs. *Journal of Medical Ethics, 20*(1), 26–30.

Thaler, R. H., & Sunstein, C. R. (2009). *Nudge: Improving decisions about health, wealth, and happiness*. Penguin.

US Department of Transportation, National Highway Traffic Safety Administration (NHTSA). (2010). *Traffic safety facts: Children*. NHTSA. Retrieved from http://www-nrd.nhtsa.dot.gov/Pubs/811387.pdf

Utrilla, D. (2021). Compulsory vaccination and European law: Balancing opposing principles. In D. Utrilla & A. Shabbir (Eds.), *EU Law in times of pandemic* (pp. 215–231). EU Law Live Press/Comares.

Voigt, K. (2017). Too poor to say no? Health incentives for disadvantaged populations. *Journal of Medical Ethics, 43*(3), 162–166.

Wald, A. (2022). Booster vaccination to reduce SARS-CoV-2 transmission and infection. *Journal of the American Medical Association, 327*(4), 327–328.

Wigham, S., Ternent, L., Bryant, A., Robalino, S., Sniehotta, F. F., & Adams, J. (2014). Parental financial incentives for increasing preschool vaccination uptake: Systematic review. *Pediatrics, 134*(4), e1117–e1128.

Wilkinson, S. (1999). Smokers' rights to health care: Why the 'restoration argument' is a moralising wolf in a liberal sheep's clothing. *Journal of Applied Philosophy, 16*(3), 255–269.

World Health Organization. (2021, April 13). *COVID-19 and mandatory vaccination: Ethical considerations and caveats: Policy brief*. World Health Organization.

Wu, K. J. (2021). We're asking the impossible of vaccines. *The Atlantic*. Retrieved November 19, 2021, from https://www.theatlantic.com/science/archive/2021/09/sterilizing-immunity-myth-covid-19-vaccines/620023/

Chapter 5
Triage: When the Tsunami Hits

5.1 Introduction

In February 2020, COVID-19 cases started to multiply in Europe. The health situation in Lombardy became untenable, despite being one of the richest regions on the continent. In the following weeks, many countries faced an extremely complicated situation. Despite the fact that there were many citizens who did not only need access to resources such as hospital beds, ventilators or ICU places but also had the right to them, health-care systems were unable to respond adequately to this challenge. In this scenario, it became clear that we did not have the right tools to respond to such a challenge. Although there was already an abundance of academic literature to construct detailed emergency triage guidelines, this effort was undertaken adequately only in a few exceptional cases, such as in the State of Maryland in the USA (Daugherty Biddison et al., 2019).

The consequence of this lack of foresight was the hasty drafting of protocols that often included criteria contrary to the fundamental values of the European Union or the Member States in which they were intended to be applied. At other times, their recommendations were empty. In many cases, they responded only to the needs of a particular health-care institution, region, profession or speciality. Worse still, they often only made sense in a hospital context, forgetting those who had not yet had access to it. This patchwork of often incoherent or contradictory responses did not help to build one of the main values needed in a situation that requires great sacrifices, namely, the trust of citizens. Nor was this helped by the lack of public information or prior debate or by the problems of transparency that many countries have still not resolved despite the time that has elapsed.

The aim of this chapter is to analyse the ethical and legal issues raised by emergency triage involving life-sustaining treatment (LST). As usual in this work, the COVID-19 crisis will be a starting point, but not the exclusive object of analysis. Instead, I will introduce elements that serve as a general framework for dealing with

I. de Miguel Beriain, *The Ethical, Legal and Social Issues of Pandemics*,
https://doi.org/10.1007/978-3-031-03818-1_5

other scenarios in which some of the key factors, such as the age of those affected, might be different. In order to enrich the debate, I will not consider that the values currently prevailing in the European Union or its Member States should determine the course of action. For example, as we already know, the withdrawal of non-functional treatments is considered a legal offence, and Article 21 of the Charter of Fundamental Rights of the European Union prohibits discrimination based on age or disability. These facts, however, should not prevent the possibility of penalising or prioritising high or low age, or of allocating LSTs on the basis of quality-adjusted life years (QALYs), from being included in the discussion. Whether these factors are compatible with these values, or whether these values should be adapted to the circumstances of a pandemic if they are not, is a different matter. This is precisely what I will try to explore here.

The chapter will be divided into several parts. In the first one, I will explain what constitutes emergency triage and what differentiates it from other forms of triage. I will also outline the cases in which I consider that triage should not be, strictly speaking, referred to as triage. I will then discuss the different criteria that have been proposed for allocating scarce resources when the situation requires rationing and the rules that should allow us to translate these criteria into practical solutions. Its culmination will be the presentation of a proposal for an allocation system in the case that we opt for a scheme that tries to reconcile efficiency and equity in some way. Given that this kind of proposal is likely to be incompatible with our legal system, I will then discuss which solutions would avoid such a contraction. Finally, I will focus on procedural questions related to determining the weighting between these values or how best to apply the selected criteria to the specific case.

Before getting into this thorny issue, let me, however, point out that the first duty of a public health official is to try to prevent triage from happening, either by increasing available resources or by reducing demand. On the former, I will say a few things below. On the latter, I will limit myself to stating that many of the measures that I have described or will describe in other chapters (confinements, prohibition of certain types of activities, health certificates, compulsory vaccination, etc.) are aimed at preventing triage. It will be up to those who manage the available resources to determine whether these policies should be implemented to protect the population in the face of a dramatic shortage of resources.

5.2   Emergency Triage: Description

Triage in a pandemic is a public health intervention authorised by a state's laws and government declarations of a public health emergencies (Gostin et al. 2012). It takes place in exceptional situations, where everybody's health is at risk. Therefore, it must be designed to achieve public health policy objectives in a scenario where the necessary resources are dramatically scarce. Normally, the criteria available include considerations of efficiency (optimising the allocation of means to optimise public welfare) and equity (distributing those resources in such a way as to favour the realisation of the postulates on distributive justice) (White & Lo, 2021). This concept, incidentally, has been adopted by the World Health Organization (Sage, W. H. O., 2020) and the National Academy of Sciences, Engineering, and Medicine (National Academies of Sciences, Engineering, and Medicine, 2020). From this general idea, the complicated task arises of establishing how to implement this reconciliation and what concrete mechanisms will allow it to be put into practice.

However, it should be noted that resource triage, which involves prioritising or even restricting access to resources, is not alien to standard medical practice. In reality, health resources are, by definition, scarce. Therefore, it is always necessary to prioritise their access and sometimes they will have to be rationed, depriving some patients of their use. Thus, if there is a single surgical team operating 8 h a day and there are dozens of patients who need the type of intervention they perform, prioritisation is inevitable. Moreover, so too perhaps will be restriction of access, that is, that some of those patients may never get the surgery at all. However, the type of triage that will be the focus of attention here is a specific one, that of a pandemic emergency. This makes it different from the triage that takes place in everyday health care in many ways.

The main difference lies in the way problems are approached. In the case of the response to a pandemic, the priority is to safeguard all citizens' health, not individual patients. Hence, public health considerations predominate over clinical care considerations. This is a complete game changer, at least from an ethical point of view (and probably also should be the case in the field of law). As Powers et al. (2006) rightly wrote:

> The ethical goals of public health differ in emphasis from those of clinical medicine, which emphasize physicians' fiduciary obligations to individual patients more than advancing population health. Moreover, although some clinicians and medical ethicists may object to allowing social (i.e., nonmedical) considerations to influence usual clinical care, doing so is the norm in public health interventions, which often seek to address the social determinants of health (Powers et al., 2006).

However, the use of health assets for emergency triage has important consequences for the population's health care as a whole. Suspending non-urgent operations has consequences. Referring health-care staff from other services to emergency or intensive care will result in harm to the patients concerned. It is important to keep this in mind when making decisions. Emergency triage is not a bubble isolated from other care services. There are also times, as in the case of COVID-19, when primary care in person suddenly becomes a scarce resource. However, in this book I will focus only on emergency triage related to life-sustaining treatments, which should be applied immediately. Issues such as prioritisation of access to resources that can be delayed are closer to the debates that arise in the management of health-care resources in general, especially when there are shortages (Bochenek et al., 2018). I will therefore leave this issue aside, despite its importance.

In the case of other scarce resources that need to be used immediately, such as drugs or emergency medical transport, it is more than likely that all of the above are perfectly applicable to them also, as the use of many of these resources usually needs to be immediate. Consequently, a delay in the allocation of the resources can often result in the death of patients. While it is true that a ventilator has temporary substitutes (such as bag valve mask for ventilation), or that a delay in the arrival of an ambulance sometimes does not make the difference between life and death, it is also true that none of these resources can tolerate prolonged delays. Hence, triage of these assets does not differ much from what is involved in triage of LSTs.

Another fundamental characteristic of emergency triage is that rationing and prioritisation converge, although conceptually they can be differentiated (Hortal-Carmona et al., 2021). While it is true that determining the order of access to the resource (prioritising) and deciding whether to deny access to it (rationing) are not the same thing, in emergency triage both actions end up merging into one, for one simple reason: delaying the administration of a resource to a patient who will not survive without it is comparable to denying it.

On the other hand, it is obvious that the implications for emergency triage health professionals are far more demanding than a delay in primary care, especially from a psychological point of view. So much so that, in fact, the only thing that really bears any resemblance to the situation in a pandemic is the scenario in organ transplant units and among patients who need such interventions to survive or, perhaps, what happens when administering a scarce vaccine to a large population (Persad et al., 2009).

Finally, it should be noted that emergency triage is not always necessary, as patients may not actually need or want that resource. It may also be possible to increase the number of units available, which would eliminate the need of prioritisation or rationing. In such circumstances, there is no need for triage at all, as I will show in the next section (De Miguel Beriain, 2020).

5.3   Distinguishing Triage from Not Triage

Triage only takes place when there are insufficient resources to look after the patients who need them. We should not invoke this concept if (a) patients do not need the resource (yet); (b) patients do not wish to be administered the resource or are willing to forgo it for altruistic reasons; (c) available resources can be increased to meet demand; and (d) it is possible to refer patients to other facilities where they can be provided with the care they need. Let us look at each of these factors.

5.3.1   Patients Do Not Need the Resource

Firstly, a resource cannot be considered scarce if patients do not need it. In other words, for a resource to be considered scarce, a clinician (or a team of clinicians) must first consider that a patient's treatment requires its use. If not, there is no triage. Of course, the lack of need may be because the clinician judges that patients will get better without using the scarce resource or because it will not benefit them. In both cases, its allocation would be superfluous, implying a waste of resources (particularly serious in these situations) and, perhaps, therapeutic overkill (providing a useless treatment instead of the one indicated).

Therefore, certainty about the timeliness of resource use is the first thing to be achieved. Multiple tools have been developed for this purpose, some of them very sophisticated, such as APACHE-II, SOFA or PELOD-2 (Barilan, 2021; Daugherty Biddison et al., 2019; Jöbges et al., 2020). In clinical practice, they are routinely used to determine whether measures such as admission to the ICU, connection to a ventilator, etc. are appropriate. The first step to take in a desperate situation is to use these same criteria. Only those who meet them should be considered as claimants of the scarce resource.

It is also interesting to note that studies show that health-care professionals are often overly optimistic about a treatment's ability to improve patients' health. This, in ordinary times, is a problem that results in excessive interventionism, leading to overuse of resources and sometimes unnecessary suffering for the patient. In a health crisis, it must be carefully avoided, as it causes harm not only to the overtreated patient but also to the patient who does not have access to the scarce resource that the former is hoarding. Hence, corrective mechanisms should be applied as far as possible, in line with the suggestions developed in the academic literature (Michalsen et al., 2021; Chang & Shapiro, 2016).

5.3.2 Patients Do Not Wish to Be Administered the Remedy or Are Willing to Forgo It for Altruistic Reasons

Secondly, there will be patients who have given strict instructions to avoid being administered the scarce resource, even though its use is the only way to provide them with a chance of recovery. These patients should not be included in triage. Their will must be respected even if it involves their death. To do otherwise would imply a breach of their autonomy, with more than likely legal consequences (it is debatable whether this would be a crime of coercion or otherwise). Fortunately, we have now left behind the paternalistic paradigms that placed the patient's well-being as the ultimate criterion for action, even above the patient's will.

Keeping this evidence in mind is particularly important in situations where we are facing unconscious patients. What respect for autonomy demands is that the medical team should ascertain if there are prior instructions on how to act in such a scenario (Atienza Macías et al., 2015). In addition, it should always be considered that a patient might change his or her views. In these cases, the later ones will take precedence. It should also be considered that many of the rules applicable to these situations have strong exceptions in the case of minors. They are particularly vulnerable and unable to express their own views. In this case, it is therefore appropriate to act in the child's best interests. This is the case under the UN Convention on the Rights of the Child (I will return to this later in this chapter).

Finally, there will be people who, in situations such as the ones we are discussing, will renounce any recourse for altruistic reasons. They should not be included in the triage either. However, these scenarios require specific and adequate information on the consequences of the waiver. It is not a matter of altering the patient's will or creating greater distress, but of ensuring that it is an act that corresponds to a real will, constructed on the basis of adequate information.

5.3.3   Available Resources Can Be Increased to Meet Demand

Thirdly, triage is not appropriate if it is possible to increase the available resources in such a way that they are able to meet the demand, either by relocating staff, creating new posts or in any other plausible way (Sprung et al., 2010). This indication often comes up against a serious practical problem: it is not possible to pool a resource in a uniform way, as its optimal use is highly nuanced. Consider, for example, the ICU. In principle, we could think of X number of positions, available to whoever needs them. In practice, this is not the case. To begin with, children's ICUs should not be used for adults, or at least, places should always be reserved for children. On the other hand, it would be unreasonable to mix in the same space those suffering from an easily transmissible viral disease with those who have not been infected, but would be susceptible to it. Hence, it is necessary to divide the resource into several sub-resources, with the paradox that some of them could end up being in short supply, while others could remain idle. It goes without saying that this is a scenario that we should try to avoid as far as possible by being as flexible as possible in the design of health care, but there are many limits to flexibility. It is worth bearing this in mind.

Finally, it should be taken into consideration that sometimes it is not possible to increase resources, but it is possible to refer patients. If these circumstances arise, it is obligatory to do so. This is demanded both by the need to optimise the number of lives saved and to ensure that belonging to a specific territory does not mean the difference between life and death. At times when triage becomes necessary, it makes more sense to place all health centres administering units of the scarce resource under a single allocation system. This makes response capacity more flexible and optimises the use of available resources. It also avoids inefficient administrative and bureaucratic procedures, as well as the lack of coordination between administrations or between public and private centres. Of course, this implies the creation of adequate monitoring and control centres capable of coordinating an efficient response to the situation, which is not easy to achieve in practice.

5.4 Different Possible Objectives

If, once all avenues to increase the supply of necessary health-care resources have been exhausted and after having done everything possible to reduce demand, it turns out that they are not sufficient, then we have to ration their allocation. In order to do this, we must be clear about the objective that we want to achieve with triage. This is essential, because once we agree on the purpose of triage, we can assign the resource accordingly. Determining the objectives will also be the justification for the difference in treatment. There may be several. The most common is usually to optimise some parameter, such as the number of lives or years of life saved or even the years adjusted for the quality of life (the famous "QALY"). There are some models that do not share this view. Indeed, if we assume that human lives cannot be weighted or that it is too complex to do so, then it is necessary to allocate resources randomly, irrespective of the patients' chances of survival or the time they would have to use them. This logic of argument is present, for example, in a classic article by John Taurek, in which he argued that, faced with the decision to rescue five people or one, we should flip a coin because it gives everyone an equal chance of saving what matters most to them: their lives. When this option cannot be given to everyone, this version of egalitarianism appeals to lotteries or other procedures to allocate resources fairly (Taurek, 1977).

However, these views do not seem to follow our intuitions. If implemented, they would lead to a truly significant increase in mortality. They would, for example, protect people with a low chance of survival from people with a high chance. This is unreasonable. It is implausible that in a position marked by a veil of ignorance, we are indifferent to the number of lives saved. Nor is it true that the Kantian criteria of dignity make it impossible for some to accept the renunciation of means of survival for the benefit of all. Nor is it true that weighing the number of lives is really irreconcilable with the idea of dignity, as Derek Parfit's classic response (Parfit, 1978) to Taurek dictates and as many authors have subsequently expressed (Adams, 2020). Nevertheless, it is true that the theoretical discussion is still alive. What is in any case undeniable is that, if we accept this idea of the impossible weighting of lives, then most of the theoretical elaboration on triage becomes absurd. Why bother to introduce rules for allocating resources if the first to arrive is the one who gets it? I will return to this issue later.

For the moment, I would like to point out that, in general, there are three broad potential objectives that triage can cover: optimising the lives saved, optimising all life years or optimising as many years of quality life as possible. Once this has been achieved, it will be time to address an issue that separates those who embrace utilitarian postulates from those who are more deontological: the nuances that are introduced into this general objective. Deontologists subject the result to be achieved to the fulfilment of some restrictions, in the interest of greater equity in the distribution of evils, even if this results in somewhat lower figures in the final expression of the parameter chosen as the objective. For example, they may choose to prioritise care for those who have not adequately protected themselves by fulfilling a mission that is essential for society to continue to function, even if this means that more people die or that fewer years of quality life are saved. What is essential, therefore, for someone who places greater emphasis on equity is not only to optimise the objective but also to introduce nuances that will prevent an optimal result from being achieved numerically, but which will be better adapted to equity parameters.

There are times, of course, when it is not easy to know whether we are talking about a purely utilitarian objective or whether it should be sifted using parameters of equity. QALYs are surely the best example. It is possible to think that the introduction of the idea of "quality of life" already has something to do with equity. On the other hand, what is certain is that some of the proposed equity parameters make no sense at all. The most notorious example is that of "giving priority to the most disadvantaged", at least in its "sickest first" aspect (Emanuel et al., 2020). In the case of patients requiring a resource such as a ventilator, for example, there is little choice of graduation by severity: they all need it within a short period of time (hours, not weeks or months, as in the case of transplants) if they are to survive. If this is not the case, they are not patients who should really enter into the distribution of the health commodity. On the other hand, just because someone is sicker does not necessarily mean that it makes more sense to provide them with the scarce resource. In fact, if this has little impact on his or her chances of survival, it makes sense to divert the resource to another patient with better prognosis.

Finally, when we have a clear objective, with the corresponding nuances, it will be time to construct practical rules that allow us to achieve it in a reasonable manner, appropriate to the circumstances in which triage takes place. The literature has developed many of them: "first come, first served", lottery, weighting, etc. If we leave aside those variables that are morally unacceptable, such as patients' economic capacities, or others that are not sufficient to meet the moral challenges at hand, such as referring exclusively to the usual criteria in medical practice, there are not too many of them. I will discuss them carefully later. For the time being, however, let us begin by outlining the three main objectives as I have described them.

5.5   The Objectives

The most common objectives of triage—optimising outcomes in terms of morbidity or mortality—owe much to utilitarian thinking. This is not surprising, because what defines triage is the replacement of the usual parameters of clinical practice, focused on the individual, with others that focus on the population. Utilitarianism provides a formidable framework for these purposes (Annas, 2010, p. 277). Its success is evidenced by the fact that such criteria have been adopted by multiple institutions (Jöbges et al., 2020). However, there is not, as I have mentioned, a single utilitarian objective, but several: optimising the number of lives saved, optimising the number of years of life to be lived or quality-adjusted life years (QALYs). They all seek to optimise population benefit, but they involve different aspects. This often means choosing one over the others or at least prioritising one over.

To begin with, let us consider a system that aims at optimising QALYs as an essential objective of triage. If we follow this criterion, the end result of the resource allocation will be different than if we try to optimise the number of years of life saved regardless of their quality. We may save the same number of people, but they will be different individuals. They will be different, among other things, because of their degree of disability, which has led to much criticism of this criterion. In fact, the use of QALYs has been considered unethical, as it discriminates against people with disabilities (Whitehurst & Engel, 2018; Sinclair, 2012; Panocchia et al., 2021). Hence, several associations have called for its discontinuation (National Council on Disability, 2019) on the basis of the International Convention on the Rights of Persons with Disabilities.

However, there will be situations where persons with disabilities are deprived of a scarce resource, without this being a direct violation of the above Convention. I am referring to scenarios where the deprivation of the resource will not be due to the disability itself, but to the consequences in connection with the short- or medium-term chances of survival or the time of use of the scarce resource that will be required for their care. It is perhaps simpler if I choose as an example a person who may end up in a coma or even in a persistent vegetative state that will require continuous use of assisted ventilation. In a context of scarcity, providing this patient with the resource will mean death for other people who could have benefited from a much shorter use of the ventilator. Hence, at least, if we accept that optimising the number of lives saved is a significant criterion, it would be necessary not to allocate the scarce resource to our protagonist, not because of his disability by any means, but because such an allocation would result in the enormous consumption of a resource that we wish to optimise. In addition to the discrimination problems involved in QALYs, if we add the difficulty in applying these criteria to a pandemic situation produced by an unknown agent (making it very difficult to predict a patient's future quality of life), it is clear why they are not the most appropriate criteria for setting the triage objective in these scenarios, although they can be taken into account as tie-breaker criteria.

Two alternative criteria are available: optimising the number of lives saved and/or the number of years of life to be lived. Both are easier to justify. In the case of optimising the number of lives saved, there is not much to say. As I have anticipated, it is intuitive to think that if we can save five people instead of one, this is the option to choose (Hsieh et al., 2006). The thesis of the imponderability of human lives does not tend to find many adherents in practice. In turn, the importance of the age of the person to be saved or, rather, of the years he or she may have left to live is a criterion frequently used in the allocation of organs for transplantation, with general acceptance in the academic literature and society, although with some obvious exceptions (Coca Vila, 2021). It seems reasonable that we grant the resource to whoever can obtain the maximum benefit as a result. Or, at least, that we demand a minimum life expectancy in order to have the same probabilities of access to the scarce resource as a healthy patient. This could be perhaps a year, following the example of lung allocation in organ donation in some countries (United Network of Organ Sharing, 2020).

The bad news, however, is that these two objectives are not always compatible with each other either. They even lead to contradictory situations when the age of the people involved is different. Giving a few extra years to many is not the same as giving them to a few (Kamm, 1993; Puyol, 2018; Hortal-Carmona et al., 2021). Imagine that we can allocate the 5 units of the scarce resource that are available either to a group of 5 people in their 70s with an 80% chance of survival each or to a group of 5 people in their 40s with a 40% chance of survival each. If we provide them to the former, four of the five will be saved. In the case of the second, only two will survive. However, the 4 survivors in the first group are unlikely to live more than 40 years between them, while the 2 in the second group are likely to live at least 60, and that is assuming a life expectancy of only 70 years. Therefore, both criteria give rise to contradictory solutions. If we adopt the maximisation of the number of lives saved, we will allocate resources to people in their 70s. If, on the other hand, we opt for the number of years of life saved, those in the 40-year age group will be the beneficiaries. Moreover, the younger the patients, the greater the need to provide them with the resource. If we were dealing with young people in their 20s, it would probably be enough for them to have a 20% chance of being saved for them to be eligible for the resource, thus giving priority to the life of a young person over that of four septuagenarians.

Which of these two objectives should we aim for? Studies of population preferences (Biddison et al., 2014, 2018), and much of the academic thinking that has dealt with emergency triage, favour implementing the criterion of optimising the number of lives saved. This is also the recommendation made by the WHO for these cases (World Health Organization, 2008). This is not surprising, as it is more in line with the idea of human dignity, which holds that it is better to choose more people than more years of life. More dubious to me is whether the goal of maximising life years should play a secondary role, i.e. serve as a way of choosing between two people with the same chance of surviving using the resource for the same length of time. My reluctance stems from the fact that this could be to the detriment of the most vulnerable groups, including people with disabilities (White & Lo, 2021). If we were to do so, we would probably have to compensate them by offering them preferential access to other resources, such as vaccines. As a preliminary conclusion, suffice it to say that, among the possible objectives of triage, the one that prescribes optimising the number of lives saved should predominate.

5.6 Equity Criteria

The introduction of equity criteria attempts to adjust the allocation of the general objectives of triage to the specific circumstances of individuals, so that their final distribution is appropriate to a set of parameters that are meaningful in terms of equity. The underlying idea is that public health strategies should not be indifferent to values such as fairness. To achieve an adequate implementation of this value, one should not only aim at optimising the benefit for all, or even at making it the response's essential objective. What must be ensured is that scarce goods are distributed according to the circumstances of the various collectives (ideally, of course, according to personal circumstances, but it is not always possible to get to that point). Hence, different criteria have been proposed that can serve as a counterweight to the purely utilitarian ones. Among all of them, the following stand out: giving preference to the vulnerable, opting for minors, considering reciprocity criteria or taking into account fair innings.

5.6.1 Preference for Socially Vulnerable People

In a pandemic, and, more generally, in the entire health-care framework, the idea of vulnerability can be understood in many ways. Some groups may show clinical vulnerability to suffer from a severe or fatal form of the disease or benefit less from the available therapeutic tools. In terms of COVID-19, this is the case for the elderly, the obese or those with chronic pathologies. In other pandemics, it may be other populations, such as children, for example, who are more affected by a virus. Nonetheless, there is another form of vulnerability that affects only those sectors of the population that suffer from social conditions and that place them at a disadvantage compared to others. In this section I will focus on this type of vulnerability, which is the one that is really relevant to equity considerations—social vulnerability.

This is particularly relevant because conditions of inequality are often severely accentuated in a pandemic. Among those who suffer its consequences are, first and foremost, some ethnic minorities who traditionally face discrimination in health care. In the case of COVID-19, data collected in the USA show that non-whites have suffered far more cases of severe illness than whites (Blackburn et al., 2021; Karaca-Mandic et al., 2021). "And it isn't that black people have failed to take the virus seriously: black survey respondents were more than twice as likely as white respondents to view Covid-19 as a major threat, to be very concerned about its impact on their health, and to take various precautions" (Cleveland Manchanda et al., 2020).

The causes of these imbalances often have to do with factors such as social structures in which structural racism and inequality still exist, leading to unequal access to housing, employment, education or health care. Both members of traditionally discriminated ethnic minorities and other socially disadvantaged groups—people with low incomes, for example—find it more difficult to protect themselves when the occasion arises. Many are unable to adopt behaviours consistent with social distancing because they share homes or because their jobs cannot be performed remotely (Centers for Disease Control and Prevention, 2020; Emeruwa et al., 2020). Others, moreover, suffer from a wider range of pollution-related diseases that cause lung impairment or chronic heart disease or diseases resulting from unhealthier diets, such as diabetes (Adams et al., 2020). To all of these should be added those in foreigners' detention centres and prisons, those without resources or homeless, migrants in an irregular situation, victims of gender-based violence and minors who are victims of abuse of all kinds in their own homes or in foster homes, elderly people living alone, single-parent families, etc. (Hortal-Carmona et al., 2021; Hick et al., 2021). Finally, it is reasonable to also include within these groups people with disabilities who are particularly vulnerable due to their social status, as this is a type of vulnerability that is often added to their clinical vulnerability. All are much more likely to be infected by a virus and much more vulnerable to subsequent illness than the majority of the population.

In this scenario, if we were to simply apply the maximisation objectives described above, we would be accentuating the injustice inherent in the discrimination that socially vulnerable groups routinely suffer (Mayr et al., 2010; White & Lo, 2020). In general, upper-middle-class white people who do not exhibit any disability and live in healthier districts will be less sick and more likely to recover from COVID-19. Hence, it makes sense to make some modifications to a resource allocation that is limited to optimising lives or years of life saved. In this way, even if we sacrifice some lives, the end result will be more equitable. Which, by the way, would also mean achieving a scenario characterised by greater social happiness (something that any utilitarian would praise, we imagine). Or, viewed from the reverse angle, "worsening inequities among disadvantaged groups may lead to loss of social cohesion, public mistrust, and societal unwillingness to follow restrictive public health measures" (White & Lo, 2021; National Academies of Sciences, 2020).

The problem is that implementing these corrective criteria in practice is complicated. In fact, health resource allocation systems rarely incorporate factors related to patient vulnerability. Isolated examples, such as the consideration of estimated glomerular filtration rate (eGFR), a surrogate for renal function to avoid ethnicity-driven distortions in organ allocation, have not worked well in the past (Cleveland Manchanda et al., 2020). Since the SARS-CoV-2 crisis, many have called for changes to allocation protocols to correct this historical deficiency (Sederstrom, 2020; Schmidt, 2020). However, achieving this is complex, especially when we are talking about resources whose administration cannot be delayed. Some, in fact, consider it impossible, advocating instead a first-come, first-served system that is more likely to avoid the biases that penalise vulnerable groups (Stone, 2020).

In my view, we should not be so prescriptive. There are some ways of introducing weights based on equity considerations that are easy to implement. For example, in the USA, the *area deprivation index (ADI)* has been used for this purpose. This is a geographical measure of socioeconomic disadvantage that is calculated at the census block level (approximately 1500 persons). The index generates an aggregate disadvantage score on a 10-point scale, based on 17 measures related to poverty, education, employment, physical environment and infrastructure within a neighbourhood. Anyone can calculate a person's index based on the district in which they live and their corresponding ADI in less than a minute, because the register is public. With this objective data, correction factors can be introduced (White & Lo, 2021). In other countries, such as Canada (Pampalon & Raymond, 2000), the UK (Phillips et al., 2016) or Sweden (Sundquist et al., 2003), there are relatively similar inequality measurement factors, which could be introduced in a similar way. The key issue will always be to involve society as much as possible in the creation of these weights, so that the necessary consensus can be reached.

5.6.2 Preference for Risky Professions

A criterion that also corresponds to the requirements of equity is the one that promotes the possibility of positively discriminating certain people, either because of their particular value to society or because of a different criterion, one of reciprocity or compensation for the risk assumed. Both factors sometimes converge. Think, for example, of an intensivist who has been subject to extraordinary risk due to the virus outbreak and has become infected as a result, but who will also be of enormous use in dealing with future cases of a disease (Biddison et al., 2014). Other times, this is not the case. Imagine this time a hard-to-replace operator of a nuclear power plant who has not had to expose himself to extraordinary risk, but nevertheless possesses a kind of wisdom that may be absolutely necessary for the safety of society. Both cases have been taken up to some extent in various guidelines produced by professional associations. For example, the document by the Spanish Society of Intensive Care Medicine, Critical Care and Coronary Units (SEMICYUC) recommends including factors such as dependents, in order to make decisions maximising the benefit of the maximum number of people (SEMICYUC, 2020).

However, we should separate the two variables. The second—value of the person for society—can only justify privileged care based on a utilitarian criterion, which does not seem acceptable in itself (Comité de Bioética de España, 2020). The first, on the other hand, combines this criterion with another based on justice, easily described in circumstances such as those that characterised the fight against SARS-CoV-2 at the beginning of the pandemic. In this case, those workers that had been subjected to extraordinary risk as a result of the shortage of protective materials should be at least compensated with priority access to the scarce resource (Ranney et al., 2020).

However, there are two nuances to this general statement. The first is that it should not refer to only the health professions nor to all its members. With regard to the latter—not all health professionals—it must be considered that, if the criterion is one of fairness, then it must be weighed whether this exposure to extraordinary risk has taken place with greater intensity than in other professions. This need not be true for all health professionals, but will depend on the conditions of their service (Daffner, 2021). On the first point—only health-care workers—it should be borne in mind that other professions are also linked to extraordinary risk exposure and contribute to pandemic response efforts. Those who work in clinical settings, even if they are not health-care professionals (cleaning staff, administrative staff, etc.), are good examples of this, as are people working in other occupations necessary to provide the rest of the population with minimum services (grocery or supermarket workers, bus drivers, police, firefighters, soldiers, etc.). In addition, given that many of those in these jobs tend to be from more socially disadvantaged backgrounds than others where working from home is feasible, such reciprocity measures would also help to prevent unfair discrimination against them. Obviously, the extension of the criteria will give rise to conflicting situations, which will call into question the true fairness of triage, fuelling the debate. However, this must be addressed. Prioritising only health workers would be unfair.

Beyond this, some sound theoretical criticisms need to be reflected. The main one is that prioritising health workers could erode citizens' trust in the system, as they would suspect privilege in the allocation of available resources. To avoid this situation, it would make more sense for prioritisation to be decided by some kind of protocol developed by government agencies unconnected to the workers involved (Sprung et al., 2020). Another compelling reason to oppose prioritisation of health workers (but not of other frontline workers) is that, in principle, it is part of their profession to assume the obligation *to* "provide emergency medical care during disasters even if they face higher than usual risks to their safety, health or lives" (Huber & Wynia, 2004). However, the argument loses much weight when they are inadequately protected to face such risks due to a general failure to prepare for such an event. Hence, at least in these scenarios, it seems reasonable to take this criterion into account to ensure a fairer allocation.

5.6.3   The Fair Innings

The "fair innings" argument was splendidly described by my good friend John Harris in his *The Value of Life*:

> The fair innings argument takes the view that there is some span of years that we consider a reasonable life [for a person to have had], a fair innings. Let's say that a fair share of life is the traditional three score and ten, seventy years. Anyone who does not reach 70 suffers, on this view, the injustice of being cut off in their prime. They have missed out on a reasonable share of life: they have been short-changed. Those, however, who do make 70 suffer no such injustice, they have not lost out but rather must consider any additional years a sort of bonus beyond that which could reasonably be hoped for. The fair innings argument requires that everyone be given an equal chance to have a fair innings, to reach the appropriate threshold but, having reached it, they have received their entitlement (...) The fair innings argument points to the fact that the injustice done to someone who has not had a fair innings when they lose out to someone who has is significantly greater than in the reverse circumstances. It is for this reason that in the hopefully rare circumstances where we have to choose between candidates who differ only in this respect we should choose to give as many as possible the chance of a fair innings (Harris, 2006).

Thus, the fair innings criterion implies that, in a triage scenario, the perspective of years lived should play a role in the allocation of resources. This should not be confused with the QALY criterion. This is not about optimising quality years of life. It is about the fact that some people have already reached the years of life that we consider sufficient or reasonable and others have not. We prioritise those who have not reached that goal yet, irrespective of the survival expectancy or QALYs of one or the other. It is true, however, that it does not seem appropriate to appeal to the fair innings argument if the life of the person to whom the scarce resource is allocated will be of poor quality indeed (e.g. think of scenarios of persistent vegetative state). In these circumstances, the basis of the argument (that younger people should have the opportunity to enjoy life as older people have had) vanishes, because there is no enjoyment as such. Therefore, it is not a criterion that has to do strictly with age, but with the idea of having the opportunity to enjoy a reasonable lifespan. Hence, it is not inconsistent to accept fair innings as a criterion and, on the other hand, not to be in favour of maximising the number of years of life saved, even more so if they are of poor quality, as an absolute criterion (it would seem even more inconsistent not to assign the "fair innings" argument any role; it is true).

The conclusion, in sum, is that the fair innings argument probably makes sense. It should not, in my view, play a role when candidates have different survival options or other fairness criteria suggest a different alternative (Altevogt et al., 2009; Rubio et al., 2020). But it should at least be taken into account if there are a priori equality scenarios between the different candidates for the award.

5.6.4 The Child's Best Interests

A related—though conceptually somewhat different—question is whether we should give children (meaning those under the age of 18) preferential access to scarce resources in accordance with the UN Convention on the Rights of the Child[1]or Article 24.2 of the EU Charter of Fundamental Rights, which states that "in all actions relating to children, whether taken by public authorities or private institutions, the child's best interests shall be a primary consideration". Note that this is a different case from fair innings, because here we are talking about the mere fact that the patient is a minor. Obviously, the two will often be lumped together, but conceptually they are not identical. In addition, the legal backing of the two criteria is different, of course. On the other hand, these positions fit well with any acceptable ethical reasoning in today's societies. We generally feel a greater need to protect our children's lives than we do our parents' or even our own. Indeed, I would find it surprising if a society that is characterised precisely by sometimes even excessive protection of minors did not adopt clauses of this kind. In fact, high infant mortality could be lethal for collective morale in the context of a pandemic. I therefore believe that there is a legal obligation, moral justification and psychological need to put children first in the prioritisation of resources.

However, one might point out that, even if all this is reasonable, one would have to conclude that age is already a criterion to be taken into account when allocating resources. This seems to contradict what I have stated elsewhere about the difficulty to choose between one criterion and another on this basis alone. My answer is that,

---

[1]See Instrument of Ratification of the Convention on the Rights of the Child, adopted by the United Nations General Assembly on 20 November 1989, BOE, No. 313, 31 December 1990, pages 38897–38904.

if we consider it particularly important to protect children, it is not because of their age, but because of their vulnerability and the fact that their existence is the consequence of a compromise. We have children—or at least we should have them—because we are prepared to guarantee them minimally satisfactory lives. This implies, among other aspects, doing all we can to ensure that they have a minimum number of years of survival. This dual circumstance—they are vulnerable persons in our care and we have a commitment towards them—is, in my view, what ultimately justifies putting their vital interests first. It is not, in short, a question of age (or, again, purely of age).

5.7   Rules for the Implementation of the Criteria

Once we have analysed the criteria that would underpin the allocation of resources, the next step is to analyse the rules, the systems that will allow us to implement them. Although they are sometimes intertwined, they are conceptually different: the criteria show us what we intend to achieve and the rules on how to do it. As I have already mentioned, this aspect is particularly important. There are several rules that have been proposed for the different criteria. The main ones, in my view, are these: preference for those who show the best ratio between the probability of salvation and the time of use of the resource, "first come, first served", strict lottery and "compensated lottery" or algorithms based on combinations of rules.

5.7.1   Preference for Those Who Show the Best Ratio Between the Probability of Salvation and the Time of Use of the Resource

The first rule to be analysed is that preference should be given to the people who have the best chance of survival using the resource for the shortest possible time. Obviously, this tool attempts to materialise an efficiency criterion that seeks to optimise the number of lives saved. This requires, firstly, the proper identification of the scarce resource(s). Secondly, it requires weighing the prospects of a cure against the time needed to use the resource needed to treat the disease. In the case of a virus affecting the lungs, this will mean accepting that the scarce asset will not only be the ICU stay or access to a ventilator but also the number of days the resource is used. The scarce asset will be, in short, the ICU/Day (or Day/Ventilation, as the case may be). Understanding this will be essential in order to optimise the number of lives saved overall (Zohny, 2020). For those who do not understand, let us think of an example (Pagel & Utley, 2020): imagine we have, on the one hand, a group of 4 sepsis patients with a 50% chance of survival who will use the scarce resource for 1 week. On the other hand, we have a group of 8 COVID patients, with a 75%

chance of survival, but who will need the resource for 2 weeks. At the end of 1 month, there will be eight sepsis patients alive if we allocate the resource to them. In contrast, only six COVID cases will have survived. Therefore, counter-intuitively, it makes sense to allocate the resource to sepsis patients, hence the importance of weighing the time of use of the resource against the likelihood of survival.

The rule has, in principle, the advantage that it is easy to implement. However, in practice, following it is not as straightforward as one might assume, because of a scientific problem. The entire efficiency calculation is based on the ability to make a more or less accurate prognosis of the patient's evolutionary course once he or she is allowed access to the scarce resource. Unfortunately, this is not always possible. At least in the early stages of a novel pathology, it is almost impossible to anticipate whether a patient will benefit from the scarce resource. Moreover, it will be extremely difficult to know how long they will need access to the scarce resource in order to reverse their condition. This, unfortunately, is essential in terms of efficiency, because it is not so much a matter of optimising the options of one patient, but of all those who need to be administered the health resource subject to rationing. Such a rule, in short, is not operational if it is not possible to specify the parameter values at stake.

5.7.2 "First Come, First Served"

The simplest and easiest rule to use in practice is the "first come, first served". Although the various guidelines often recommend against its use (Herreros et al., 2020; Ruiz-Hornillos et al., 2021), it is often used in practice, because it allows facilities to avoid many moral or legal problems. In fact, an analysis of the criteria used by a large sample of US hospitals (66 institutions in 28 states) to allocate *remdesivir* when it was a scarce resource showed that almost half (47%) used this criterion (Mun et al., 2021).

Its popularity does not mean, however, that it is an efficient or fair system, for several reasons. It is not efficient because it allocates the resource to patients regardless of their chances of survival or how long they will need it. As a consequence, the number of victims increases considerably. Moreover, it is also clearly unfair. To begin with, it violates the principle of temporal neutrality, which states that the time at which an event occurs cannot in itself be a morally relevant factor, since the instant at which something happens does not make a moral difference (Hare, 1981; Cameron et al., 2020). This shortcoming, which already disqualifies this rule, is even more accentuated if we consider that the order in which a person arrives at a health resource is not free of determining factors that are important from the point of view of ethics. It is not true that whether or not to go to a health centre—or to go in a concrete moment—during a pandemic is a matter of chance. There are factors that influence whether some have an advantage over others in this regard. Eberl (2020) put it well:

Such a policy may not fairly allocate resources insofar as it could unjustly disadvantage individuals who lack ready access to health care services, especially those without their own means of transportation, live in rural areas, or otherwise experience access dispari- ties. Also potentially disadvantaged by such a policy are those who practice measures to safeguard themselves from infection but nevertheless become ill later on, or persons who, for whatever reason, experience a longer incubation period between infection and the onset of illness.

In addition to the factors that Eberl points out, there are others that could be added to this lack of equity. People from certain minorities are less able to access health resources, either because of poorer education or because there are biases in the system itself that work against them. In the case of the COVID-19 pandemic, health workers in nursing homes often decided who was eligible for hospital trans- fer. Sometimes those patients who had relatives who were concerned about their situation were chosen over others. The same was true for patients on the ward wait- ing for a place in the ICU. Consequently, applying a "first come, first served" rule would be victimising those who are already victims of the system. In short, this criterion could end up discriminating (even more) against patients belonging to vul- nerable groups (Wassemann et al., 2020; Persad, 2020). In addition, of course, it does not allow for the introduction of efficiency correction criteria in favour of efficiency or equity.

Adding it all up, it is necessary to conclude that the "first come, first served" system is a terrible system of resource allocation, unless one considers that it is not for humans to make decisions that involve life or death for other humans or that weighing one life against another is immoral, as I have explained in previous sec- tions. The clear advantage for health professionals and crisis managers, however, is that it circumvents many of the problems that characterise their main alternatives. It is easy to apply, provides a rapid response and avoids moral conflicts. This is no mean feat, of course. This, however, should not be a decisive factor in its success, but rather an incentive to preserve these advantages without taking on board its shortcomings. Let us now turn to the third alternative, the draw.

5.7.3   The Draw

A fortune-blind allocation rule consists of something as simple as allocating a num- ber to those who need the scarce resource and then awarding it to lottery winners. This has some advantages over much more elaborate mechanisms, such as reducing the stress levels of health professionals or hopefully improving social cohesion. As opposed to a "first come, first served" rule, it gives patients a sense that everyone has a chance at some point, especially if we agree to reallocate the scarce resource (Dufner, 2021).

This rule, however, also presents substantial problems. To begin with, it com- pletely sacrifices the objectives of maximising the number of lives saved, as resources are sometimes allocated to those who have little chance of survival.

Moreover, it also fails to guarantee a fair outcome. The reason is obvious: a pure lottery does not introduce any correction in the allocation, no counterweight to compensate people who have already suffered from a previous inequity problem (e.g. people who have become ill because they cannot be isolated from others who have been infected).

5.7.4   The Compensation System: The "Weighed Lotteries"

There is a rule, obviously linked to the previous one, which tries to reach an equitable result, lessening the impact of social inequalities in access to resources: compensated lotteries. These are based on introducing equity criteria into the allocation of resources, without disregarding a factor of fortune. In this way, no-one would be absolutely excluded from access, but neither would we all be given the same probability of obtaining it. In principle, it is assumed that this would allow for a good reconciliation of all the various fairness criteria. Since the starting point will probably be to optimise the outcome on efficiency considerations, the system as a whole would in reality result in a mix of the main criteria for distribution in emergency triage.

The COVID pandemic saw some concrete proposals in this regard. In 2020, authors such as White and Angus (2020) proposed a peculiar form of lottery for the allocation of remdesivir, a drug approved for the treatment of COVID-19 patients. Their model attempted to allocate the compound by combining pure chance with other factors, such as therapeutic benefit maximisation, which assigned a higher probability of winning the resource to those under certain conditions. This model has had some reflection in practice. Pennsylvania approved it in 2020 (White et al., 2020), and it was used to allocate remdesivir in two dozen hospitals in 2021. A central system conducted a daily lottery, allocating the resource based on its results. The distribution corresponded fairly well to what it would be expected from a weighting that gave 25% more chances to patients belonging to these groups while reducing by 50% those of patients whose death was expected in the following year or those who required mechanical ventilation or extracorporeal membrane oxygenation (ECMO). Overall, the probabilities of receiving the resource ranged from 28% to 88%.

In principle, this rule is reasonable if one believes that it is necessary to introduce equity considerations into the allocation of scarce resources. However, it is more feasible for a resource that is administered in batches and allows for some delay, such as a drug, than for a health resource that needs to be provided urgently and is of continuous use, such as any of the components of life-sustaining treatment. In these cases, it is not possible to group cases together, as they have to be dealt with on the spot. In addition, the resources do not increase as they are produced, but those that are available are simply the only resources available and do not usually increase too much. That is why it is difficult to think of a mechanism such as a lottery with compensation, unless we are willing to reallocate resources, when we are talking about life-sustaining treatment.

One of the great experts in disaster ethics, Michael Barilan, has attempted to develop a model to adapt the compensated lottery rule to the kind of scenario we are dealing with now—a pandemic crisis with a respiratory virus—by constructing an algorithm to aid decision-making, including in the equation the possibility of real-locating the scarce resource (Barilan, 2021):

> Within this framework, whenever a patient arrives, the algorithm will determine whether he or she gets a ventilator by the pre-set chances correlated to his or her score. For example, a patient with excellent prognosis may have a 95% chance. One in a lower prognostic decile will have 85% and so forth. Thus, when rejection of curable candidates is inevitable, every patient, even the most promising one, will be subjected to a combination of medically justified criteria and lottery. Patients with excellent prognosis will have an excellent chance to gain the respirator, whereas those with relatively poor prognosis will have a low chance. The personal experience of patients and healthcare providers will be similar for all. It will constitute solidarity in fate and in promise. The whole population is at risk. Everybody faces scarce resources and everybody has a chance. Chances are a matter of prognosis with a component of luck. The absence of discrete categorization, such as absolute thresholds by age or other dominant parameter, is expected to ease the moral distress of healthcare professionals and might avert a sense of social disruption by the public.

Barilan's alternative is based on dual triage, i.e. a set of criteria that apply not only to gaining access to a resource but also to its withdrawal. However, in the latter case, he recommends not to use games of chance but to base the decision on the deterioration of the patient's prognosis, not necessarily to the point where treatment is futile, but a real decline in any of the parameters that recommended admission. As he adds:

> The way in and the way out are not symmetric. Whereas a tiny gap in scoring may justify allocation of a respirator, disconnecting one may require a pre-set and significant deterioration in one's score. When the score gap is very narrow, it makes sense to allocate resources by the logic of sheer luck. Yet, disconnecting patients must not be chance-guided. Reintroducing chance into ongoing medical care will obfuscate clinical practice and invite bias and moral distress. Society cannot expect healthcare professionals to risk their lives and stretch their personal resources for care that is subjected to arbitrary interruptions.

This criterion certainly seems more than sensible. To take life-sustaining treatment away from a person who can benefit from it (even if to a lesser extent than another) on the basis of a lottery seems inhumane to me. Indeed, my criticism of models that interweave fortune into decision-making is that, in my view, lotteries are a poor resource. They are a sign of failure, of an abdication of moral responsibility for a decision (Puyol, 2018). Therefore, they should only be used if all other options have failed. Hence, we can conceive of proposals that exclude them, except as a way of deciding a tie-breaker that resists the staggered application of other criteria, without dismissing the weightings between one criterion and another.

5.8 Should the Reservation or Reallocation of Resources Be Accepted or Even Promoted?

In previous sections, I have tried to express the different criteria that guide the allocation of resources, as well as the rules that have been proposed to translate them into health-care practice. However, there is a discussion in this regard that I have not yet addressed, that is, when to consider the distribution of scarce resources. This is an essential question in moral terms, as it has a profound impact on the choice of both the objective and the rule or rules to be applied in triage. It is not possible to decide on one scenario or the other without first determining whether the access criteria will be applied to those who have not yet been allocated the resource or whether they should be extended to all patients who could benefit from it, regardless of whether they are already doing so or not. Bearing in mind that this debate implies the possibility of withholding, or even withdrawing, life-sustaining treatment from one patient in order to provide it to another, the seriousness of the case and the consequences of adopting one position or the other will be understood. If we decide that neither is acceptable, the "first come, first served" rule will become the only acceptable criterion. There will be no other option. Rules such as those that attempt to optimise lives saved, or introduce postulates of equity in distribution, will be inapplicable. This is for a simple reason: if a treatment cannot be reallocated until it becomes futile, nor can its application be delayed, then those who need it when it becomes available will be the recipients, simply because they are in the right place at the right time. But is such conduct permissible? In this section I will explore this question. To do so, I will start with what seems to be the simplest question, i.e. whether a delay in the allocation of the resource is acceptable. Then it will be time to talk about reallocation.

5.8.1 The Reservation of Resources Is Unacceptable

The most common way to avoid allocating the resource to the first person that needs it is to delay its application, reserving it for patients who are more likely to survive than those who might be allocated it at the moment it becomes available. This is feasible in practice, not least because the concept of need itself knows certain margins, especially depending on which resource is involved. There are times when it is not clear whether the patient can still survive without access to a resource, so it is possible to optimise its use without omitting a treatment or even reallocating it.

However, if at some point it is clear that this is no longer the case, that is, if we are dealing with a patient who is clearly in need of life support and as a result is likely to survive the pathology, it must be administered. Any other criteria would be irrational, immoral and illegal. Reserving the resource would be irrational because it is possible that during the time we are waiting for other patients, other resources may become available. Or indeed, the health centre concerned may not receive any more patients. Therefore, not allocating the scarce resource would be clearly immoral, as it would condemn to death a person for whom there is a remedy, at least momentarily. Moreover, if we compare a system that allows a resource not to be administered to one that institutionalises its reallocation, I believe that the latter is much more rational and, of course, more humane. In this case at least, the affected patient would have the hope (and the opportunity) to keep using the resource if other scarce assets are released in the meantime or if no other patient appears that requires it, obviously, a faint hope, but something better than no hope at all.

Finally, opting for the reservation of resources would also be illegal in the same sense that any omission of treatment is illegal, a conduct punishable in most Member States, as I will reiterate later. Depriving a person of a life-saving resource that is available (even temporarily) would be a crime committed by omission, a crime hardly justifiable on the basis of necessity, at least under the kind of liberal criminal law paradigm now predominant. Let us bear in mind that, in this case, we could not even speak of a specific, identifiable patient whose life would be the greater good to be preserved at the time of the omission.

In summary, all these reasons point to the fact that patients in need of help must be provided with the right resources when the situation requires it, without it being possible to reserve them for others. If this is true, then, we seem to be doomed to the rule of "first come, first served" (Eberl, 2020), except for what has already been said concerning the flexibility that doubt about a patient's real need gives us. There is, however, an alternative: accepting the reallocation of resources. It is time to tackle this thorny issue.

5.8.2 To Reassign Is to Kill?

Contrary to what is often thought, resource reallocation is not usually considered immoral in the bioethical discussion. Most authors who have studied the issue (NCBC Ethicists, 2020; Truog et al., 2020; White & Lo, 2020; Emanuel et al., 2020; Daly, 2020) argue that such an action would be not only acceptable, but advisable because it is the only way to optimise the number of lives saved. It has also been included in the guidelines by relevant institutions and associations, such as the *Società Italiana* di Anestesia, Analgesia, Rianimazione e Terapia Intensiva-SIAARTI (Vergano et al., 2020). Other organisations (the Swiss organisation of intensive care physicians or some German medical organisations, such as the intensive care society and the society of medical ethics) or institutions (MedStar Georgetown University Hospital, 2020) have opted for a hybrid approach, with asymmetrical conditions for withholding and withdrawing treatment, recommending withdrawal in some cases (Dufner, 2021). Even with these variants, however, it is clear that all of the above consider that the reallocation of a scarce commodity may be morally acceptable and even advisable, if it is in order to optimise the number of lives saved, albeit under certain conditions. Therefore, there are prima facie grounds for considering such conduct not only admissible but ethically necessary.

In contrast to these positions, there are other voices that consider the reallocation of resources to be profoundly immoral, because it involves causing the death of the patient who is using it. This is the perspective adopted by the German National Ethics Council (2020). This is despite the fact that, on the other hand, many of those who hold this position have no problem accepting that it is morally acceptable not to administer the resource to a patient (and, consequently, to let him die) in conditions of scarcity (Sulmasy & Sugarman, 1994; Tham et al., 2021). The justification for such a different solution comes from the fact that, in their view, not administering the resource to a patient and withdrawing it from him when he or she is already using it (in both cases to benefit a third party with better prospects or ratios for equitable allocation) are actions that raise different moral judgements. While the former may be permissible, insofar as it simply involves letting someone die, the latter will not be, because it involves killing someone directly (Tham et al., 2021). In short, there are authors who consider that there are substantive moral differences between action and omission in these cases (Shah et al., 2011).

This argument has been rejected, however, by many authors and institutions that consider omission also equivalent to denying access to a resource or to withdrawing a unit that has already been allocated (Wilkinson & Savulescu, 2014; Beauchamp & Childress, 2001; Harris, 1994; American Medical Association, 2020; British Medical Association, 2020; Cameron et al., 2020). To focus on the difference between action/omission is a mistake. The reasonable thing to do would be to move away from this position, opting for a normative interpretation of the act itself, as has been done in German criminal doctrine (Coca Vila, 2022; Tomás-Valiente, 1999). This fits the circumstances of the case much better, if we leave aside the pitfalls of an excessively naturalistic approach to the facts. If we want to understand why, let us conduct a mental experiment. Let us think that much of the reluctance to suspend treatment is due to the fact that we are talking about resources that have to be administered continuously, such as respirators or ICU beds in the case of COVID-19. However, if we were to think of other pathologies, where the scarce resource might well be a drug rather than a continuously used medical device, the scenario would probably give a different impression. Let us imagine a case where we have four doses of a drug that protects the patient against a lethal pathology. Let us also imagine that we only have four doses and that, for the treatment to be efficient, we have to give at least three doses to the patient. Finally, let us design a scenario in which we already have a patient in the health centre to whom we have already given a dose, despite the fact that his chances of survival (even with correct administration of the resource) are low. In such circumstances, what would we do if a new patient appears with a much better chance of survival? We would have two possibilities: either continue to give the treatment to the first patient, which would mean denying it to the second, or give it to the second, interrupting the treatment of the first. My intuition is that it would be much easier for a health professional to opt for the second patient in this case, for the simple reason that he would not have to proceed to directly remove a scarce resource from a human body.

If so, we would have one piece of evidence: the fact that we are talking about a resource that is administered continuously or discretely may be of essential importance in determining permissible or advisable behaviour. Nevertheless, if this is true, then we are giving too much weight to factors that should not be given so much importance. In fact, much of the debate on this issue is reminiscent of what has already been discussed at length in the field of euthanasia, particularly with regard to the distinction between active and passive euthanasia, an issue that is a dead end. There is no way to maintain this distinction without getting into seemingly absurd dilemmas. If we think, for example, in the case of the respirator, we will conclude that the ideal would be to have devices that work on a timer that turns them off with a certain frequency (let us say daily). In this way, if a health-care professional wanted to reassign it to another patient, he or she would not have to disconnect the device from the power supply, but simply not update the timer (an omission), immediately proceeding to provide the patient with palliative care so that he or she would not suffer as a consequence. This is precisely what was considered at the time in Israel to satisfy the requirements of the Hebrew tradition (Halperin, 2002; Ravitsky, 2005). It appears to be an unconvincing solution, even a trick to obviate a moral problem (Barilan, 2003). In fact, it is an obvious proof of the absurdity of being guided by purely naturalistic considerations.

The reasonable thing to do, therefore, is to apply a normative perspective to the facts, which avoids concluding that withdrawing a resource is killing. In fact, withdrawal of life support from a patient who requests it is common in our hospitals and many bioethicists consider that it does not amount to "killing" the patient at all (Emanuel et al., 2020). Even many who believe that action and omission are not equivalent accept this (Ursin, 2019). Obviously, I understand that it is not the same to speak of a consented or, even more so, requested renunciation of a treatment as it is to speak of depriving a patient who wants to keep an essential element of a treatment. Nevertheless, this should have no bearing on the cause-effect relationship between the withdrawal of the device and death. If removal is killing, it is killing with or without the patient's acquiescence. As McGee says, "Consent does indeed make the difference between homicide and legitimate treatment withdrawal, but that is an ethical or legal difference, and has nothing to do with the cause of the patient's death, which is the same in both cases" (McGee, 2014, p. 32).

My impression, therefore, is that removing recourse from a sick person is not normatively equivalent to causing death, but more to returning the situation to its natural state. The patient will probably die after losing his or her ventilator, not as a consequence of the withdrawal, however, but as a consequence of the underlying pathology (Dufner, 2021). Withdrawal of the resource will not interfere in this sense with the causal relationship. Under this mentality, Phillipa Foot's lapidary statement in 1984 ("the use of 'kill' is not important: what matters is that the fatal sequence resulting in death is not initiated but is rather allowed to take its course" (Foot, 2004)) is widely accepted.

However, this does not mean that the removal of a ventilator does not cause harm. In fact, it prevents the patient from retaining the possibility of overcoming the underlying pathology. Moreover, this is precisely where the circumstances come into play that may or may not justify the conduct of the person who proceeds to deprive the patient of the resource, despite being able to do so. Firstly, it is obvious that if it is the patient who wishes to renounce treatment, the person who proceeds to follow the patient's instructions will be exempt from liability (criminal lawyers draw many distinctions depending on whether a health professional does so (Tomás-Valiente, 1999), but in moral terms, this does not seem important). If, on the other hand, this withdrawal of recourse occurs against their will, it is much more difficult to qualify the action from a legal point of view. In my view, the essential thing to consider is that, in the midst of a pandemic that has killed thousands of people, it is reasonable to abstract from the usual conceptual framework that we use to configure the state of necessity. This is often indebted to the principle of double effect and the necessary comparison between the evil caused and the evil to be avoided (which, by the way, leads to very debatable results from an ethical point of view). This, which in ordinary times is reasonable, loses its relevance when it is no longer a question of preserving individual rights, but of optimising the results of a policy in population terms. In these circumstances, it is necessary to know how to replace the liberal schemes that feed, among others, our criminal laws, whose mission is not to protect through their rules the aggregate interests of any collective entity formed by the aggregation of particular interests, but to guarantee a harmonious separation of spheres of freedom administered autonomously by each citizen (Coca Vila, 2021).

In fact, if we change to a system in which the legal assets to be preserved are collective and population-based, concepts such as those of consent lose all validity, because the usual clinical care scheme no longer governs, but it is the public health mentality itself that has to pave the way. If the aim of intervention is to optimise the number of lives saved (with whatever restrictions we may wish to introduce from the point of view of equity), it is appropriate to disregard any consideration of the will of the individual patient when it comes to allocating the scarce resource. The appropriate way to reinforce this belief is to rescue the conception of scarce resources as strictly collective assets in times of pandemic. It would be appropriate here to quote St. Thomas Aquinas himself, who in his wonderful *Summa Theologica* already points out that "in case of necessity all things are common, and thus it does not seem to be a sin if one takes a thing from another, because necessity makes it common" (Aquinas 2021, IIa-IIae, q. 66, a. 7). The key is to keep in mind that a patient should not obtain a right to keep a health resource until it ceases to be of any use to him merely because it was initially assigned to him. Such a "right to retain possession" is not justified by any just reason when public health considerations prevail.

Accepting this conceptual framework, what would exonerate both the decision-maker and the person depriving the patient of the resource would be the will to act in the best interests of the group, on the basis of properly considered objective reasons. This is what would differentiate, on the other hand, the conduct of the professional who withdraws the resource in order to reassign it from that of the patient or his relative who takes the resource away from another patient in order to administer it to himself or to another relative whose health is compromised. In this case, the defence of acting in the best interests of the group would not be applicable at all. Therefore, he would have to be tried for depriving a person of any chance of survival, without any defence.

5.8.3 Other Arguments

What about the patient's right to physical integrity? Is this not another factor to be taken into account, and if we remove the resource from their body without their consent, would we not be violating that fundamental right? This is a relevant issue, which has already been analysed in the academic literature (Gedge et al., 2007; Breslin & Oliver, 2021). It is necessary to start by making some nuances in this regard. As Dufner explains:

> A fully worked out position on this issue might partly depend on whether the ventilator has to be viewed as part of the patient's body, as is arguably the case for pacemakers. A further question might be whether a ventilator has to be viewed as functioning autonomously, or whether its proper functioning requires constant attendance by medical staff (Dufner, 2021).

Other authors, such as Coca Vila, present somewhat similar arguments, when they point out that, in reality, the impossibility of reallocating the resource "is due to the validity in our (criminal) legal system of the principle of casum sentit dominus, as a general defective principle of distribution of misfortune. Given that the first patient, from a normative perspective, ceases to be a patient in need at the very moment in which the doctor in need starts treatment, it is the second patient in need who is the only dominus called upon to bear the costs of his or her misfortune. There is thus an essential normative difference between ex ante and ex post triage situations. In the first scenario, the interests of two needy subjects are at stake, both are in danger; in the second, on the other hand, the interest of a needy person is at stake, who can only be saved at the expense of someone who, normatively, is no longer a needy person" (Coca Vila, 2021, p. 195).

The biggest problem implicit in this type of arguments is that, as I have mentioned, the circumstances surrounding a pandemic diametrically change the underlying ethical framework and, if we are reasonable, should also alter the framework underpinning the applicable regulations. When we are in an extreme situation, we should no longer think in terms of individualised health care, in which the individual's consent must take precedence over the general interest. Hence, it is sometimes possible to impose a treatment, even if this involves an attack on an individual's physical integrity, as is the case with coercive vaccination. The same could be stated regarding the allocation of resources and the doctor-patient relationship: at a time when public health considerations prevail, it no longer makes sense to think that patients acquire a preferential right to enjoy a resource: everything belongs to everyone and must be available to everyone.

Nevertheless, I concede that it is true that the physical—and psychological—relationship that a sick person or his or her relatives have with the resource that has already been allocated to him or her is very powerful. In this sense, not allocating a resource is not the same as reallocating it, even if, in reality, the provisional allocation gave it a lifespan that the original non-allocation would have denied it. This, in my view, means that we should only proceed with such reassignment when the patient has been adequately informed of the conditionality of the resource allocation from the outset and only in discrete cases where the chances of salvation are clearly different, as I will insist later.

There is, however, another argument against the reassignment of life-sustaining treatments that should not be ignored. As recently expressed by Tham et al.: "A morally relevant doctor-patient relationship includes the doctor's responsibility to continue proportionate care with a reasonable likelihood of success. To end proportionate care willfully is to betray the doctor's duty for his patient's wellbeing" (Tham et al., 2021).

The problem with this additional criticism, again, is that it ignores the fact that, in times of pandemic, public health considerations must take precedence over clinical health-care considerations. Hence, while it is true that the doctor-patient link is sacred in the scheme of health care, we should try to overcome it, without compromising it, when circumstances recommend other courses of action. Allocating the decision on reassignment to a committee rather than clinicians, as many protocols already do, should be the appropriate response to this problem (Dufner, 2021). I will return to this later.

5.8.4 Reallocating Resources: Final Considerations

On the basis of the above, in summary, I believe that there is good reason to consider that the difference between not allocating and reallocating a scarce resource is not morally significant when delaying the assignation of the resource will undoubtedly cause irreparable harm to the individual. Moreover, contrary to general opinion, I suspect that the latter is far more acceptable than the former, for all the reasons I have already explained. The choice, therefore, will be limited to deciding whether to reallocate resources. If we do not, there will be only one hard and fast rule to apply: "first come, first served". If we choose the latter, we are making it possible to allocate the available resources in the way that best satisfies the maximisation and equity criteria described above.

I am fully aware that our liberal legal systems are not prepared to deal with the second scenario. There would be criminal liability nowadays if, for example, a physician refused to provide the remedy to a person in need, despite being available, because it was reserved for another potential patient whose certainty of therapeutic benefit was greater. The question of withdrawal from a remedy that is administered on an ongoing basis to a patient who did not provide consent is even clearer. Indeed, a practitioner who took such an action could be charged with manslaughter (Eastman et al., 2010; Hurford, 2020; Liddell et al., 2020; Coca Vila, 2021). If the clinician was aware that removing the ventilator would result in the patient's death, the applicable charge would surely be murder, at least in countries such as the UK, as expressed in R (Burke) v General Medical Council (2005)[2] per Lord Phillips MR)

---

[2] EWCA Civ 1003, at [53].

(Hurford, 2020; Cameron et al., 2020). These charges could, of course, be extended to other health-care professionals involved in the withdrawal of the remedy (Cohen et al., 2020).

I am aware that to step outside the liberal axiological framework is to step over the precipice, but not to do so may likewise push us over it. In the absence of change, defensive medicine will play its great role in decision-making. If withholding or withdrawing a ventilator from a patient who has some chance of survival, however slim, raises legal issues, it is likely that the decision-maker will not make that choice (Cohen et al., 2020). The most reasonable solution, in short, would be to consider temporary regulatory modifications, which would only apply for as long as a crisis scenario remains in force. If we accept that circumstances force us to radically change our criteria for action, giving priority to public health over health care, it is reasonable to introduce regulations that are consistent with this change. In this way, we would be able to escape from the narrow margins of action granted by markedly liberal penal codes. And this would undoubtedly help enormously in achieving the objectives of optimising the number of lives saved and of equity in their distribution, if we opt for them.

This is not so complex to assimilate if we accept for a moment the metaphor that equates a pandemic with a war. With such a frame of mind, it would probably not be so difficult to set aside forms of resource allocation that put the individual above the collective. However, it would be absurd to deny that, for many health professionals, there is indeed a relevant difference between withdrawing a treatment and simply not providing it (Ursin, 2019; Sandman & Liliemark, 2019). Or they find withdrawing a still useful resource unbearable. Hence, imposing protocols that oblige them to proceed in this way would be highly conflictive, and it is at least appropriate to consider whether a right to conscientious objection should be recognised, although authors such as Wicclair seem to reject this (Wicclair, 2020). I cannot help recognising that perhaps Ravitsky (2005) was right when she stated that, if this is the best way to reconcile the demands of ethical thinking with the emotions and convictions of health-care professionals or a large part of the community, introducing timers in ventilators or even ICU stations is surely not an absurd scenario.

In any case, if reallocation of resources is accepted, the key issue is to find a way to carry it out without causing unnecessary emotional harm to all involved. In my view, the conception of a temporary allocation as something similar to a clinical trial, as proposed by some authors (Dufner, 2021; Wilkinson & Savulescu, 2014), is a reasonable idea. In this way, we could introduce conditions to treatment maintenance that go beyond mere continuationism.

Finally, two important points remain to be mentioned. The first is that such constant redistribution should by no means be limited to patients to whom the resource was first administered when the period of scarcity began. There is no reason to exclude those who used such means on previous occasions. The fact that one person had been using the resource for much longer than another, or had started using it before a pandemic appeared, should not be a reason to exclude them from fair reallocation (Hope et al., 2012). Second, at the very least, the difference in the expected benefit to the patient deprived of the resource and the patient receiving it should be clear and substantial. Reassigning a resource is a terrible decision, which undermines the expectations of a patient, who can only take refuge in the fact that his or her alternative may be even worse. If this evidence is not clear, it is better not to proceed in this way.

5.9 A Combined Resource Allocation Model: Mixing Equity and Efficiency

On the basis of the considerations made in the previous sections, it is also possible to think, as a plausible alternative, of triage based on a pure criteria weighting rule, with no place for luck, as an alternative to one governed by the "first come, first served" rule. In this section I show an example, which is far from being a firm proposal. It is simply a generic model that should be adapted to a particular society's understanding of the objectives of triage or the weight to be given to the different factors involved.

The proposal is set out in Table 5.1, which is indebted to that developed by Douglas White and Bernard Lo (2020). Column one sets out the criteria tentatively used to determine resource allocation. The patient would be assigned points based on these criteria. Of these, a patient's survival expectancy and time of resource use play the role of the target to be optimised in this case. In order to show how the outcome could be made fair, I have introduced several criteria that give a weight to the outcome. Some of them—such as a very low quality of life expectancy—subtract points towards obtaining the resource. Others, on the other hand, add points, while further criteria are used to break ties. The scores assigned to each of the parameters are, I repeat, merely illustrative. If we were to consider implementing an

Table 5.1 Criteria to determine resource allocation

Criteria/points	4	3	2	1
Expectation of survival	75–100%	50–75%	25–50%	1–25%
Time of use of the resource (or units)	X (4 days)	2X	3X	4X
Minority	Three extra points			
Belonging to a vulnerable group	An extra point			
Belonging to a leading collective	An extra point			
Severely reduced quality of life (persistent vegetative state)	Three points less			
Very short life expectancy (less than 1 year)	Two points less			
First tie-breaking criterion	Vaccination/non-vaccination			
Second tie-breaker	Fair innings			
Third tie-breaking criterion	Very low quality of life			
Fourth tie-breaking criterion	Chance/luck			

algorithm of this type, the allocation of corrective points would require a great deal of discussion.

The advantage of this proposal is that, once the parameters have been established, it is reasonably simple to operate. Let us imagine that the resource is needed by a minor with an expected cure rate of 50–75% in exchange for use of the resource for $2x$ days; a frontline person in their 40s, who also belongs to a vulnerable group and has an expected cure rate of 2–25% in exchange for use of the resource for x days; and a vaccinated 75-year-old person who has an expected cure rate of 75–100% in exchange for use of the resource for $2x$ days. The points for each of these would be:

Case 1: 3 (50–75%) + 3 ($2x$) + 3 points for minor. Total, 9 points.
Case 2: 1 (2–25%) + 4 (x days) + 1 point per vulnerable group + 1 point per frontline
      group. Total: 7 points.
Case 3: 4 (75–100%) + 3 ($2x$). Total: 7 points.

The order of allocation of available resources would therefore be, firstly, the youngest person. After that, there would be a tie between the 40-year-old and the 75-year-old, which would be broken in favour of the former by the vaccination criterion, which is higher than the *fair innings* criterion.

5.10   Operational Standards: Who Is to Control the Allocation of Resources? How to Decide Which Criteria Are to Be Applied?

5.10.1   Response Planning in General

Throughout this chapter, I have discussed many of the criteria to be considered when dealing with a situation requiring triage. None of them, however, can be considered absolute. It is therefore necessary to strike a balance between them, which is what weighted systems provide, whether or not they include an element of fortune. In any case, it is best to undertake this weighting well before the emergency situation is already present, for a number of reasons. It is not only that haste does not help. It is also the case that before a crisis scenario arises we are still subject to a veil of ignorance that falls away when we know the circumstances of the case. SARS-Cov-2, for example, attacks older people to a much greater extent than other age groups. This is not always the case. The Spanish flu wreaked particular havoc among the young. In some places, such as Maryland, USA, commendable efforts have been made to reach this kind of consensus. Their promoters involved both the community at large and representatives of emergency response services and health professionals in this effort. As a result, it was possible to reach some consensus that was eventually translated into a resource allocation protocol (Biddison et al., 2018; Daugherty Biddison et al., 2019). We could probably learn a lot from these preliminary attempts.

However, it is not easy to delimit each and every aspect of triage a priori because the scarce resource can change substantially from one crisis to another. If in the case of COVID-19, it was a question of life-support treatments or ICU stations, in other cases, the health resource to be rationed may be antibiotics or retrovirals, for example. In addition, the resource itself may have many nuances that require adaptation on the fly. If we are faced with a contagious agent, an isolated ICU is not the same as one that is not isolated, and this has consequences depending on the number of people infected. In fact, at the beginning of the COVID-19 pandemic, patients went to these isolated ICUs. Later on, these ICUs had to be allocated to those who were not infected because the numbers were reversed. So, in practice, we should speak of two types of resources (isolated, non-isolated) and two types of patients (infected, non-infected). The picture is therefore often considerably complicated. This needs to be borne in mind when planning a triage response in the context of a pandemic.

In any case, what is undeniable is that a model that seeks to optimise the criterion of equity, even if it has to yield in some of its postulates, requires that the representatives of the groups potentially susceptible to discrimination participate in its design. Ideally, the construction of the weightings should be the result of negotiation between the different groups concerned. It is also necessary to consider that some of the measures to be adopted may clash head-on with existing legal frameworks. If this is the case, it is advisable to reach social agreements in time to undertake the necessary reforms. What is clear is that transparent procedural aspects are absolutely essential to justify the decisions taken (Hower, 2020).

5.10.2   Decision-Making on the Individual Patient

One criterion that is generally considered universally valid is that the decision on who should allocate scarce resources should not rest with the clinicians who care for patients. This is, firstly, because health-care professionals have obligations towards their patients that they do not have towards everyone else. On the other hand, it is obvious, as already mentioned, that making some decisions—such as reallocating scarce resource—could be very difficult for them to make (Truog et al., 2020). This would create a huge psychological burden on them (Craxì et al., 2020). Hence, it seems a good idea to shift the final responsibility for decisions, and perhaps their implementation, to other people.

Just as important is the fact that by placing the responsibility for decision-making on a body other than the clinicians, we would avoid undermining the bond of trust on which the doctor-patient relationship is based. This is essential in order to avoid one of the main—and most reasonable—arguments against reallocation of resources. If it is up to clinicians to make such a decision, the patient may feel betrayed by his or her doctor. If, on the other hand, the decision is made by someone else, this will not be the case. It goes without saying that this, in turn, would reinforce the discharge of professional responsibility that I mentioned in the preceding paragraph. Thus, "There may also be a role for scrutiny of individual decisions by a second physician or, where appropriate, by duly constituted clinical ethics committees, when time permits" (BMA, 2020). It is, at last, reasonable that in this decision-making process, the patient or his or her relatives should be given the possibility to express their opinion or even to appeal a decision to a different body, provided that the circumstances make this possible.

Who, then, should make the decision? Probably the best idea is to form committees that can tackle this difficult task (Emanuel et al., 2020; Sprung et al., 2020). Circumstances permitting, there should probably be an intensivist among their members. For example, a document produced by the German Society for Intensive Care (Marckmann et al., 2020) suggests the involvement of two intensive care physicians, one representative of the nursing staff and one person with another background, such as clinical ethics, ideally, *senior* professionals with triage experience, but also nurses, palliative care experts, social workers, lawyers and bioethicists (Sprung et al., 2020). In this way, clinicians would on the one hand be relieved of the burden of having to choose between their patients and on the other hand be strengthened by the authority of such a committee. In turn, it makes sense to create a *triage officer*, who would be distinguished by his or her clinical expertise, leadership skills and ability to communicate effectively. This person would not only form part of the committee, but would also be in charge of communicating the case to the patient's relatives, explaining all the circumstances and responding to their doubts, suggestions or complaints. However, one must be aware that these mechanisms would only operate reasonably well in a hospital context. It is much more complex to think about how to solve problems that take place outside of this context, such as in nursing homes, for example. New proposals on how to deal with such scenarios are urgently needed, I am afraid.

Finally, I think it is reasonable to envisage monitoring of the triage decisions made by these committees, which would operate at the level of the centre, by an independent body made up of advisors directly appointed by the corresponding administrative authority. This committee would be responsible for unifying criteria as far as possible, resolving doubts, advising where necessary and collecting suggestions for modifying protocols, for example. In no case should it be seen as an appeal body for decisions taken, but rather as an entity dedicated to the coordination and improvement of protocols (Christian et al., 2014; Daugherty Biddison et al., 2019).

References

Adams, J. (2020, October). The disrespectfulness of weighted survival lotteries. In *Proceedings of the Aristotelian Society* (Vol. 120, no. 3, pp. 395–404). Oxford University Press.

Adams, M. L., Katz, D. L., & Grandpre, J. (2020). Population-based estimates of chronic conditions affecting risk for complications from coronavirus disease, United States. *Emerging Infectious Diseases, 26*(8), 1831.

Altevogt, B. M., Stroud, C., Hanson, S. L., Hanfling, D., & Gostin, L. O. (2009). *Committee on guidance for establishing standards of care for use in disaster situations, Institute of Medicine. Guidance for establishing crisis standards of care for use in disaster situations: A letter report.* National Academy Press.

American Medical Association (AMA). (2020). *AMA code of medical ethics.* Retrieved October 1, 2020, https://www.ama-assn.org/delivering-care/ama-principles-medical-ethics

Annas, G. J. (2010). *Worst case bioethics: Death, disaster, and public health.* Oxford University Press.

Aquino, T. (2012). Suma Teológica. In English: Aquinas, T. (2021). *Summa theologica* (pp. 324–329). De Gruyter. Accesible en: https://hjg.com.ar/sumat/c/c66.html#a7

Atienza Macías, E., Armaza Armaza, E. J., & de Miguel Beriain, I. (2015). Aspectos bioético-jurídicos de las instrucciones previas o testamento vital en el contexto normativo español. *Acta bioethica, 21*(2), 163–172.

Barilan, Y. M. (2003). Revisiting the problem of Jewish bioethics: The case of terminal care. *Kennedy Institute of Ethics Journal, 13*(2), 141–168. https://doi.org/10.1353/ken.2003.0008

Barilan, Y. M. (2021). Allocation of respirators in the coronavirus crisis in Israel: An ethical analysis and a scheme for triage. *The Israel Medical Association Journal: IMAJ, 23*(5), 274–278.

Beauchamp, T. L., & Childress, J. F. (2001). *Principles of biomedical ethics.* Oxford University Press.

Biddison, E. L. D., Gwon, H. S., Schoch-Spana, M., Regenberg, A. C., Juliano, C., Faden, R. R., & Toner, E. S. (2018). Scarce resource allocation during disasters: A mixed-method community engagement study. *Chest, 153*(1), 187–195.

Biddison, L. D., Berkowitz, K. A., Courtney, B., De Jong, C. M. J., Devereaux, A. V., Kissoon, N., Roxland, B. E., Sprung, C. L., Dichter, J. R., Christian, M. D., & Powell, T. (2014). Ethical considerations: Care of the critically ill and injured during pandemics and disasters: CHEST consensus statement. *Chest, 146*(4), e145S–e155S.

Blackburn, J., Yiannoutsos, C. T., Carroll, A. E., Halverson, P. K., & Menachemi, N. (2021). Infection fatality ratios for COVID-19 among noninstitutionalized persons 12 and older: Results of a random-sample prevalence study. *Annals of Internal Medicine, 174*(1), 135–136.

Bochenek, T., Abilova, V., Alkan, A., Asanin, B., de Miguel Beriain, I., Besovic, Z., Bonanno, P. V., Bucsics, A., Davidescu, M., De Weerdt, E., Duborija-Kovacevic, N., Fürst, J., Gaga, M., Gailīte, E., Gulbinovič, J., Gürpınar, E. U., Hankó, B., Hargaden, V., Hotvedt, T. A., … Godman, B. (2018). Systemic measures and legislative and organizational frameworks aimed at preventing or mitigating drug shortages in 28 European and Western Asian countries. *Frontiers in Pharmacology, 8*, 942.

Breslin, J., & Oliver, J. (2021). Ventilator withdrawal for reallocation during a COVID-19 surge needs a deeper discussion. *University of Toronto Medical Journal, 98*(2), 18–21.

British Medical Association (BMA). (2020). *COVID-19—Ethical issues. A guidance note.* Retrieved December 14, 2021, from https://www.bma.org.uk/media/2360/bma-covid-19-ethics-guidance-april-2020.pdf

Cameron, J., Savulescu, J., & Wilkinson, D. (2020). Is withdrawing treatment really more problematic than withholding treatment? *Journal of Medical Ethics, 47*(11), 722–726.

Centers for Disease Control and Prevention. (2020). *Health equity considerations and racial and ethnic minority groups.* Centers for Disease Control and Prevention (CDC).

Chang, D. W., & Shapiro, M. F. (2016). Association between intensive care unit utilization during hospitalization and costs, use of invasive procedures, and mortality. *JAMA Internal Medicine, 176*(10), 1492–1499.

Christian, M. D., Sprung, C. L., King, M. A., Dichter, J. R., Kissoon, N., Devereaux, A. V., & Gomersall, C. D. (2014). Triage: Care of the critically ill and injured during pandemics and disasters: CHEST consensus statement. *Chest, 146*(4), e61S–e74S.

Cleveland Manchanda, E., Couillard, C., & Sivashanker, K. (2020). Inequity in crisis standards of care. *New England Journal of Medicine, 383*(4), e16.

Coca Vila, I. (2021). Triaje y colisión de deberes jurídico-penal Una crítica al giro utilitarista. *Indret: Revista para el Análisis del Derecho, 1*, 10.

Coca Vila, I. (2022). La justificación penal de la desconexión letal de aparatos médicos. A propósito de la reasignación de respiradores en contextos dilemáticos (triaje *ex post*). *Revista Penal*, (49), 7–25.

Cohen, I. G., Crespo, A. M., & White, D. B. (2020). Potential legal liability for withdrawing or withholding ventilators during COVID-19: Assessing the risks and identifying needed reforms. *Journal of the American Medical Association, 323*(19), 1901–1902.

Comité de Bioética de España. (2020). *Informe del Comité de Bioética de España sobre los aspectos bioéticos de la priorización de recursos sanitarios en el contexto de la crisis del coronavirus.* Retrieved from http://assets.comitedebioetica.es/files/documentacion/Informe%20 CBE-%20Priorizacion%20de%20recursos%20sanitarioscoronavirus%20CBE.pdf

Craxì, L., Vergano, M., Savulescu, J., & Wilkinson, D. (2020). Rationing in a pandemic: Lessons from Italy. *Asian Bioethics Review, 12*(3), 1–6. https://doi.org/10.1007/s41649-020-00127-1. Advance online publication. Retrieved December 29, 2021.

Daffner, K. R. (2021). Point: Healthcare providers should receive treatment priority during a pandemic. *Journal of Hospital Medicine, 16*(3), 180–181.

Daly, D. J. (2020). Guidelines for rationing treatment during the COVID-19 crisis: A catholic approach. *Health Progress, 101*(2). Retrieved December 19, 2021, from https://www.chausa.org/publications/health-progress/article/pandemic-coverage/guidelines-for-rationing-treatment-during-the-covid-19-crisis-a-catholic-approach

Daugherty Biddison, E. L., Faden, R., Gwon, H. S., Mareiniss, D. P., Regenberg, A. C., Schoch-Spana, M., Schwartz, J., & Toner, E. S. (2019). Too many patients…a framework to guide statewide allocation of scarce mechanical ventilation during disasters. *Chest, 155*(4), 848–854.

De Miguel Beriain, I. (2020). Triaje en tiempos de pandemia: un análisis a partir de las limitaciones del marco jurídico español. En: Elena Atienza Macías y Juan Francisco Rodríguez (Dir.). In *Las respuestas del derecho a las crisis de salud pública* (pp. 229–242). Dykinson.

Dufner, A. (2021). Withdrawal of intensive care during times of severe scarcity: Triage during a pandemic only upon arrival or with the inclusion of patients who are already under treatment? *Bioethics, 35*(2), 118–124.

Eastman, N., Philips, B., & Rhodes, A. (2010). Triaging in adult critical care in the event of overwhelming need. *Intensive Care Medicine, 36*(6), 1076–1082.

Eberl, J. T. (2020). Ethics as usual? Unilateral withdrawal of treatment in a state of exception. *The American Journal of Bioethics, 20*(7), 210–211.

Emanuel, E. J., Persad, G., Upshur, R., Thome, B., Parker, M., Glickman, A. Zhang, C., Boyle, C., Smith, M., Phillips, J. P. (2020). Fair allocation of scarce medical resources in the time of Covid-19.

Emeruwa, U. N., Ona, S., Shaman, J. L., Turitz, A., Wright, J. D., Gyamfi-Bannerman, C., & Melamed, A. (2020). Associations between built environment, neighborhood socioeconomic status, and SARS-CoV-2 infection among pregnant women in New York City. *Journal of the American Medical Association, 324*(4), 390–392.

Foot, P. (2004). Killing and letting die, repr. In B. Steinbock & A. Norcross (Eds.), *Killing and Letting Die* (pp. 280–289). Prentice Hall.

Gedge, E., Giacomini, M., & Cook, D. (2007). Withholding and withdrawing life support in critical care settings: Ethical issues concerning consent. *Journal of Medical Ethics, 33*, 215–218.

German National Ethics Council. (2020). *Solidarity and responsibility during the corona virus crisis.* Retrieved December 24, 2021, from https://www.ethikrat.org/en/press-releases/2020/solidarity-and-responsibility-during-the-coronavirus-crisis/

Gostin, L. O., Viswanathan, K., Altevogt, B. M., & Hanfling, D. (Eds.). (2012). *Crisis standards of care: A systems framework for catastrophic disaster response: Volume 1: Introduction and CSC framework* (Vol. 3). National Academies Press.

Halperin, M. (2002). Clinical experiment in secured systems that transform ventilation into discrete medical treatment—Ethical introduction. *Report submitted to the Israeli Ministry of Health by the chief officer of medical ethics [in Hebrew].* Ministry of Health.

Hare, R. M. (1981). *Moral thinking: Its levels, method, and point.* Clarendon Press/Oxford University Press.

Harris, J. (1994). Are withholding and withdrawing therapy always morally equivalent? A reply to Sulmasy and Sugarman. *Journal of Medical Ethics, 20*(4), 223–224.

Harris, J. (2006). *The value of life: An introduction to medical ethics.* Routledge.

Herreros, B., Gella, P., & De Asua, D. R. (2020). Triage during the COVID-19 epidemic in Spain: Better and worse ethical arguments. *Journal of Medical Ethics, 46*(7), 455–458.

Hick, J. L., Hanfling, D., Wynia, M. K., & Toner, E. (2021). Crisis standards of care and COVID-19: What did we learn? How do we ensure equity? What should we do? *NAM Perspectives, 2021,* 10.31478/202108e.

Hope, T., McMillan, J., & Hill, E. (2012). Intensive care triage: Priority should be independent of whether patients are already receiving intensive care. *Bioethics, 26*(5), 259–266.

Hortal-Carmona, J., Padilla-Bernáldez, J., Melguizo-Jiménez, M., Ausín, T., Cruz-Piqueras, M., de la Vieja, M. T. L., Puyol, À., Rodríguez-Arias, D., Tamayo-Velázquez, M.-I., & Triviño, R. (2021). La eficiencia no basta. Análisis ético y recomendaciones para la distribución de recursos escasos en situación de pandemia. *Gaceta Sanitaria, 35*(6), 525–533.

Hower, E. G. (2020). What we should learn from the COVID-19 pandemic. *The Journal of Clinical Ethics, 31*(3), 197–208.

Hsieh, N. H., Strudler, A., & Wasserman, D. (2006). The numbers problem. *Philosophy & Public Affairs, 34*(4), 352–372.

Huber, S. J., & Wynia, M. K. (2004). When pestilence prevails… physician responsibilities in epidemics. *American Journal of Bioethics, 4*(1), 5–11.

Hurford, J. E. (2020). The BMA COVID-19 ethical guidance. A legal analysis. *New Bioethics, 26*(2), 176–189.

Jöbges, S., Vinay, R., Luyckx, V. A., & Biller-Andorno, N. (2020). Recommendations on COVID-19 triage: International comparison and ethical analysis. *Bioethics, 34*(9), 948–959.

Kamm, F. M. (1993). *Morality, mortality: Death and whom to save from it* (Vol. 1). Oxford University Press on Demand.

Karaca-Mandic, P., Georgiou, A., & Sen, S. (2021). Assessment of COVID-19 hospitalizations by race/ethnicity in 12 states. *JAMA Internal Medicine, 181*(1), 131–134.

Liddell, K., Skipek, J. M., Palmer, S., Martin, S., Anderson, J., & Sagar, A. (2020). Who gets the ventilator? Important legal rights in a pandemic. *Journal of Medical Ethics, 46,* 421–426.

Marckmann, G., Neitzke, G., Schildmann, J., Michalsen, A., Dutzmann, J., Hartog, C., … Janssens, U. (2020). Entscheidungen über die Zuteilung intensivmedizinischer Ressourcen im Kontext der COVID-19-Pandemie. *Medizinische Klinik-Intensivmedizin und Notfallmedizin,* 1–9.

Mayr, F. B., Yende, S., Linde-Zwirble, W. T., Peck-Palmer, O. M., Barnato, A. E., Weissfeld, L. A., & Angus, D. C. (2010). Infection rate and acute organ dysfunction risk as explanations for racial differences in severe sepsis. *Journal of the American Medical Association, 303*(24), 2495–2503.

McGee, A. (2014). Does withdrawing life-sustaining treatment cause death or allow the patient to die? *Medical Law Review, 22*(1), 26–47.

MedStar Georgetown University Hospital. (2020). *Ethical principles of resource allocation in the event of an overwhelming surge of COVID-19 patients.* Retrieved December 14, 2021, from https://kennedyinstitute.georgetown.edu/wordpress/wp-content/uploads/2020/03/CovidEthics-MGUH.pdf

Michalsen, A., Neitzke, G., Dutzmann, J., Rogge, A., Seidlein, A. H., Jöbges, S., Burchardi, H., Hartog, C., Nauck, F., Salomon, F., Duttge, G., Michels, G., Knochel, K., Meier, S., Gretenkort, P., & Janssens, U. (2021). *Overtreatment in intensive care medicine-recognition, designation, and avoidance: Position paper of the ethics section of the DIVI and the ethics section of the DGIIN*. Medizinische Klinik, Intensivmedizin und Notfallmedizin.

Mun, F., Hale, C. M., & Hennrikus, E. F. (2021). A survey of US hospitals' criteria for the allocation of remdesivir to treat COVID-19. *American Journal of Health-System Pharmacy, 78*(3), 235–241.

National Academies of Sciences, Engineering, and Medicine. (2020). Encouraging participation and cooperation in contact tracing: Lessons from survey research.

National Council of disability quality-adjusted life years and the eevaluation of life with disability. (2019, November 6). Retrieved December 19, 2021, from https://ncd.gov/sites/default/files/NCD_Quality_Adjusted_Life_Report_508.pdf

NCBC Ethicists. (2020). *Ethical concerns with COVID-19 triage protocols*. National Catholic Bioethics Center. Retrieved December 19, 2021, from https://ncbcstore.org/s/NCBC-Concerns-with-Triage-Protocols-Final.pdf

Pagel, C., & Utley, M. (2020). Covid-19: How to triage effectively in a pandemic. *British Medical Journal*. Retrieved December 19, 2021, from https://blogs.bmj.com/bmj/2020/03/09/covid-19-triage-in-a-pandemic-is-even-thornier-than-you-might-think/

Pampalon, R., & Raymond, G. (2000). A deprivation index for health and welfare planning in Quebec. *Chronic Diseases in Canada, 21*(3), 104–113.

Panocchia, N., D'ambrosio, V., Corti, S., Presti, E. L., Bertelli, M., Scattoni, M. L., & Ghelma, F. (2021). COVID-19 pandemic, the scarcity of medical resources, community-centred medicine and discrimination against persons with disabilities. *Journal of Medical Ethics, 47*(6), 362–366.

Parfit, D. (1978). Innumerate ethics. *Philosophy & Public Affairs, 7*(4), 285–301.

Persad, G. (2020). Disability law and the case for evidence-based triage in a pandemic. *Yale Law Journal Forum, 130*, 26.

Persad, G., Wertheimer, A., & Emanuel, E. J. (2009). Principles for allocation of scarce medical interventions. *The Lancet, 373*(9661), 423–431.

Phillips, R. L., Liaw, W., Crampton, P., Exeter, D. J., Bazemore, A., Vickery, K. D., Petterson, S., & Carrozza, M. (2016). How other countries use deprivation indices—And why the United States desperately needs one. *Health Affairs, 35*(11), 1991–1998.

Powers, M., Faden, R. R., & Faden, R. R. (2006). *Social justice: The moral foundations of public health and health policy*. Oxford University Press.

Puyol, Á. (2018). Del derecho a la salud a la ética del racionamiento sanitario. In *Anales de la Cátedra Francisco Suárez* (Vol. 52, pp. 43–65).

Ranney, M. L., Griffeth, V., & Jha, A. K. (2020). Critical supply shortages—The need for ventilators and personal protective equipment during the Covid-19 pandemic. *New England Journal of Medicine, 382*(18), e41.

Ravitsky, V. (2005). Timers on ventilators. *British Medical Journal (Clinical research ed.), 330*(7488), 415–417. https://doi.org/10.1136/bmj.330.7488.415. Retrieved December 21, 2021.

Rubio, O., Estella, A., Cabre, L., Saralegui-Reta, I., Martin, M. C., Zapata, L., Esquerda, M., Ferrer, R., Castellanos, A., Trenado, J., & Amblask, J. (2020). Recomendaciones éticas para la toma de decisiones difíciles en las unidades de cuidados intensivos ante la situación excepcional de crisis por la pandemia por COVID-19: revisión rápida y consenso de expertos. *Medicina Intensiva, 44*(7), 439–445.

Ruiz-Hornillos, J., Hernández Suárez, P., Marín Martínez, J. M., Miguel Beriain, Í. D., Nieves Vázquez, M. A., Albert, M., Abián, M. H., Pacheco-Martínez, P. A., Trasmontes, V., & Guillén-Navarro, E. (2021). Bioethical concerns during the COVID-19 pandemic: What did healthcare ethics committees and institutions state in Spain? *Frontiers in Public Health, 9*, 737755.

Sage, W. H. O. (2020). *WHO SAGE values framework for the allocation and prioritization of COVID-19 vaccination.* World Health Organization.

Sandman, L., & Liliemark, J. (2019). Withholding and withdrawing treatment for cost-effectiveness reasons: Are they ethically on par? *Bioethics, 33*(2), 278–286.

Schmidt, H. (2020). Vaccine rationing and the urgency of social justice in the Covid-19 response. *Hastings Center Report, 50*(3), 46–49.

Sederstrom, N. (2020). The "give back:" Is there room for it. *The American Journal of Bioethics.*

Shah, S. K., Truog, R. D., & Miller, F. G. (2011). Death and legal fictions. *Journal of Medical Ethics, 37*(12), 719–722.

Sinclair, S. (2012). How to avoid unfair discrimination against disabled patients in healthcare resource allocation. *Journal of Medical Ethics, 38*(3), 158–162.

Sociedad Española de Medicina Intensiva, Crítica y Unidades Coronarias (SEMICYUC). (2020). *Recomendaciones éticas para la toma de decisiones en la situación excepcional de crisis por pandemia covid-19 en las unidades de cuidados intensivos.* Retrieved December 29, 2021, from https://semicyuc.org/wp-content/uploads/2020/03/%C3%89tica_SEMICYUC-COVID-19.pdf

Sprung, C. L., Joynt, G. M., Christian, M. D., Truog, R. D., Rello, J., & Nates, J. L. (2020). Adult ICU triage during the coronavirus disease 2019 pandemic: Who will live and who will die? Recommendations to improve survival. *Critical Care Medicine, 48*(8), 1196.

Sprung, C. L., Zimmerman, J. L., Christian, M. D., Joynt, G. M., Hick, J. L., Taylor, B., Richards, G. A., Sandrock, C., Cohen, R., & Adini, B. (2010). Recommendations for intensive care unit and hospital preparations for an influenza epidemic or mass disaster: Summary report of the European Society of Intensive Care Medicine's Task Force for intensive care unit triage during an influenza epidemic or mass disaster. *Intensive Care Medicine, 36*(3), 428–443.

Stone, J. R. (2020). Social justice, triage, and COVID-19: Ignore life-years saved. *Medical Care, 58*(7), 579–581.

Sulmasy, D. P., & Sugarman, J. (1994). Are withholding and withdrawing therapy always morally equivalent? *Journal of Medical Ethics, 20*(4), 218–224.

Sundquist, K., Malmström, M., Johansson, S. E., & Sundquist, J. (2003). Care need index, a useful tool for the distribution of primary health care resources. *Journal of Epidemiology & Community Health, 57*(5), 347–352.

Taurek, J. M. (1977). Should the numbers count? *Philosophy & Public Affairs, 6*(4), 293–316.

Tham, J., Melahn, L., & Baggot, M. (2021). Withdrawing critical care from patients in a triage situation. *Medicine, Health Care, and Philosophy, 24*(2), 205–211. https://doi.org/10.1007/s11019-020-09999-4. Retrieved December 19, 2021.

Tomás-Valiente Lanuza, C. (1999). *La disponibilidad de la propia vida en el Derecho Penal.* Boletín Oficial del Estado.

Truog, R. D., Mitchell, C., & Daley, G. Q. (2020). The toughest triage—Allocating ventilators in a pandemic. *New England Journal of Medicine, 382*(21), 1973–1975.

United Network of Organ Sharing. (2020). *A guide to calculating the lung allocation score.* United Network of Organ Sharing. Retrieved from https://unos.org/wpcontent/uploads/unos/lung-allocation-score.pdf

Ursin, L. Ø. (2019). Withholding and withdrawing life-sustaining treatment: Ethically equivalent? *American Journal of Bioethics, 19*(3), 10–20.

Vergano, M., Bertolini, G., Giannini, A., Gristina, G., Livigni, S., Mistraletti, G., & Petrini, F. (2020). *Clinical ethics recommendations for the allocation of intensive care treatments, in exceptional, resource-limited circumstances.* Retrieved December 12, 2021, from http://www.siaarti.it/SiteAssets/News/COVID19%20-%20documenti%20SIAARTI/SIAARTI%20-%20Covid-19%20-%20Clinical%20Ethics%20Reccomendations.pdf

Wassermann, D., Persad, G., & Millum, J. (2020). Setting priorities fairly in response to Covid-19: Identifying overlapping consensus and reasonable disagreement. *Journal of Law and the Biosciences, 7*(1), 1–12.

White, D. B., & Angus, D. C. (2020). A proposed lottery system to allocate scarce COVID-19 medications: Promoting fairness and generating knowledge. *Journal of the American Medical Association, 324*(4), 329–330.

White, D. B., & Lo, B. (2020). A framework for rationing ventilators and critical care beds during the COVID-19 pandemic. *Journal of the American Medical Association, 323*(18), 1773–1774.

White, D. B., & Lo, B. (2021). Mitigating inequities and saving lives with ICU triage during the COVID-19 pandemic. *American Journal of Respiratory and Critical Care Medicine, 203*(3), 287–295.

White, D. B., Schmidhofer, M., McCreary, M., et al. (2020, May 28) *A model hospital policy for fair allocation of scarce medications to treat COVID-19*. Retrieved December 12, 2021, from https://ccm.pitt.edu/node/113320

Whitehurst, D. G., & Engel, L. (2018). Disability discrimination and misdirected criticism of the quality-adjusted life year framework. *Journal of Medical Ethics, 44*(11), 793–795.

Wicclair, M. (2020). Allocating ventilators during the Covid-19 pandemic and conscientious objection. *The American Journal of Bioethics, 20*(7), 204–207.

Wilkinson, D., & Savulescu, J. (2014). A costly separation between withdrawing and withholding treatment in intensive care. *Bioethics, 28*(3), 127–137.

World Health Organization (WHO). (2008). *Pandemic influenza preparedness and mitigation in refugee and displaced populations* (2nd ed.). WHO. Retrieved from http://www.who.int/diseasecontrol_emergencies/HSE_EPR_DCE_2008_3rweb.pdf.

Zohny, H. (2020). COVID-19 and the moral community: A nursing ethics perspective. *Journal of Medical Ethics* blog.

Index

Printed in the United States
by Baker & Taylor Publisher Services

Printed in the United States
by Baker & Taylor Publisher Services